Stories of our
Mormon Hymns

June 17, 1977.

Happy Birthday to Bobby —
May our dear Lord bless you as you
lead and teach the songs of Zion;
for He has said:
"My soul delighteth in the song of the
heart; yea the song of the righteous
is a prayer unto me, and it shall be
answered with a blessing on their heads,
wherefore, lift up your heart and
rejoice —" Doc and Cov. 25: 12
In His wonderous love.
Willard

EMMA SMITH

Compiler of the first Latter-day Saint Hymnbook

Stories of our Mormon Hymns

BY

J. SPENCER CORNWALL
Author and Compiler

Enlarged Fourth Printing

Published by
DESERET BOOK COMPANY
Salt Lake City, Utah

1975

SBN No. 87747-245-9

Lithographed in U. S. A.
by
Stanway/Wheelwright Printing Co.

FOREWORD

Hymns should be in accord with gospel truths.

"To my mind the musician who pays little or no attention to the words of the song destroys half the value of his or her singing. . .The more beautiful the music by which false doctrine is sung, the more dangerous it becomes. I appeal to all Latter-day Saints and especially to our choirs, never to sing the words of a song no matter how beautiful and inspiring the music may be, where the teachings are not in perfect accord with the truths of the gospel.

"No individual singer or organization of singers in the Church should ever render a selection unless the words are in harmony with the truths of the gospel and can be given from the heart of the singer. In other words, our songs should be, in very deed, 'Prayers unto the Lord.' If we are careful to sing only such songs, then we are sure of such blessings as are promised by the Lord, because his promises are 'true and faithful and will be fulfilled.' "

—President Heber J. Grant.

v

Acknowledgements

Sincere appreciation is hereby expressed to the Heber J. Grant family for use of material found in George D. Pyper's "Stories of Latter-day Saint Hymns": to Dr. William Leroy Wilkes, Jr. for quotations from "Borrowed Music in Mormon Hymnals" (a noteworthy volume): to the Historian's Office of The Church of Jesus Christ of Latter-day Saints for free access to the Church Library files and the assistance of the librarians: to the Public Library, Fort Worth, Texas, for access to its library files, and to all others who have contributed pictures and information.

PREFACE

A thoughtful man once said, as he contemplated his worth in the world, "I should like to create something by which I could be honorably remembered, after I die." He tried many ventures in the creative field, one of which was the laudable undertaking of the writing and preaching of sermons, but it was not until he penned a hymn that he touched the hearts of men and endeared himself to all subsequent generations. Such a man was the Reverend Henry F. Lyte, the author of "Abide with Me; Fast Falls the Eventide."

No matter what its degree of excellence, every hymn extant, and there have been almost as many hymnals published as Bibles, was written with a worthy motive. Religious beliefs, except in scriptures themselves, have never been sustained on a higher level than in hymnology. Hymnology is the terse essence of the religious life coupled with the enhancement of reverential song.

The contents of this compilation is devoted to telling the stories of the hymns in the Latter-day Saint hymnal together with the available information concerning the lives of the authors and composers of these hymns.

The compilers have had only one objective in searching out and bringing forth this information and that is to make the reader more conscious of the beauty and import of the hymns and also make his singing of them more meaningful.

Those hymns in the Latter-day Saint hymnal which have been written and composed by Latter-day Saint authors and composers represent a distinct religious heritage to the members of the Church of which they can be justly proud.

INTRODUCTION

Hymnology

Hymnology holds a very respectable place in human cultural, and religious endeavors. Poets, preachers, even laymen, together with musicians of all ranks, have set their hands to writing and composing hymns. Every hymn creation is the result of an idea, a circumstance, an experience, an event, or some other motivating influence. Naturally then, the greatest and most worthy hymns are those with the most imposing or significant background, out of which has come a lofty expression, in immortal lines, of the significance of that motivating influence. The elegance and loftiness of these lines are the reflection of the stature of the creator of the hymn.

The creators of great hymns are not mediocre persons. They are they who have the ability to think clearly and feel deeply. Their lives are dominated by thorough-going religious motives. It is natural and proper for us to revere them.

A recent survey declares that some 400,000 hymns have been identified in the countries across the water and 40,000 have been published in books in America. Charles Wesley, an English hymnist, alone, is credited with writing 6500 hymns. No religious movement has ever started without the aid of religious song. In fact music has always been the handmaiden of religion.

All great religious leaders unite in paying homage to the powers of music in its influence on church goers. Each great religious movement has brought forth its contribution to hymnology. In so far as these hymns represent a universal faith and belief, they have become a medium of exchange between the various religious denominations. Hymns of the churches do not excite controversy as do the tenets of the various faiths.

In a well-known collection of fifty best hymns, fifteen were written by Episcopalians - six by Congregationalists - five by Methodists - five by Presbyterians - two by Baptists - two by Quakers - four by Unitarians - five by Roman Catholics, and six were anonymous.

A recent publication of Christmas Carols included the Catholic "O Come All Ye Faithful," the Unitarian "It Came upon the Midnight Clear," the Episcopal "O Little Town of Bethlehem," the Congregational "Joy to the World," the Methodist "Hark, the Herald Angels Sing."

Music has peculiar powers unmatched in the other fine arts to illuminate thought. Its chief power lies in the fact that it is not fixed or statuesque. It is panoramic. It does not give a single impression but rather a series of unfolding impressions. It is like writing in the water-the letters disappear as fast as they are formed. Music goes beyond words and carries one into the realm of mute feeling-which is so true of hymn music. The content of hymn texts has been a subject of much controversy and evolution. John Calvin held that "only God's own word is worthy to be used in praising Him," therefore in the early days of the Reformation the scriptures, predominantly the Psalms were used almost exclusively in hymn texts.

Thousands of versifications of the scriptures are to be found in the various hymnals. Much modern hymnology however, has gone far afield in both words and music from the classic hymn with its "Praise to the Lord" text and its one-beat tones in the music.

A glance at the topical index of any hymnal will show the great variety of subjects used in modern hymns. One well-known hymnal has forty-six topics. However, the true hymn still stands and will always be the model or ideal in hymnology.

Academically speaking it is axiomatic that some hymns are better than others. The sophisticated critic would insist that all hymns used in the Church have lofty literary merit and classic musical excellence. If such a standard were exacted, a large number of hymns now in common use, taking Christendom as a whole, would be discarded. The fact that hymn singing is a cherished religious practice of both the high and the lowly, as far as taste and understanding is concerned, precludes any such rigidity. However, the aim of all forward looking church movements should be to improve the taste of the congregations. Hymns of lesser excellence must be supplanted by hymns of greater excellence through an educative process. The opinions and advice of those who set the standards in hymn excellence should be sought and heeded.

Choir Hymns

The large number of hymns in the Latter-day Saint Hymnal written expressly for choirs of select voices rather than for congregation, sets this hymnal apart from almost every other hymnal in America. The hymns designated as choir hymns in the Latter-day Saint Hymnal numbers (223-299) are characterized by their being too intricate for congregational singing: too high in many cases and often containing solo, duet, and trio passages.

Some of the Latter-day Saint choir hymns, because of their form, could be classified as miniature anthems. No such hymns are found in other hymnals.

Most of the choir hymns in the Latter-day Saint Hymnal were written for the Tabernacle Choir—thirty being composed by four men—Evan Stephens, George Careless, Ebenezer Beesley, former Tabernacle Choir conductors, and Joseph J. Daynes, the first organist at the Tabernacle. They were written for the most part under a directive from President John Taylor, President of the Church of Latter-day Saints (1880-1887), who asked these composers to write some new hymns for the church.

Since the texts of the choir hymns are completely Latter-day Saint or in harmony with Latter-day Saint doctrine, they can be grouped together in one category - that of Latter-day Saint hymns.

We can safely add to the choir hymns *some* congregational hymns which are distinctly Latter-day Saint. These are they which are based on Latter-day Saint doctrine and are composed by Latter-day Saint composers. These hymns differ from the distinctive choir hymns in only one particular-that of the hymn form. They are patterned after traditional hymn forms extant throughout Christendom. Latter-day Saints could not rightfully claim originality in this particular. It must be said, however, that many of these hymns are as fine from any point of view, as hymns of like nature found in other hymnals.

The Hymn Anthem

The hymn-anthem is a decidedly controversial creation. The theory propounded for its existence, which is that of establishing a point of contact with the listener by building upon something with which he is already familiar, is controverted by many people when they simply say, "I do not like them."

When a hymn is elaborated by an arrangement, it no longer can be performed by the people of the congregation. Its simplicity has been set aside, and intricacy has been imposed on it. This is the basis of some folk's resistance to the hymn-anthem. Many prefer to sing the hymn themselves rather than listen to special singers perform an arrangement of it. However, there are those, and they are in substantial numbers, who enjoy elaborations of hymns, especially is this true when the elaboration is consistent and serves to make the hymn text more impressive than did the simpler music of the hymn tune.

It is to these listeners that the arranger of hymn anthems directs his efforts.

No arrangement of a hymn is consistent if it diverts the attention of the listener to itself, rather than to the original intent of the hymn text. If the arranger uses a hymn tune on which to build an elaborate musical creation which becomes in itself the most imposing part of the composition, then the hymn is made to serve an ulterior end and in doing so, of course, loses its original intent and purpose. A good example is found in a recent arrangement of "A Mighty Fortress" wherein the arrangement all but demolishes the stronghold.

In conclusion it is safe to say that with most of the hymn-anthem creations, fine and all as they may be, the hymn will last longer than the arrangement.

A Statistical Classification of the Hymns

An analysis of the Latter-day Saint Hymnal reveals that there are one hundred twenty-five numbers which could be classified as true hymns, five which are chorales, eleven Christmas carols, thirty-five gospel songs, thirty-seven songs with texts which are closely allied to real hymn-texts but are not hymns in the true sense, such as "Kind Words Are Sweet Tones of the Heart," six patriotic songs, and seventy-nine numbers classified as choir hymns.

The topical index of the hymnal contains fifty-four categories into which the various hymns and songs are also classified.

Music in the Church

Mr. William B. Bradbury, in a letter which is in the Library of Congress, has the following to say about Music in the Church:

1. "I believe it is to be the privilege and duty of *all* to unite in singing in the Church as an act of worship.

2. I believe that from the congregation at large, a number possessing more musical talent than the rest should be organized into a separate body with a competent leader and occupy a place by themselves.

3. I believe that this choir so organized should not only serve in the capacity of *leader to the congregation* but that a part of each service may and should be performed entirely and exclusively by themselves, the congregation at such times being silent listeners. That in such services new and beautiful music appropriate to the occasion, may be performed with such taste and skill as by attentive study and practice they can command.

4. I believe that for *congregational singing* only such tunes as are simple in their structure and very easy of execution should be introduced and that these should consist chiefly of old familiar tunes such as the congregation generally can sing; that in each service one such congregational tune should be selected, and when introduced by the choir all the people should arise and sing it to the best of their ability without reference to *art* or musical effect, but simple and solely as an act of worship before their Maker."

Mr. Bradbury composed the following hymns found in the Latter-day Saint Hymnal:-

"God Moves in a Mysterious Way." "Sweet Hour of Prayer."

"Farewell all Earthly Honors."

This letter reflects, in large measure, the views of the General Music Committee.

Sermons in Hymns

The best sources for hymn text material are the same as those which provide texts for sermons. The difference is found in the style of the composition. A sermon is prose while the hymn strives for rhyming verse. Poetry is succint while prose is elaborately explanatory. A whole sermon can be created from one line of a hymn. Take for example, the terse sentence in the chorus of the hymn "Do what is right; let the consequence follow." No more complete admonition on proper conduct can be found than in these eight words. Elaborations on this text could be multiplied indefinitely.

And then consider the compassionate plea in "Come, come, ye Saints, no toil nor labor fear; but with joy wend your way," a great example of wholesome encouragement. "I'll go where you want me to go, dear Lord," is a fearless statement of trusting obedience - a perfect text for a sermon.

The heart of the hymn writer's genius lies in his ability to create thought-laden lines which are beautifully complete but compact. Flowing combinations of choice words, teeming with meaning spring from his gifted pen.

The essence of a great hymn is in its striking lines. Thought conceptions of all grades of subtlety cannot be expressed better than in the words of the poet. The great hymn writer couches religious conceptions in *his* lines with striking impact. Note the poignancy in the following examples from the Latter-day Saint Hymnal:

"A mighty fortress is our God"
"The rock of my refuge is thee"
"Ere you left your room this morning, did you think to pray?"
"God be with you till we meet again"
"God moves in a mysterious way"
"High on the mountaintop a banner is unfurled"
"Hope of Israel"
"How great the wisdom and the love"
"Time flies on wings of lightning; we cannot call it back."
"I need thee every hour."

Every great hymn has its great lines, otherwise it has no claim to greatness. The many fine hymns in the Latter-day Saint Hymnal are worthy contributors to our cultural and religious heritage.

CONTENTS

Stories of our Mormon Hymns

The First Latter-day Saint Hymnbook

Compiled by Emma Smith

Among the messages delivered to Emma Smith, wife of the Prophet, is the following from a revelation given July, 1830, just three months after the organization of the Church:

> And verily I say unto thee that thou shalt lay aside the things of this world, and seek for the things of a better. And it shall be given unto thee, also, to make a selection of sacred hymns, as it shall be given thee, which is pleasing unto me, to be had in my church. For my soul delighteth in the song of the heart; yea the song of the righteous is a prayer unto me, and it shall be answered with a blessing upon their heads. (Doctrine and Covenants, 25:10-12.)

Though there are numerous references in holy writ to the use and value of music and song, this is the only instance on record where the Lord, by revelation, has directed the compilation of hymns and recognized the power of song. And the honor of compiling the first Latter-day Saint hymnbook was given to the "elect lady," Emma Smith.

The work of collecting suitable hymns for the Church, a hundred years ago, was no easy task; but Emma Smith was earnest and diligent in complying with the divine message, and within two years had succeeded in selecting a goodly number of hymns. In the *History of the Church,* recorded on May 1, 1832, we read:

> It was also ordered that W. W. Phelps correct and print the hymns which have been selected by Emma Smith in fulfilment of the revelation.

A number of these hymns were published in the *Evening and Morning Star* during 1832 and 1833, but in July, 1833, the printing press was destroyed and much of the material lost. It seems that whenever anything good is projected by the Lord the power of evil are always on the alert to retard its progress. However, the work did not stop. The Saints continued to sing, and in 1835, at a meeting of the Presidency and High Council, held at Kirtland,

> It was further decided that Sister Emma Smith proceed to make a selection of sacred hymns according to the revelation and that President W. W. Phelps be appointed to revise and arrange them for printing.

These two again applied themselves faithfully to the work. William W. Phelps wrote twenty-nine or more poems for the proposed volume. Parley P. Pratt and Eliza R. Snow, and others contributed from their gifted pens. Emma Smith also gleaned from the published hymnbooks, songs by Isaac Watts, the Wesleys, Dr. Rippon, Samuel Medley, Bishop Ken, and other early hymnists, making up a list of ninety favorite hymns which were published in 1835. The preface to that volume was as follows:

> In order to sing by the Spirit, and with the understanding, it is necessary that The Church of he Latter-day Saints should have a collection of "Sacred Hymns," adapted to their faith and belief in the gospel, and, as far as can be, holding forth the promises made to the fathers who died in the precious faith of a glorious resurrection, and a thousand years' reign on earth with the Son of Man in his glory. Notwithstanding the church, as it were, is still in its infancy, yet, as the song of the righteous is a prayer unto God, it is sincerely hoped that the following collection, selected with an eye to his glory, may answer every purpose till more are composed, or till we are blessed with a copious variety of the songs of Zion.

Following is a list of the 90 hymns contained in Emma Smith's compilation with the names of the authors as far as known. The asterisk indicates that the hymns so marked (27 in number) are included in the latest edition of Latter-day Saint hymns:

Author

Adieu, my dear brethren, adieu	
Alas, and did my Savior bleed	*Isaac Watts*
An angel came down from the, etc.	*Wm. W. Phelps*
And did my Savior die	
*Arise, my soul, arise	*Wesley*
Awake, for the morning is come	
Awake, my soul, and with the sun	*Thomas Ken*
Awake, O ye people! the Savior is, etc.	*Phelps*
Before the earth from Chaos sprung	
Behold the Savior of mankind	*Hastings*
*Come, all ye sons of Zion	*Phelps*
Come, all ye saints who dwell on earth	*Phelps*
*Come, let us sing an evening hymn	*Phelps*
Come, ye children of the kingdom	
*Earth with her ten thousand flowers	*Phelps*
Ere long the veil will rend in twain	*P. P. Pratt*
Farewell our friends and brethren	*Phelps*
*From Greenland's icy mountains	*Heber*

It is said that the character of a people may be judged by the songs they sing. If this be true then an examination of those selected by Emma Smith prove that the Latter-day Saints were a reverential, peace-loving, worshipful, God-fearing people. After a hundred years it is acknowledged that the songs selected for that first Latter-day Saint hymnbook are among the best of all Christian hymns.

Stories of Mormon hymns with biographies of
authors and composers in the order they
appear in the current hymn book of the
Church of Jesus Christ of Latter-day Saints

Come Rejoice

Words and music by Tracy Y. Cannon

The Hymn

Tracy Y. Cannon comments on this hymn in the following lines: "The reason for writing this hymn was that I desired to compose a hymn on the restoration of the gospel. It has always been easier for me to write music than words. The music of this hymn kept filling my mind and I, therefore, wrote words that seemed to me to suit the spirit of the music."

The Composer and Author

Tracy Y. Cannon was born July 23, 1879 in Salt Lake City, son of George Q. Cannon and Caroline Young Cannon. When he was fifteen years old he joined the Tabernacle Choir, which was directed by Evan Stephens. He was appointed choir leader of Cannon Ward when sixteen years of age and shortly thereafter began studying piano and organ, and composition with John J. McClellan and later with noted teachers in Ann Arbor, Berlin, Paris, New York, and Chicago. The Chicago Musical College conferred upon him the honorary degree, Master of Music, in 1930.

In 1909 he was appointed assistant organist, Salt Lake Tabernacle, serving in this capacity for twenty-one years. Just prior to his release, in 1930, he had the honor of playing for the great pageant, *The Message of the Ages,* presented in the Tabernacle in commemoration of the one hundredth anniversary of the Church. It was during his term as Tabernacle organist that the choir and organ began broadcasting over the national network, and he was featured in many of these programs.

When the General Music Committee of the Church was organized in 1920 he was appointed as one of the members. In 1930 he became second assistant to Melvin J. Ballard and in 1939 was sustained as chairman. Under his chairmanship the committee compiled and published the 1950 edition of *Hymns,* Church of Jesus Christ of Latter-day Saints, the *Recreational Songs,* and *The Children Sing* — three standard books to meet the needs of all types of congregational singing in the Church.

In 1925 he was appointed Director of the McCune School of Music and Art, a Church-sponsored music conservatory. He served

Tracy Y. Cannon

in this capacity for twenty-five years. While serving as director, in 1935, he inaugurated a program to educate Church music conductors and organists. This program, now under the General Music Committee, serves hundreds of Church musicians each year. Up to the present time (1961) approximately 25,000 conductors and organists have availed themselves of this Church-wide program.

His music compositions include hymns, anthems, and art songs.

He is also the author of the widely used textbook, *The Organist's Manual.* He died November 6, 1961.

No. 2

Abide with Me, 'Tis Eventide

Words by Lowrie M. Hofford   **Music by Harrison Millard**

The Hymn

"Abide with Me, 'Tis Eventide" is a frequently used hymn in Latter-day Saint assemblies. The lilt of the melodic line is largely responsible for its popularity. However, it is never sung as it is written. It is the opinion of this author that the note values at the ends of the various lines should be elongated to agree with the common way of singing them.

5

The Composer

Harrison Millard was an American composer and teacher of vocal music. He was born in Boston, Massachusetts. As a child he joined the Handel and Haydn Society. On reaching adulthood he studied in Europe and on his return, taught singing in New York City. Later he joined the Union forces in the Civil War. Mr. Millard was wounded in the battle of Chickamauga.

During his lifetime he published over three hundred songs, a Grand Mass, and a four act opera, *Deborah*. "Abide with Me, 'Tis Eventide" is typical of the sentimental gospel song.

The Author

No information is available concerning the life of author Lowrie M. Hofford.

No. 3

A Mighty Fortress Is Our God

Words and music by Martin Luther

The Hymn

"A Mighty Fortress Is Our God" has often been termed the Marseillaise of the Reformation. It was written originally as a rally song against the Roman Catholic Church, but it has served in many other capacities as well, for in 1631 Gustavus Adolphus ordered it sung by his Army before the battle of Leipzig. It was also the victory battle hymn in 1632 at Lutzen. This song has been a part of numerous celebrations which called for sustaining power. Effective performance of "A Mighty Fortress" demands tremendous volume with a determined word by word accent.

The composition of "A Mighty Fortress Is Our God" is usually credited to Martin Luther, but there is ample evidence that some thematic items used by Luther existed before his time and that he made free use of them in building the great tune. Variants of the melody as recorded in the Latter-day Saint Hymnal are to be found in other printings of the famous chorale. Its drive and impact and ruggedness are not surpassed by any other chorale. The tune has been used by Meyerbeer, Mendelssohn, Wagner, and Bach in larger works.

Composer and Author

Martin Luther, who was both author and composer of this hymn, was the founder of congregational singing in the church. One of his great contributions to the Reformation was to take from the clergy and put into the mouths of the layman of the church, singing in the church service. Martin Luther was the leader of the revolution

6

Martin Luther

against the tyranny of papal dominion of the Catholic Church. The selling of indulgences, absolving people from sin, to build the Church of Saint Peter in Rome, was the culminating indiscretion. It was then that Luther nailed the ninety-five theses of protest on the door of Wittenburg Castle church. Through a providential series of circumstances Luther escaped death, and ultimately established the church which bears his name. The Lutheran Church gave to the people of Germany, in their own language, "the Bible, the Catechism, and the hymnbook so that God might speak directly to them in His Word, and that they might answer Him directly in their songs."

Making the hymnbook available to the lay church man was the greatest gift of Luther to the worshiper. Congregational singing as practiced in Luther's church represented the greatest emancipation of the common man from clerical domination, of the time.

No. 4

All Creatures of Our God and King

Words by St. Francis of Assisi   **Music Anonymous**

The Hymn

St. Francis of Assisi, 1182-1225. Translation 1910 by William Henry Draper, 1850-1933.

This hymn was not written originally in Latin as were most hymns of the day but rather in what was known as the "vulgar tongue." This language was used by the common people. The famous poet Dante wrote his verses in this tongue. From this language, combined with numerous other barbaric dialects, the Italian language was generated. History records that St. Francis was blind in his later years. During all of that time he received much consolation from conversations with his sister, Clara.

One day, as he sat at the table with her, he seemed suddenly to be rapt in ecstasy. It was then that he uttered the various caption phrases of the "Hymn to the Sun." The literal translation of the first stanza by Mathew Arnold is as follows: "Praise be my Lord God with all His creatures, and especially our brother the sun, who brings us the day and who brings the light; fair is he and shines with a very great splendor; O Lord he signifies to us, Thee." William Henry Draper versified the hymn and added the repetitive "Allelulias."

This magnificent hymn, when sung by the congreation, should be performed in unison. As a choir number it is most effective if the four parts are well sustained. The phrasing is impressive when breath is taken at the ends of all word phrases and after each "Allelulia" except the next to the last one on the bottom line. At this point sing, "Allelulia! O Praise Him" with one breath. A vigorous tone in legato style will give the type of dignity required to bring out the meaning of this fine music.

The Composer

The tune found in the Latter-day Saint Hymnal is of German origin dating back to the sixteenth century. It is a hymn melody of pleasing lilt and builds to an impressive climax. Many built-up arrangements are to be found of this famous tune. One is by Leroy Robertson, a well known Latter-day Saint composer.

The Author

St. Francis of Assisi was born in the Italian town of Assisi — the son of a wealthy cloth merchant. In his youth he ran with a gang of young outlaws. After serving a prison term for his offenses, he suddenly experienced what he claimed to be a vision. It turned him to the better life and he became a wandering preacher. A group of twelve young men joined him and together they went to the Pope of Rome to gain permission "to live a life of absolute conformity to the preaching and precepts of the gospel."

Francis and his band began a life of preaching tours.

The gospel he preached was practical in admonishing all who

8

would listen to give up their ill-gotten gains and in their place substitute the love of fellow men. The church finally took over the movement and deprived St. Francis of his power. At the early age of forty-five years, he died. Many of the events of his life are clothed in mysticism.

No. 5　　　　　　　As Swiftly My Days

Unknown　　　　　　　　　　　　　　　　　　　　　　Unknown

"As Swiftly My Days" is an anonymous gospel song. Its six-eight measure form has an attractive flow which gives to people real enjoyment while singing it. The song cannot be classified as dignified but rather it is in the category of pleasant or mildly satisfying. It is not stirring as are many revival gospel songs. Its text is paraphrased from 2nd Samuel, 22: wherein God is declared to be the "Rock of our Salvation."

No. 6　　　　　Beautiful Zion for Me

Words by Charles W. Penrose　　　　　　Music by John Rogers Thomas

Arr. by Evan Stephens

A mood of Charles W. Penrose is shown in his song "Beautiful Zion for Me."* An arrangement from the original tune by J.R. Thomas was made by Evan Stephens and is found in the *Latter-day Saint Hymnal*. President Heber J. Grant, who was very fond of the song and its borrowed melody, is authority for the following story and its origin.

Brigham Young, Jr., had presided over the European Mission and was coming home. Brother Penrose had been editing the *Millennial Star* and expected to return with Brother Brigham, but was requested to remain longer, he being such a capable man. He said to Brigham, "Oh, Brigham, Brigham, Brigham, beautiful Zion for me. I wish I were going with you." Then he said, "Brigham, do you know the song 'Beautiful Isle of the Sea'?"

Brother Young said, "Yes."

"Well," said Brother Penrose, "I will write you a hymn, 'Beautiful Zion for Me,' and when you are on the ocean you can sing it and think of me. I will write it so that it can be sung to the melody of 'Beautiful Isle of the Sea'."

The hymn was written as promised.

The adapted tune for "Beautiful Zion for Me" has the lilt of a ballad. However, the mood of the words of Charles W. Penrose are somewhat in harmony with this music.

---

*From George D. Pyper's *Stories of Latter-day Saint Hymns*.

Behold the Royal Army

Words by Fannie Crosby   **Music by Adam Geibel**

The Hymn

Many hymns of exhortation have in them a militant connotation to establish an atmosphere of conquering determination in worshipers. Such an one is "Behold the Royal Army" with its "Victory, Victory," chorus. This hymn is unique in that it was written and composed by a blind author and a blind musician.

The Composer

Adam Geibel was numbered with the blind composers. He was American born. Among the numbers he wrote are "Stand up for Jesus" and the ever popular male quartette "Kentucky Babe."

The Author

Fanny Crosby's favorite saying was, "I think that life is not too long and therefore I determine that many people read a song who will not read a sermon." Many of Fanny Crosby's popular hymns are written to music already composed. Instead of writing a poem for someone else to set to music, she wrote quite a few of her stanzas to fit somone else's tunes. Many composers of note came to her for her poems.

Born in a little cottage in Southeast, Putnam Co., N.Y., March 1820, she was permanently blinded when six years old because of the ignorance of a country doctor who applied hot poultices to inflamed eyes. During her ninth year, as she played in the field one beautiful spring day, she wrote her first poem. It has been considered one of the most beautiful in literature in the realm of children authors.

> O what a happy soul am I!
> Although I cannot see;
> I am resolved that in this world
> Contented I will be.
> How many blessings I enjoy,
> That other people don't;
> To weep and sigh because I'm blind,
> I cannot and I won't.

God worked miracles through Fanny Crosby. Before her death in 1915 at the age of ninty-five, she had written more hymns, songs, and poems than anyone else since the beginning of the Christian era. Her first hymn was written at the age of forty-four years, but she turned out over five thousand more before her death.

God, Our Father, Hear Us Pray

Words by Annie Malin   **Music by Louis Gottschalk**

The Hymn

"God, Our Father, Hear Us Pray" is a favorite sacramental song. The lovely arched melody seems to give the fine words of Annie Malin, buoyancy and meaning.

The Composer

Louis Morean Gottschalk 1829-1869 was the first American pianist to win renown in Europe. He was born in New Orleans, schooled in Paris, concertized in France, Switzerland, and Spain, and in other European countries, and in North and South America.

His concert tours were always highly successful. As a composer, he ranked among the best during his lifetime but most of his music has now gone into discard. The exquisite melody in his piano number "The Last Hope" has been perpetuated in the hymn, "God, Our Father, Hear Us Pray."

The Author

Annie Pinnock Malin was born in London, England, in May, 1863. Her parents, Williams and Sarah Ann Pinnock, who were Latter-day Saint converts, set sail for America when little Annie was

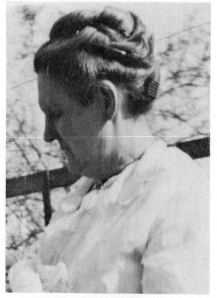

Annie Malin

11

only six years old. The sea voyage lasted seven weeks. The latter part of their journey to Salt Lake City, Utah, was made by ox-team. Mrs. Malin had literary talent. She was trained at the St. Mark's Academy where she graduated. In 1884 she married Millard Fillmore Malin. Along with raising a family of five children, she devoted much time to writing. Her stories and poems were published in the Latter-day Saint church magazines. When she was asked to contribute a sacramental hymn to the 1948 edition of the Latter-day Saint Hymnal, she found she had already written "God, Our Father, Hear us Pray." It was selected out of all of her poems for the book. Annie Malin was loved by all who knew her. She died at her home in the Ninth Ward in Salt Lake City, March 20, 1935.

No. 9

In Hymns of Praise

Words by Ada Blenkhorn   **Music by A. Beirly**

"In Hymns of Praise" is the form of a gospel song with its verse and chorus, but is much better musically than the average. The text is rather good having a distinct element of dignity.

Nothing can be found by your author concerning A. Bierly.

Ada Blenkhorn was a nineteenth century author who had several gospel songs published by E. O. Excell. See No. 74.

No. 10

Christ the Lord Is Risen Today

Words by Charles Wesley   **Music Anon**

The Hymn

"Christ the Lord Is Risen Today" is the most popular of all Easter hymns. The Latter-day Saint people have accepted its recent inclusion in the hymnal with the same enthusiasm with which it was greeted in the protestant churches when it was first published.

When this tune was first published in *Lyra Davidica* in 1708, its Allelulia measures caused a furor among the advocates of the pure hymn whose tradition forbade the inclusion of notes shorter than the beat note. It was justified, however, by the following explanation:-

"There is a desire for a little freer air than the grand movement of the psalm tune" said the editors. Its ready acceptance brought in a new form to hymn music. Notwithstanding the criticisms of the purists who declared it to be "frivolous and vulgar" it soon gained world-wide popularity.

The Author

*This song is credited by some hymnologists with being one of the four best hymns in English hymnology. It was written by Charles Wesley who was born at Epworth, Lincolnshire, England, December 18, 1708. Charles was the youngest of eighteen children, a son of Reverend Samuel Wesley, an English clergyman. His mother, who is credited with being the more gifted of his parents, was Susannah Annesley, daughter of Reverend Samuel Annesley, a non-Conformist minister of London. Charles is described by one writer as "the greatest hymnist of all ages." He is said to have written sixty-five hundred hymns. Four thousand of them were published before he died and

Charles Wesley

twenty-five hundred manuscripts signed by Charles, John, and Samuel Wesley, were found among his belongings. Though in straitened financial circumstances his parents managed to send him to Oxford. At the age of twenty-seven he came to America with his brother John and lived in Georgia, but on account of ill health he was obliged to return to England within a year. Soon after their return to England the brothers came in contact with a Moravian to whom John gave

---

*From George D. Pyper's *Stories of Latter-day Saint Hymns.*

lessons in English. As a result of this contact the brothers received a tremendous spiritual awakening. They went through some unusual experiences and laid the foundation for Methodism. John preached and Charles sang; and for forty years they stirred up old England. Charles formulated many of his hymns as he rode along on a little pony. The inspiration would come to his mind, and at the first resting place he would call for pen and paper in order to perpetuate his thought. One time the horse stumbled and fell, and Charles sprained his hand, and the inspiration for that day, he said, was lost. He died March 29, 1788.

No. 11

Come, All Ye Saints and Sing His Praise

Anon   **Music by Lorin F. Wheelwright**

The Hymn

Lorin Wheelwright, the composer gives his own account of the hymn. The text "Come, All Ye Saints, and Sing His Praise," was supplied by the General Music Committee. This hymn was written to express a joyful sentiment of praise. The melody is on the same descending scale line as "Joy to the World" and attempts to capture the same spirit. The second phrase evolves from the first and is a variation of the same melodic line.

When writing this hymn tune, I wanted every voice to have an interesting line, to be able to sing a melody in its own range. Also, I wanted a spirit of "onwardness" to carry the thought right through to the end. This is not a chorale, it is more in the spirit of other Latter-day Saint hymns which move without hesitation, among which are "Far, Far Away on Judea's Plains" and "Redeemer of Israel," both of which express a certain flavor of directed movement and action.

When singing this hymn, keep it spirited and alive. In the words of Hollis Dann, "Never halt the march of a song." Of course, it should not run with the wind — but rather move with determination. I like to think of its being sung at a dedication of a chapel, or at the opening of an inspirational worship service where the gospel message stirs men's hearts to thanksgiving. In this spirit, all voices join in an anthem of praise and dedication. Let there be no smothering of determination, rather a kindling of renewed zeal. This is the spirit of the hymn as I conceived it, and a spirit we all need when we renew our covenants to serve Christ in word and deed.

The Composer

Five days before Christmas in the year 1909, a little immigrant mother from Denmark bore her third son, Lorin, and prayed that he might someday hold the Holy Priesthood in the restored church. As he grew, she played hymns on a little reed organ and sang them to him at home and in the family car as they traveled on many family outings. His father, David R. Wheelwright a contractor said, 'If my boys are to receive a musical education they shall study only with the best teachers.' He made this resolution come true.

One day while Lorin was practicing at the piano, his father opened the Deseret Sunday School Songbook and asked him to play a hymn. Faltering fingers led to a phone call to Mona Smith, the boy's piano teacher. After that, every lesson contained a hymn, and it was not long until the young lad was playing for Junior Sunday School, then Senior Sunday School, then the ward choir. Under the leadership of Reed Gammell, he accompanied the Ogden Twelfth ward choir in the 'Restoration' and other cantatas.

Paralleling this church service, he studied pipe organ from his brother, D. Sterling Wheelwright, and later from Edward P. Kimball, Alexander Schreiner, Horace Whitehouse, and others. He studied piano from Mona Smith, Sybella Clayton Bassett, William Peterson, Charles Haight, Alton Jones, and Percy Grainger. He studied composition at Columbia University and the Julliard School of Music.

Following a teacher career, he completed research studies in

Lorin F. Wheelwright

15

music reading at the University of Chicago (M.A.) and Columbia University (Ph.D.) He headed the music department at the Oswego Teachers Collegs, N.Y., and later succeeded J. Spencer Cornwall as music supervisor for the Salt Lake Public Schools, where he served for thirteen years. He also taught at the Branch Agricultural College of Cedar City and as guest professor at a number of higher institutions.

During the centennial year of 1947 he served as manager for the Arts Division under President David O. McKay. He was responsible for the creation and production of *Promised Valley* and a host of musical, literary, dramatic, and parade events. He was president of the California Western Music Educators Conference and brought the convention to Salt Lake City for the first time. He retired from the schools and formed his own publishing company. At the time of this writing he is sales director and vice-president of the Wheelwright Lithographing Co. and president of Wheelwright Publications Inc., also a member of the Utah Legislative Council, and a member of other civic groups. He is a Seventy and member of the General Sunday School Union Board where he serves on the music committee and is chairman and associate editor of the *Instructor* magazine.

Among his writings is a research study, "The Perceptibility and Spacing of Music Symbols" published by Columbia University, "Go Down Moses" a symphonic and choral paraphrase published by Witmark and Co., "Festival Songs," "My World," "The Things We Love," "Breathes There a Man," "Symbols," and a number of other octavo works, published by Pioneer Music Press of Salt Lake City.

No. 12
Come All Ye Saints Who Dwell On Earth

Words by W. W. Phelps   **Old Tune**

"Come All Ye Saints Who Dwell on Earth" is a hymn of exhortation to all Saints to praise our Heavenly Father.

The composer of this hymn is not known, but its rhythmical form makes it attractive. The three measure first phrase of the first and third lines, followed by a two measure phrase is intriguing. It is the opinion of this author that the rhythm of this hymn tune is the musical reason for its inclusion in the 1950 edition of the Latter-day Saints Hymnal.

The Author — W. W. Phelps (See No. 213)

Sweet Is the Hour When Thus We Meet

Words by Evan Stephens   **Old Tune**

The Hymn — See No. 213

"Sweet Is the Hour When Thus We Meet" is a hymn depicting the joys of religious communion.

The Author — Evan Stephens (See No. 144)

No. 13

Come, Come, Ye Saints

Words by William Clayton   **Old English Tune**

The Hymn

Although it has been generally believed that the writing of "Come, Come, Ye Saints"* took place on the Pioneer journey between Winter Quarters and Salt Lake City, the hymn really was written while the company of Brigham Young, of which William Clayton was a member, was at or near Locust Creek, about forty-three days out on the journey from Nauvoo to Winter Quarters. William Clayton's diary has a very brief note concerning it under the date of Wednesday, April 15, 1846: "This morning I composed a new song—All is Well."

The Author

As far as known this is the only reference to the origin of the hymn recorded in any of the writings of the author or other Pioneers. In the *Relief Society Magazine* (Vol. 8, page 57, 1921), the following story is told:

> President Young, feeling great anxiety because there were murmurings in the camp of Israel, called Elder William Clayton aside and said: "Brother Clayton, I want you to write a hymn that the people can sing at their campfires, in the evening; something that will give them succor and support, and help them to fight the many troubles and trials of the journey. Elder Clayton withdrew from the camp and in two hours returned with the hymn familiarly known as "Come, Come, Ye Saints." His personal testimony is to the effect that ". . . it was written under the favor and inspiration of the Lord."

This story, or something like it, has been published many times, but some have questioned its authenticity, because William Clayton made no mention of it in his diary, and because there seems to be no original record of the incident. But whether or not it is authentic,

---

*From George D. Pyper's *Stories of Latter-day Saint Hymns.*

17

the song served the purpose named in President Young's purported request: it was sung in the evening at the campfires; it gave succor and support to the pioneers, and helped them to lay aside useless cares and to "fight the many troubles and trials of the journey."

Many pathetic incidents have been told of the Pioneer treks. President Heber J. Grant, in an article on "Our Favorite Hymns," published in *The Improvement Era*, volume 17, part 2, 1914, writes that Oscar Winters, his father-in-law, related to him the following story:

> One night, as we were making camp, we noticed one of our brethren had not arrived and a volunteer party was immediately organized to return and see if anything had happened to him. Just as we were about to start, we saw the missing brother coming in the distance. When he arrived he said he had been quite sick; so some of us unyoked his oxen and attended to his part of the camp duties. After supper, he sat down before the camp-fire on a large rock and sang in a very faint but plaintive and sweet voice, the hymn "Come, Come, Ye Saints." It was a rule of the camp that whenever anybody started this hymn all in the camp should join, but for some reason this evening nobody joined him. He sang the hymn alone. When he had finished I doubt if there was a single dry eye in the camp. The next morning we noticed that he was not yoking up his cattle. We went to his wagon and found that he had died during the night. We dug a shallow grave and after we had covered the body with the earth we rolled the large stone to the head of the grave to mark it—the stone on which he had been sitting the night before when he sang: "And should we die before our journey's through—Happy day! All is well, . . ."
>
> I noticed tears in my father-in-law's eyes when he finished relating this incident, and I imagined the reason he did not relate to me another far more touching incident to him was the fear that he might break down. I subsequently learned that after he had been located for some time in Pleasant Grove, he came to Salt Lake with his team and with a cheerful heart to meet his mother. When the company arrived he learned that she, too, had died before her journey's end and was sleeping in an unknown grave on the vast plains between here and the Missouri River. Some years later when engineers of the Burlington Railroad were surveying the route in Nebraska, they ran across a piece of wagon tire sticking in the ground with the word "Winters" chiseled upon it. They immediately surmised, knowing they were on the Old Mormon Pioneer trail, that the piece of wagon tire must mark the grave of one of the Pioneers, so they very considerately went back several miles and changed the line of the road so as to miss the grave, and sent an account of what they had discovered to the *Deseret News*, asking if any one knew about the grave. The railroad company has since built a neat little fence about the grave, and the Winters family have erected a little monument of temple granite on which is chiseled the fourth verse of "Come, Come, Ye Saints."

18

"Come, Come, Ye Saints," within the small space of its four stanzas, epitomizes the wearying hardships, the unfaltering faith, the indomitable courage, the unconquerable spirit of the Mormon Pioneers.

Stanza I is a challenge to the courage of the Pioneers: though the journey may be hard, the grace of God will strengthen them; useless cares will be thrown aside; murmurings will cease. As a recompense, joy! All will be well!

Stanza II spiritualizes the Pioneer endeavor: why mourn? Why expect a reward if they falter? Why shun the fight? "Gird up your loins, fresh courage take, Our God will never us forsake" — another call for fortitude with a glorious promise.

Stanza III gives assurance of temporal joys: that the Saints will find a resting place in the West as foretold by their Prophet. There they will be safe from mobs and violence; there they will swell the air with music and praises to God their king.

Stanza IV dedicates anew their lives to their task. Living or dying they will be true; if the latter, they will find a celestial home with the just, free from toil and sorrow; if the former, their lives spared, they will shout praises to God, and make the chorus swell with—"*All is well! All is well!*"

Truly, "Come, Come, Ye Saints" is worthy to be classed among the great hymns of Christian literature, because the poet has caught the spirit and sentiment of an oppressed people and crystallized them into simple verse which arouses the interest of the multitude.

When the Salt Lake Tabernacle Choir was in Europe in 1955,* they sang a hymn anthem arrangement by J. Spencer Cornwall, of "Come, Come, Ye Saints," in every concert. Notwithstanding the difficulties in languages, it was encored every time it was sung. The repetitive phrase "All is well" seemed to be understood in each country and even by the refugees in Berlin where the people before whom the choir sang were without home, work, food, and even citizenship. Nothing was "well" with them, yet they encored the grand old hymn.

The tune to "All is Well" is of English origin, and was brought down by oral tradition until its appearance in *Union Harmony and Original Sacred Harp*, early Southern publications. In 1844, two years before the exodus, J. T. White, of Georgia, revised the song, giving it more emotional vigor. The first verse of the old version runs as follows:

---

*See also, A *Century of Singing* by J. Spencer Cornwall.

What's this that steals (that steals) upon my frame—
Is it death? Is it death?

That soon will quench (will quench) this mortal flame—
Is it death? Is it death?

If this be death, I soon shall be
From every pain and sorrow free;
I shall the king of glory see—
All is well! All is well!*

No doubt it was from this source that William Clayton got the tune and "Mormonized" it to fit "Come, Come, Ye Saints."

William Clayton, a native of Penwortham, Lancashire, England, first saw the light of day, July 17, 1814. The earliest missionaries who visited England in 1837 found an ardent convert in young Clayton and he was soon baptized, ordained to the priesthood and set apart as a missionary. In March, 1838, upon the return of Apostles Heber C. Kimball and Orson Hyde to America, William Clayton became second counselor to President Joseph Fielding, holding that position until 1840. In the meantime he closed up his private business and devoted himself to missionary work in Manchester, where at the end of eighteen months he reported 240 members in the branch he had established there. He emigrated to America September 8, 1840, sailing on the good ship *North America*, arriving in New York October 11, and in Nauvoo November 24, 1840. He first located on the west bank of the Mississippi River and in July, 1841, became clerk of the high council of Iowa. His ability was soon recognized and moving to Nauvoo he succeeded Willard Richards as the Prophet's secretary, became clerk and recorder of the Nauvoo Temple, and was elected treasurer of the city of Nauvoo. The *L.D.S. Biographical Encyclopedia* contains the following:

> He . . . was an intimate associate and tried and trusted friend of the Prophet to whom he continued to act as private secretary up to the time of the latter's martyrdom. While laboring in that capacity he transcribed the revelation on celestial marriage and other revelations under the Prophet's dictation and direction.

With President Young's company he left Nauvoo in 1846, became one of the original pioneers of 1847 under the leadership of Brigham Young, and was clerk of the camp. He returned east the same year and in 1848 came back to the valley where he resided until his demise, which occurred December 4, 1879.

---

*"Twelve Folk Hymns: From the old Shape Note Hymn Books and from Oral Tradition." Published by J. Fischer & Bro., 119 West 40th St., N. Y. 1934.

Various offices of confidential and public trust were held by William Clayton, notably treasurer of Z. C. M. I., Territorial Recorder of Marks and Brands, and Territorial Auditor of Public Accounts. All offices were conducted with the skill and integrity characteristic of the man.

Musically inclined, he was prominently connected with the Nauvoo Brass Band and played second violin in the first Salt Lake Theatre orchestra. This divine art has manifested itself to a large degree in his large and talented posterity. In addition to "Come, Come, Ye Saints" he wrote another song beloved by the Latter-day Saints: "When First the Glorious Light of Truth," familiarly known to Saints as "The Resurrection Day." Of this hymn, President Grant in the article already referred to says:

> As long as I live I shall never forget the wonderful impression and the spirit that accompanied the singing of this hymn at the funeral of Brother Clayton in the Fourteenth Ward when Brother John Lewis, a writer of music of some of our hymns, led the choir and the Saints. The congregation arose and sang this hymn and I felt the inspiration of the Lord and of the man who wrote it (whose remains were lying before us), was there with us. I had never before, nor have I since, been so impressed with any other congregational hymn or with this one as at Brother Clayton's funeral.†

The *Journal* of William Clayton, published in 1921, though long delayed, is among the most valuable documents of Pioneer history.

William Clayton

†Gleaned from sketches of William Clayton's life in the L. D. S. *Biographical Encyclopedia* and William Clayton's *Journal*.

Come, Follow Me

Words by John Nicholson   **Music by S. McBurney**

The Hymn

"Come, Follow Me" is a hymn of exhortation - gentle in its entreaty but positive in its promise of the rewards to one who will follow the teachings of the Savior.

The Composer

S. McBurney: While nothing has come to hand of the life of McBurney, his music in this hymn and in "While of These Emblems" bespeaks an academic background.

The Author — John Nicholson (See No. 217)

No. 15

Come Go with Me, Beyond the Sea

Words by Cyrus Hubbard Wheelock   **Music Arr. by Thomas C. Griggs**

The Hymn

The hymn "Come Go with Me" envisions the land of "Zion" in the everlasting hills. This song should be sung with just a little nostalgic sentimentality.

The Composer

The tune of "Come Go With Me, beyond the Sea" is probably of secular origin from the nineteenth century. Thomas G. Griggs 1840-1903, an assistant conductor of the Tabernacle Choir and composer of the radio theme song of the Tabernacle Choir "Gently Raise the Sacred Strain," arranged this song for inclusion in the 1889 Latter-day Saint Psalmody.

The Author

Cyrus Hubbard Wheelock, president of the Northern States Mission from 1878 to 1879, was born February 28, 1813, in Henderson, Jefferson County, New York, a son of Asa Wheelock and Lucy Hubbard. He was baptized in 1839 and filled a mission in Vermont, and other missions in the states in the early days. His labor with Governor Ford in behalf of the Prophet Joseph Smith and the other brethren, while they were incarcerated in Carthage Jail, is a matter of history. He was a gifted orator and was set apart in 1878 as president of the Northern States mission then comprising Michigan, Wisconsin, Minnesota, Iowa, and Illinois. He returned in August 1879 and died October 11, 1894 in Mount Pleasant, Utah.

Come, Hail the Cause

Words by Bertha Kleinman   **Music from a German Christmas Song**

The Hymn

"Come, Hail the Cause of Zion's Youth" is a Mutual Improvement Association rally song. As a typical example of the way tunes came into the hymnody by uncritical folk choice, the quotation below is a paraphrase of an account of the creation of a Mormon hymn with a borrowed tune as told to Leroy Wilkes, author of a "Thesis on Borrowed Music" in the Latter-day Saint Hymnal. Mrs. Bertha A. Kleinman in an interview on December 23, 1936 in Mesa, Arizona said:

> Around the year 1935 President Oscar A. Kirkham of the First Council of Seventy of The Church of Jesus Christ of Latter-day Saints, visited in Mesa to preside over a Mutual Improvement Association convention held in the Maricopa Stake. A spontaneously musical person, Elder Kirkham suggested in the morning session of the convention, "Let's have a song of our own for Maricopa Stake. Some of you writers go home and write some songs and bring them back to us for the afternoon session. Never mind about the music, just adapt your words to some well-known melody and we'll sing it. I started to write "Come, Hail the Cause of Zion's Youth, M.I.A. Our M.I.A." After writing the first line or two, the tune "Maryland, My Maryland" came to mind, and from that point on, I conceived the rest of the poem, as set to that melody.
>
> Elder Kirkham met with a committee before the afternoon session of the convention to hear the three or four songs which we had written. He became enthusiastic about "Come, Hail the Cause of Zion's Youth." In the convention, he had everyone sing it, then he sang it alone. After the meeting, he told me that he wanted to take the song with him to Salt Lake City and make it a song for the general MIA. The next I saw it, it was printed in the MIA *Recreational Song Book*.

Mrs. Kleinman says of this song,

> I have other songs I much prefer, but—so it is.

The Composer

When the evergreen tree became a Christian symbol as a part of the Christmas festivities in the time of Martin Luther, there also came into existence songs or carols about the tree—most notable of which was "O Tannenbaum" (O Christmas Tree). The tune for this carol was of German folk song origin. The state of Maryland uses it for their State song - "Maryland, My Maryland."

The Author

Mrs. Bertha Kleinman had her first poem published when she was only twelve years old. She has written hundreds of poems, hymns, short stories, dramas, and pageants since then. Her work has been published in such magazines as *Ladies Home Journal, Musician,* the *Quarterly Review, Arizona Highways, Harper's Bazaar, Business Outlook.* Poems have appeared in five national anthologies. Last year saw the publication of her book of poems, *Through the Years.*

Message of the Ages, her first pageant, written in 1930, has been followed by ten others. A Thanksgiving ode won third place in the nation over 2500. Her "Ode to the Danish Flag" won acknowledgement and praise from King Carl Christian X, of Denmark.

Civic consciousness has also had a place in Mrs. Kleinman's busy life. She served as publicity chairman for the Musicians club, as the city librarian; as legislative and education chairman for the Women's club; as stenographer for the Rotary Club. These activities came to an end when she was appointed assistant recorder in the Arizona Temple, Church of Jesus Christ of Latter-day Saints, a position she has held for twenty-six years until her recent retirement. Mrs. Kleinman has been the recipient of several honors—the Rotary Award for outstanding citizenship in 1957; Gov. McFarland's proclamation on her 80th birthday, of Bertha Kleinman Day in Arizona; the first David O. McKay Humanities Award from BYU.

In 1958 the Fine Arts committee of the Mesa writers club presented her with a plaque and named her the Club's Artist of the year.

Bertha A. Kleinman

Come Let Us Anew

Words by Charles Wesley   **Music by James Lucas**

The Hymn

This hymn is used widely as a New Year's hymn which, due to the import of the words, was first published in 1750 in a penny tract entitled "Hymns for New Year's Day." It is used throughout the world by the Methodists in their Watchnight and Covenant Services.

The Composer

The Latter-day Saint Hymns ascribe the tune of "Come, Let Us Anew" to a James Lucas-1726.

This is also the opinion of a few other hymnologists but certainty in the matter cannot be established. In the American Tune Book, the title of the hymn is Lucas', but it is not known whether this has to do with the composer or something else.

The rhythm of the hymn is altered in "Latter-day Saint Hymns" from that printed in "The American Tune Book" and several fermatas have been interpolated. The soprano and alto duet in measures 16-20 is now joined by the bass and tenor doubling with it one octave lower.

The Author — Charles Wesley (See No. 10)

No. 18

Come, Ye Disconsolate

Words by Thomas Moore   **Music by Samuel Webbe**

The Hymn

This hymn was written in 1816 and revised in 1831 by Thomas Hastings. "Come, Ye Disconsolate" is an invitation to pray. The final line is positive assurance of the goodness of the Lord to those who will seek him! "Earth has no sorrow that heaven cannot heal."

The Composer

Samuel Webbe 1740-1816 was the composer of this music. Lowell Mason and Thomas Hastings arranged it for a four-part hymn tune. They published it in 1831.

The Author

Thomas Moore 1779-1852 was born in Dublin and became a lawyer. He wrote a great deal of poetry which he recited in fashionable homes in London among the elite social set. Finally financial difficulties made a wreck of his life, and he died in poverty. "Come, Ye Disconsolate" is the only hymn which survives him.

Come Along, Come Along

Words by William Willes   **Music by A. C. Smyth**

The Hymn

"Come Along, Come Along" is a hymn of exhortation written in the form of the rhythmical gospel song, with a verse and chorus. This song should be sung joyously with a measured tread.

The Composer — A. C. Smyth (See No. 136)

The Author

William Willes was born July 5, 1814 in Woolwich, London, England. His father was a plumber, painter, and glazier. William entered school at the age of three and continued until the age of 12 when his father died. It was planned that William would become a seaman on a whaler. However, these plans were altered by the death of his brother, which necessitated William's carrying on his father's business. William later attended a normal school and at the age of 22 was placed in charge of a boys' school in Cardiff, Wales. He continued to teach in different parts of Britain until he was baptized into The Church of Jesus Christ of Latter-day Saints in 1848.

He was baptized in the Thames River at night, and his dismissal as master of Woolwich British and Foreign School followed. After failing in three more attempts to open schools, William left on his first mission for the Church to India. He later filled another mission in India and one in Britain. In India the missionaries had to travel by foot to the interior carrying all their belongings on their backs. Other hazards also awaited them in India, namely wild beasts such as leopards and tigers, and they depended entirely upon "the guardian care of our Heavenly Father." They performed many baptisms in India, and at Mirzapari William baptized a Brahaman priest. William's companion during these travels was Elder Joseph Richards.

Following his mission to India in 1853 William Willes migrated to the U.S. where he became a "pillar in the Sunday Schools." He was called as a Sabbath School Missionary in the 1870's, where, with a companion, George Goddard, they became known as "the Sunday School Twins." Their stories, songs, and long beards were familiar to Sunday School children from one end of the Territory of Utah to the other. In the words of George D. Pyper: "It was a gala day when these two men visited a Sunday School. They sang 'Who's

On the Lord's Side, Who?' and 'A Mormon Boy.' These two men,
I venture to say, by their songs and stories, had a greater influence
in indoctrinating the boys and girls in the Word of Wisdom than
any other medium."

In the mountains of Zion William Willes became known for
his teaching, singing, and song writing. In 1882 he completed a seven
year Sunday School Mission.

William Willes died in 1890, but the good he did among the
Sunday Schools of the Church echoes still. It always will so long as
members sing his well-known words in the song, "Thanks For the
Sabbath School."

No. 20

Come, O Thou King of Kings

Words by Parley P. Pratt   **Music Anon.**

The Hymn

Parley P. Pratt and twelve hundred men, women, and children
had been driven from their homes in Jackson County, Missouri, in
the autumn of 1833, by a murderous mob. Two hundred homes were
burned and families separated. Many of the Saints were killed and
others brutally flogged. Cattle were either shot or confiscated, hay and
grain burned, and the people forced across the river into Clay County.

It was amid such trying and perilous times, no doubt, that Parley P. Pratt wrote "Come, O Thou King of Kings." It was a fervent
cry to the God of Israel to come and set his people free; an appeal to
the mighty King of kings to make an end of sin which was gripping
the world, and to cleanse the world by fire; a prayer that the time
might soon come when the Saints in happier songs and rejoicings,
might enjoy a reign of peace. The hymnist looked forward to the day
when all the ransomed throng would join in singing a new triumphant
song, filling the heavens with anthems from Zion's Hill. The hymn
ends in a paean of praise to the Prince of Life and Peace, the Lord
and Savior, before whom all nations shall bow the knee and every
tongue give praise.

Parley P. Pratt's life was full of trials and persecutions. He rarely
found the peace his soul desired and finally gave up his life for the
cause. That he had a premonition of his death is evidenced by a statement written by him in the preface to the second edition of the *Voice
of Warning* printed in 1846, as follows: "Should the author be called
upon to sacrifice his life for the cause of truth, he will have the consolation that it will be said of him, as it was said of Abel, 'He being

27

dead yet speaketh'." Not only will Parley P. Pratt, though dead, speak through his *Voice of Warning*, but even more powerfully will he be heard through the voice of song.

Just when this hymn was written is not known except that it was during the time of dire persecution experienced by the Saints and in which he shared. It was included in Emma Smith's ninety favored selections which were published in 1835.*

The Composer

The hymn "Come, O Thou King of Kings" has been sung to many tunes including "Arise, my Soul, Arise," (Careless), Giardini's "Italian Hymn" and a fine tune by John Goss. The present tune was called "Sanford" and has been used since 1889. Its composer is unknown. The hymn is essentially a choir hymn and calls for good base and tenor sections to give it musical completeness. Its climactic fifth phrase is impressive.

The Author

Parley Parker Pratt, the author of "An Angel from on High," was one of the most fruitful hymn writers and dynamic personages of the early history of the Church of Jesus Christ of Latter-day Saints. He was born April 12, 1807, at Burlington, Otsego County, New York, the son of Jared and Charity Pratt. His forebears, seven generations before him, were among the first settlers of Hartford, Connecticut, having arrived there in 1639.

Like his parents, Parley was of a serious frame of mind, and was an intelligent searcher after truth. Of a religious nature, he early joined the Baptist Church. At nineteen he left his New York home and settled thirty miles West of Cleveland, Ohio. In 1827 he returned to Canaan, New York, where he married Thankful Halsey, and the couple moved to Parley's home near Cleveland; eighteen months later attracted by the preaching of Sidney Rigdon, who came into his neighborhood, he joined the "Disciples" and decided to devote his life's work to the ministry.

However, the Lord had a work for Parley P. Pratt to do, and while en route to visit his relatives in New York, Parley stopped at Newark and there first heard of the Book of Mormon. It thrilled him, and he went to Palmyra to investigate. In quick succession he met Hyrum Smith and Oliver Cowdery, believed and was baptized by Cowdery in Senaca Lake, New York, and ordained an elder. Soon after, Parley baptized his brother Orson. In 1831 he met the Prophet Joseph Smith by whom he was ordained a high priest. From then on

---

* From George D. Pyper's *Stories of Latter-day Saint Hymns.*

until his tragic death by assassination, May 13, 1857, he was one of the most active leaders of the Church.

Parley P. Pratt began the writing of hymns and poems early in life. The first we have record of were included in the Latter-day Saint Hymnbook, published in 1835, assembled by Emma Smith, pursuant to a revelation given through her prophet-husband. The preface to this collection is interesting, and reads as follows:

> In order to sing by the spirit and with the understanding it is necessary that The Church of the Latter-day Saints should have a selection of "sacred hymns" adapted to their faith and belief in the gospel, and as far as can be holding forth the promise made to the Fathers who died in the faith of a glorious resurrection and a thousand years reign on earth with the Son of Man in his glory.
>
> Notwithstanding the Church, as it were, is still in its infancy, yet as the song of the righteous is a prayer unto God, it is sincerely hoped that the following collection, selected with an eye single to his glory may answer every purpose till more are composed, or till we are blessed with a copious variety of the songs of Zion.

In the preface to his poems, copyright in New York in 1839, Parley P. Pratt gives us a graphic recital of conditions under which most of his hymns were written.

> When these poems were written the author had no intention of compiling them in one volume. They sprang into existence one after another as occasion called them forth, at times and in places and under circumstances widely varying. Some came forth upon the bank of the far-famed Niagara, and some were the plaintive strains poured from a full heart in the lonely dungeons of Missouri where the author was confined upwards of eight months during the late persecution. Some were poured forth from the top of the White Mountains in New Hampshire, and other were uttered while wandering over the flowery plains and wide extended prairies of the West, and some in the forest; some were the melting strains of joy and admiration in contemplating the approaching dawn of that glorious day which shall crown the earth and its inhabitants with universal peace and rest; and others were produced on the occasion of taking leave of my family, friends, or the great congregation, on a mission to other and distant parts, and some were wrung from a bosom overflowing with grief at the loss of those who were nearest and dearest to my heart.

An interesting story is told in *The Life of John Taylor* of a conversation between Brother Taylor and Brother Pratt. It seems that when Brother Taylor arrived in New York on his way to England he landed there with only one cent in his pocket. Asked as to his circumstances he replied that he had plenty. Brother Pratt, hearing this and being much in need of means to publish his writings, approached Brother Taylor, and said: "Brother Taylor, I hear you have plenty of money." "Yes, Brother Pratt, that's true," responded Brother Taylor. "Well," said Parley, "I am about to publish my *Voice of Warning* and *Millennial Poems;* I am very much in need of money, and if you will furnish me two hundred dollars, I will be much obliged."

"You are welcome to all I have," said Brother Taylor, and pulling his hand out of his pocket handed Parley his copper cent.

"But I thought you gave it out that you had plenty of money," said Brother Pratt.

"Yes, and so I have," replied Brother Taylor. "I am well clothed; you furnish me with plenty to eat and drink and good lodging. With all these things and a penny over, as I owe nothing, is not that plenty?"

History does not tell us how Parley P. Pratt got the money, but he was not a man to be discouraged and the books were published.

The first issue of the *Millennial Star* was published in March, 1840, with Parley P. Pratt as editor. Referring to this in his autobiography he says:

> While engaged in editing the *Star.* I . . . also assisted my brethren in selecting, compiling and publishing a hymn book. In this work were contained near fifty of my original hymns and songs, composed expressly for the book and most of them written during the press of duties which then crowded upon me.

The following story is also typical of many which could be written of the illustrious man;

He was crossing the Atlantic on one of his missions to England. Owing to a lack of means he was in the steerage. The Fourth of July occurred in mid-ocean, and the passengers on the upper deck, wishing to celebrate, were looking around for an orator. Someone suggested the Mormon apostle on the lower deck. He was sent for and came up.

It happened that Elder Pratt was then rather shabbily dressed, for reasons which are not given. His looks greatly disappointed the elite who were to listen to him. But they said nothing, and he was introduced as the "orator of the day." His oration entranced his audience, for Elder Pratt had a real gift of eloquence. After it was over, the men carried him about the deck on their shoulders. They said it was the finest speech they had ever heard. Another Mormon elder, who had listened to him on this occasion, said the same thing.

On the strength of that speech Parley P. Pratt was invited to ride first class for the rest of the voyage. His poor clothes were forgotten in view of his eloquent tongue.

No. 21
Think Not, When You Gather to Zion
Words by Eliza R. Snow   **Music by John Tullidge**

The Hymn

"Think Not, When You Gather to Zion" is not in any sense a hymn. Rather, it is a poem of warning to Saints who assemble in Zion. The problems of community living are told poetically by Eliza R. Snow but in realistic terms.

The Composer — John Tullidge (See No. 224)

The Author — Eliza R. Snow (See No. 139)

No. 22
Come unto Jesus
Words and Music by O. P. Huish

The Hymn

"Come unto Jesus" is a hymn of entreaty and encouragement to live in accordance with the teachings of the Savior.

The Author and Composer — O. P. Huish (See No. 85)

No. 23
Come, Ye Children of the Lord
Words by James H. Wallis   **Spanish Melody**

The Hymn

"Come, Ye Children of the Lord" is a favorite hymn with Latterday Saint congregations because of lively rhythm and buoyant text.

The Composer

Benjamin Carr, 1768-1831, arranged this tune from a Spanish Melody, according to W. L. Wilkes in "Borrowed music in Mormon hymnals." It was a four stanza setting of "Far, Far o'er Hill and Dell," popular as a parlor piece.

The Author

James Hearknett Wallis, bishop of the Vernal 1st ward, Uintah Stake, Utah, from 1927 to 1930+, was born in April, 1861 in London, England, a son of James Wallis and Jane Sarah Booth. He was baptized May 20, 1877, and came to Utah in 1881. He was ordained an elder in 1880 by John Nicholson, filled several missions; was ordained a high priest in 1913 by Francis M. Lyman; was ordained a bishop in October 1928, by George Albert Smith.

No. 24
Behold Thy Sons and Daughters

Words by Parley P. Pratt   **Music by Alexander Schreiner**

The Hymn

The music of this hymn was composed in response to assignment by the General Music Committee. It is intended to be sung by choir or congregation at times following baptism, when candidates are confirmed into the church. The hymn is completely one of our own, in authorship, and more important, in doctrine.

The Composer

Alexander Schreiner, organist of the Tabernacle, Salt Lake City, is the son of John Christian and Margaret Schwemmer Schreiner. His parents joined the Church in 1903 and soon thereafter offered their home to the members of the branch of the Church for regular Sacrament services, Sunday School, and choir rehearsals. This afforded their son opportunity to hear church music at an early age. When only five, at a Christmas program, he played in public for the first time. He was baptized at the age of eight, at which time he was also appointed organist for the Sunday School, Sacrament meeting, choir rehearsal, and the midweek Bible hour. At this time he studied the piano and violin.

At the age of twenty he played his first recitals on the Tabernacle organ. In 1921 he left for a mission in California. His fame was well-established by then. During his first year of missionary work eight different organist's positions were offered him, greatly to the pride and astonishment of his missionary companions. Of course these offers of professional engagements could not entice him away from his missionary work, and so all were refused. However, with the permission of his mission president, he played a number of concert engagements dedicating new organs in various denominational churches, one of which was the large organ in Angelus Temple, Los Angeles. During the last part of his mission he presided over the Los Angeles Conference of thirty-five missionaries. He was released in March, 1924.

Upon his return to Salt Lake City he was appointed to the position of organist at the Tabernacle. In September 1924 he left for Europe, and for two years in Paris he studied harmony and counterpart with Henri Libert, and organ with Charles Marie Widor and Louis

Vierne, the latter being organist at Notre Dame Cathedral. He was invited frequently to play various organs, and thus had good opportunity to study their design and construction.

For nine years, 1930-39, Alexander Schreiner divided his time between the Salt Lake Tabernacle and the University of California at Los Angeles at which latter institution he was a member of the faculty. He was also director of music at Wilshire Boulevard Temple which belongs to one of the most important Jewish congregations in the world. At the Fox Motion Picture Studios he assisted John Mc-Cormack, the great Irish tenor, in the making of one of his motion pictures.

Alexander Schreiner has not only been an organist in the Church all his life, but has held various other offices. Before he was twelve years of age he was ordained to the office of a deacon. At one time he was superintendent of the Sunday School in Cannon Ward, Pioneer Stake. He was a member of the high council in Hollywood Stake. He believes that everyone should train himself to be of some service in the Church, and that when the call comes to fill an office he should work faithfully and joyfully for the Lord and his Church.

He is a fervent believer in liberal education. He believes that faithfulness to the Church together with a thorough education is a good guarantee of a successful life. He believes that children should learn to do many good things early in life. His two sons, at the ages of seven and nine respectively, learned to use a typewriter with the correct fingering. One son has been organist for junior Sunday School since he was seven years old.

Alexander Schreiner is greatly interested in improving the music in the chapels of the Church. He believes that the sacred music of a church organ is one of the strongest means of leading the minds of worshipers to lofty thoughts. To help ward and Sunday School organists in choosing suitable sacred music, he has written a book of devotional music entitled *Organ Voluntaries*. This book is in use in many of our chapels, and is used in thousands of churches throughout the United States.

Alexander Schreiner, Ph.D., F.A.G.O., is organist of the Tabernacle in Salt Lake City. Millions of people have heard him broadcast over the Columbia Network and have heard his recitals in the Tabernacle. He has been listed seven times among the nation's top radio artists in the *Musical America* radio polls. He is in demand throughout the continent for concerts which require part of his time each year. Dr. Schreiner played his first recitals in the Tabernacle at the age of twenty and was appointed to the position of organist in 1924.

He is Fellow of the American Guild of Organists; author of three volumes of organ music, published by J. Fischer & Bros., New York, and has three additional volumes in preparation. He is a member of honor societies Phi Beta Kappa and Phi Kappa Phi. He is listed in *Who's Who in America* and *International Who's Who*.

Dr. Schreiner is married and has four children. The critics have said of him:

Exhibition of magic at keyboard and pedals. As a master of footwork, he probably stands supreme.

— Toronto

Took listeners up into high regions by sheer power and grandeur.

— Los Angeles

Draws throng. Largest audience ever gathered here for organ concert.

— Portland

The Author — Parley P. Pratt (See No. 20)

Alexander Schreiner

34

Come We that Love the Lord

Words by Isaac Watts   **Music by Aaron Williams**

The Hymn

"Come We that Love the Lord" is not one of Isaac Watts' greatest hymns, but its phraseology shows a master hand.

The Composer

There is some doubt as to who the composer of "Come We that Love the Lord" is, but in the Latter-day Saint hymnal it is ascribed to Aaron Williams. For a short hymn, it is academically well-written and has a certain amount of appeal. Aaron Williams was born in 1731 and died in 1776.

The Author — Isaac Watts (See No. 168)

Dear to the Heart of the Shepherd

Words by Mary B. Wingate   **Music by William J. Kirkpatrick**

The Hymn

"Dear to the Heart of the Shepherd" is a very popular gospel song with Latter-day Saints.

Its appeal comes largely from the form of its musical setting, with a duet verse and a four-part chorus.

The Composer

"Dear to the Heart of the Shepherd" was composed by a leader of the gospel song movement, James Kirkpatrick. It is made of a duet verse, and a four-part chorus. It first appeared as a Latter-day Saint incorporation in the 1909 Deseret Sunday School book. The duet was arranged for tenor and alto in the 1909 printing, but when it was transferred to the Latter-day Saint Hymnal of 1950, the duet was set for soprano and alto, a much less effective arrangement but more practical.

For additional information see No. 71.

The Author

The year of the birth of Mary B. Wingate is all the information concerning her that can be found. She was born in 1899.

Do What Is Right

Words anonymous   Music E. Kaillmark Arr. F. Smith

The Hymn

This Mormon hymn was not among those selected by Emma
Smith.* As far as known it is not of Latter-day Saint origin, but is
one of those soulful poems adopted by the Church—a waif in the
realm of song. How it came to be included in our hymnbook is told
by Assistant Church Historian, A. William Lund. He says that in a
conversation with the late Duncan M. McAllister, which occurred
just before Brother McAllister's death, the latter said that while
George Q. Cannon was presiding over the British Mission, on one
occasion he attended a conference in Scotland and there heard sung
for the first time, the hymn "Do What Is Right." He was so impressed
with it that when the twelfth edition of the Latter-day Saints' hymnbook was published in 1863 under George Q. Cannon's direction,
this hymn was included in the collection, but no one had any knowledge of who wrote it.

"Do What Is Right" cannot be classified as a sacred hymn, and
is doubtful if the author ever considered it as such. It is not a "sacred
poem expressive of devotion or spiritual experience." But if it is not
a message of divine truth, there never was one written. It is a simple
sermon and contains admonitions that appeal to the Mormon heart.
George Q. Cannon recognized its value when he heard it in that
Scottish conference. He saw in it a message of hope; a song of promise;
an urge to be "faithful and fearless," and one that fitted in with Mormon philosophy.

This song must have been written by one who had been in the
shadows, but was now bursting the shackles of ignorance and beginning to see the light.

The last stanza is a call to remain true and press forward to the
coveted goal, where blessings attend those who are faithful to the end.

It is a beloved, adopted child in Mormon hymnody.

The Tune

The tune used in "Do What Is Right," is adapted from the popular son, "The Old Oaken Bucket," words of which were written by
Samuel Woodworth who was born in Greenbush, in the township of
Scituate, Massachusetts, January 13, 1785. He was of humble birth,
his people belonging to the farmer and plantation class. "The Old

---

*From George D. Pyper's *Stories of Latter-day Saint Hymns*

Oaken Bucket" was among the first American songs—the kind that appealed to the popular fancy in that day. It was written in the summer of 1817. The well referred to is still there, it is asserted, but the bucket no longer hangs in it. Samuel liked urban communities and early became apprenticed to a printer in Boston named Benjamin Russell. From there he went to New Haven, then to New York, where he conducted weekly papers named *The War, The Halcyon* and *The Ladies' Gazette.* In 1823 when thirty-eight years of age, with George P. Morris he established the *New York Mirror* which for many years was the leading dramatic authority in America. He was the author of a romance of the War of 1812 entitled *Champions of Freedom.* He died December 9, 1842.

Though Woodworth was not a Southerner, his song became very popular, especially in the South, where the well and oaken bucket were about the only means of obtaining good water. Out of the many songs written by Woodworth, "The Old Oaken Bucket" is the only one to place his name on the pages of history.

It is regrettable that such a forthright, positive challenge as is found in this hymn could not have been traditionally associated with more worthy music and a less ignoble connotation. "Do What Is Right, Let the Consequence Follow" has no counterpart in religious admonition.

The tune was probably written by an E. Kaillmark.

No. 28

The Lord Be with Us

Words by John Ellerton   **Music by Tracy Y. Cannon**

The Hymn

Tracy Y. Cannon comments as follows on this hymn:

"The words of this hymn were written by John Ellerton, and I chose them because I felt there was need for hymns suitable for use at the close of an evening sacrament meeting."

The Composer — Tracy Y. Cannon (See biographical sketch No. 1)

The Author

John Ellerton was born in London in 1826, and received his education in King Williams College and Trinity College, Cambridge, where he was given both a B.A. and M.A. degree.

He began his career as author by writing hymns for children. Many of his hymns appeared in the *Churchman's Family Magazine* and later in *Hymn Collections.* Ellerton was a consultant during his life for every noteworthy English Hymnal. He died in 1893.

37

Come, Ye Thankful People, Come

Words by Dean Henry Alford **Music by Sir George Job Elvey**

The Hymn

"Come, Ye Thankful People, Come," is a very pleasant hymn to sing or hear. It is widely used in America as a Thanksgiving hymn. It is the second hymn to be sung to Elvey's tune, the first being "Hark! the Song of Jubilee."

The Composer

George J. Elvey was an English organist and composer. In 1835 he became organist and chorister at St. George's Chapel in Windsor, succeeding his teacher, Highmore Sheats. He received a Doctorate of Music from Oxford University in 1840 and was knighted in 1871.

He composed many sacred works, including a number of hymns. Some of his larger works were performed in America. He was born in 1816 and died in 1893.

The Author

Henry Alford's instincts were literary. He edited a paper known as *The Contemporary Review*, published a volume of *English Poetry*, and another on the Queen's English.

He revised the *New Testament"* in 1881 in collaboration with a committee, edited an edition of *Homer*, and wrote a four volume critical commentary on the *Greek Testament*. He translated and wrote many hymns.

His unsatisfied longing to visit the Holy Land accounts for the inscription on his tombstone, "The Inn of a Pilgrim Traveling to Jerusalem." He was born in 1810 and died in 1871.

Earth with Her Ten Thousand Flowers

Words by W. W. Phelps **Music by Thomas G. Griggs**

The Hymn

In the hymn "Earth with Her Ten Thousand Flowers" all of the beauties of the earth, the songs of the birds and the hopes of the human heart bear only one record-"God Is Love." Truly W. W. Phelps has given us an uplifting message in this hymn-"God Is Love."

The Composer — Thomas G. Griggs (See No. 92)

The Author — W. W. Phelps (See No. 213)

No. 31
Ere You Left Your Room This Morning

Words by Mrs. M. A. Kidder   **Music by William Oscar Perkins**

The Hymn

No other hymn in any hymnal is quite as cogent in reminding one of his daily religious duty as "Ere You Left Your Room This Morning, Did You Think to Pray?" Daily prayer is a commandment from the Lord "Evening, and morning, and at noon will I pray, and cry aloud; and he shall hear my voice." Psalm 55-17.

The Composer

W. O. Perkins was an American composer and teacher who was born in Stockbridge, Vermont in 1831. He studied first in Boston and later in London and Milan, Italy. He made his home in Boston where he taught music until his death in 1902. Mr. Perkins was given a Doctorate of Music in 1879 by Hamilton College. He composed and published over forty collections of songs and anthems. He died in 1902.

The Author

Mary A. Kidder was a native of Boston, being born in 1820, but resided in New York for forty-six years. She belonged to the Methodist Church and was a faithful worker.

She died at the age of eighty-six years in Chelsea, Mass. in 1905.

No. 32
Come, Sing to the Lord

Words and Music by Gerrit de Jong, Jr.

The Hymn

The following was written by Gerrit de Jong, Jr., about this hymn:

> When an edition of hymns was going to be printed, Tracy Y. Cannon, chairman of the Church Music Committee, asked me to send him a congregational hymn. I wrote it in a few minutes after Sunday School and had a quartet sing it in Sacrament meeting that night in the Highland Park Ward.

The Composer and Author

Gerrit de Jong, Jr. was born in 1892 in Amsterdam, Holland. He came to America in July, 1906 and joined the Latter-day Saint Church in 1908. He received his education in Holland and America. In 1920 he graduated from the University of Utah, received a Master's degree in 1925, and a Ph.D. at Stanford University in 1933.

He is a professional musician and studied in Germany, France, Austria, and Mexico.

Professor de Jong is an ardent church worker. He is a member of the general board of the Sunday School, former member of the General Music Committee, is also former Dean of Fine Arts at Brigham Young University, and is the author of several books; *Greater Dividends from Religion; Living the Gospel; The Gospel Plan;* and Sunday School manuals. He is a gifted linguist having preached the gospel in six languages.

No. 33

Far, Far Away On Judea's Plains

Words and Music by John M. Macfarlane

The Hymn

John M. Macfarlane found a need for more Christmas carols so he wrote "Far, Far Away on Judea's Plains," the popularity of which has reached far beyond our own church bounds. It is best sung when all four voice parts are well sustained.

The Composer and Author

The words and tune of "Far, Far Away on Judea's Plains" were the work of John Menzies Macfarlane, son of John and Annabella Sinclair Macfarlane, born October 11, 1833, at Sterling, near the city

John M. Macfarlane

40

of Glasgow, Scotland. His father was a duke's coachman and when the Queen of England visited Scotland, he was assigned as her coachman. The father died when John was quite young. John came to America with the family and settled in Cedar City, Utah, in 1851 or 1852, where he married Ann Chatterley. He organized a choir, and when St. George was settled, he took his choir there and gave a concert to cheer up the people. After the concert Erastus Snow said to him: "We need a choir in St. George. You go home, sell out, and come down here to live." This he did. In the meantime, he helped settle Toquerville and built the first house there.

When the late Bishop Scanlan of the Catholic Church visited Silver Reef, a flourishing mining camp in those days, he expressed a desire to hold mass in St. George. The Latter-day Saint authorities, with a liberality for which they are noted, consented, and Brother Macfarlane trained his choir for six weeks learning the Latin Mass. It was given in the St. George Tabernacle.

Brother Macfarlane was a valuable citizen in a pioneer community. Besides being a district judge, a surveyor, a builder, he was able to play on almost any musical instrument. He died in 1892.*

No. 34
Father in Heaven
Words by Agnus S. Hibbard   **Music by Friedrich F. Flemming**
The Hymn

"Father in Heaven" is one of several part songs composed by Friedrich Ferdinand Flemming.

It was originally a men's chorus setting of a famous ode by Horace, *Integer Vitae*. It is the opinion of your author that the time signature of this hymn should be changed to two half measure, "Father in Heaven" is a fervent prayer for peace.

The Composer

Nothing more of Friedrich F. Flemming has come to hand except the year of his birth and death, 1778 and 1813.

The Author

In many early hymn Collections this tune is used with a text by John Greenleaf Whittier called "At Last."

Agnus S. Hibbard, who wrote "Father in Heaven" is an obscure author about whom nothing seems to be available.

---

*From George D. Pyper's *Stories of Latter-day Saint Hymns*.

Farewell, All Earthly Honors

Words by Mary W. Bone   **Music by William B. Bradbury**

The Hymn

"Farewell, All Earthly Honors" is a funeral hymn written in the form of the typical gospel song.

The Composer — William B. Bradbury (See No. 166)

The Author

Mary Wagstaff Bone, daughter of Isaac and Mary Bethsheba Gillions Wagstaff was born the 25th of February 1811 at Upper Caldecote, Bedfordshire, England, and grew to womanhood in this vicinity.

December 5, 1833 she married William Bone at North Hill, Brookend, England, and was the mother of seven children.

Hearing and being converted to the new religion by Mormon missionaries, she was baptized into The Church of Jesus Christ of Latter-day Saints, March 22, 1854 by Elder John Sears.

Loyal to their hearts' conviction, that it was a duty and a privilege to come to Utah, live with the Saints, and help to build up Zion, they crossed the plains in the year 1861, little realizing where they were going and the trials and hardships of pioneer life. They arrived in Salt Lake City in August or September, and went to Lehi, Utah, where their son, John, had settled two years earlier, and made their home there.

She was always cheerful, neat, and thrifty.

In later life she became very ill. In her severe suffering she never lost hope nor doubted her trust in God and faith in the life hereafter. At this time she composed the words of the song "Farewell, All Earthly Honors" which was published in the LDS Hymnbook and for many years was a great favorite for funeral services.

She passed away at her home in Lehi, Utah October 29, 1875 and is buried at Lehi.

God of Power, God of Right

Words by Wallace F. Bennett   **Music by Tracy Y. Cannon**

The Hymn

"God of Power, God of Right" is a fervent prayer to the God of power, right, wisdom, truth, mercy, and love.

Elder Bennett gives an account of the writing of his hymn in the following paragraphs:

There isn't a very dramatic story to tell about my writing the words to the hymn "God of Power." I was very conscious of the project under way at that time to produce a new church hymnal for adult use. I cannot remember who encouraged me to turn my hand to writing words for a hymn. At any rate, the idea intrigued me, and I worked at it casually. However, one Sunday morning, I woke up with the feeling that I could sit down and write the whole text. There was no set of words clearly in my mind, but rather a string of ideas. Within an hour, the text of this hymn was written, and I struggled only over one word. The word "kindliness' at the end of the first verse is the one thing in the text with respect to which I still feel somewhat uncertain.

I am not prepared to go so far as to say this was inspiration, but certainly the hymn almost wrote itself, and I didn't struggle over it as I have done over many of the other things I have written.

This hymn is not sung very frequently, though it has been scheduled once or twice by the Sunday School as the song of the month. I am always thrilled to hear it, however, and I have one delightful memory that when in 1950 I was assigned to conduct the Sunday School Convention in the Hawaiian Islands, I went out on a Sunday morning and visited a number of Sunday Schools. Undoubtedly my presence was known, because when in the middle of the service I walked into one, they were very consciously singing my hymn. I was very touched by their thoughtfulness.

The Composer — Tracy Y. Cannon (See No. 1)

The Author

Sen. Wallace F. Bennett, Republican Senator of Utah, is the son of a pioneer of the Old West. His father, John Bennett, was brought across the plains as a child in a covered wagon in 1868 with a group of Mormon pioneers. In 1896, he and others bought a bankrupt paint business; as its manager he built it into a thriving paint manufacturing and glass distributing organization.

Wallace F. Bennett entered the firm as office clerk in 1920, and became successively production manager, sales manager, treasurer, general manager, and, in 1938, president. The business expanded steadily, and now has about 250 employees.

In 1939, with three partners, he founded Bennett Motor Company, a Salt Lake Ford dealership, and in addition has been on the boards of directors of a number of Western companies.

43

After serving in the '30's as President of the National Glass Distributors Association, and Vice President of the National Paint Varnish & Lacquer Association, he was elected President of the National Association of Manufacturers in 1949. He was the first representative of small business to serve as president of the NAM.

In 1950 he ran as a Republican candidate against Democratic Sen. Elbert D. Thomas, who for years had been a pillar of the New Deal in the Senate. He won the election, and in 1956 was re-elected by a substantial majority.

During his eight years in the Senate, Senator Bennett has been most closely identified with problems of government finance. He is a member of the Banking and Currency Committee, and the powerful Finance Committee, which writes the nation's tax laws. During the past two years, he has been recognized as an Administration spokesman in the Senate on fiscal and monetary policies.

Senator Bennett considers inflation to be our No. 1 domestic problem, and as a result of his work in the Finance Committee, has discussed the problem before many audiences both in and out of govement.

He has always been active in the Church of Jesus Christ of Latter-day Saints, and since 1935 has served as national treasurer of the

Wallace F. Bennett

Church's Sunday School organization. In addition, he teaches a weekly Sunday School class in the Mormon Church in Chevy Chase, Maryland.

Senator Bennett is co-chairman of the Conference of Western Senators, and is a member of the Republican Senatorial Campaign Committee. He is author of two books, *Faith and Freedom* and *Why I Am a Mormon*.

No. 37
Up, Awake, Ye Defenders Of Zion

Words by Charles W. Penrose   Music Red, White, and Blue

The Hymn

This hymn was evidently written to stir the Saints against the intrusion of Johnston's Army in 1856, which came to put down the purported rebellion of the Pioneer settlers in the "Territory of Utah."

The Composer

The words of "Up, Awake, Ye Defenders of Zion" were fitted to the early American patriotic song "Columbia, the Gem of the Ocean."

Complete confusion exists as to the authorship of the song. One printed edition has "Composer and Author-David Shaw" while a later one gives Thomas a' Becket as composer and author with David T. Shaw as the arranger. Years prior to these American publications, the song was popular in England under two titles "Britannia, the Pride of the Ocean" and "The Red, White, and Blue."

It seems, according to one account, that a' Becket wrote the song and asked Shaw to sing it in the theatre where Shaw was the soloist. Shaw did so and the song became popular at once. Then a'Becket told Shaw not to have it published but Shaw secretly did so, giving his own name as the composer and author, Then a'Becket sued the publishing company which to make amends, put out a second publication with Thomas a'Becket as the author and composer and David T. Shaw as the arranger.

Both Shaw and a'Becket lived in the City of "brotherly love" Philadelphia.

The above account still does not clear up the mystery of who composed the tune and how it appeared in England so many years previous to the Shaw-a'Becket controversy. Paul Ward, in *Notes and Queries* July 1870 said, "Either the American version of 'Columbia, the Gem of the Ocean' came from England or the English version of 'Britannia the Pride of the Ocean' or the 'Red, White, and Blue' came from America." Certainly this is a statement of fact without declaration.

The Author — Charles W. Penrose (See No. 145)

No. 38

Each Cooing Dove

Words by Robert Morris　　　　　**Music by Horatio R. Palmer**

The Hymn

"Each Cooing Dove" is a gospel song in the form of reiterated word phrases in the alto, tenor, and bass parts arranged to act as accompaniment for the prolonged notes of the melody line. This arrangement gives a kind of antiphonal effect and is widely used in gospel songs.

The Composer — Horatio Richmond Palmer (See No. 106)

The Author

Robert Morris wrote "Each Cooing Dove" as he sat near the ruins of Capernaum on the banks of Lake Genneseret. He was born August 31, 1818 and became a distinguished scholar and expert in many scientific lines. In 1868 he was sent to Palestine by the United Order to work on historic and archeological research. Being a religious man, he served in the church in every way possible. His Christian ballad "Each Cooing Dove" secured him a lasting place in the memory of many a devout church goer. He died in 1888.

No. 39

The First Noel

Words Anonymous　　　　　**Traditional Christmas Carol**

The Hymn

"Noel, Noel" in France is a Christmas greeting which means "A joyous Christmas." The word "Noel," however, is the Latin for birth or birthplace. Therefore it refers to the Nativity. The poetry and rhythm in the various lines of this popular carol are by no means perfect, but this fact does not in any way detract from their charm.

The text of this carol is based on scriptures found in Luke second chapter, verses 8-20 and in Matthew second chapter, verses 2-9-10.

The Composer

"The First Noel" is claimed by both England and France. It appeared in print in England in 1833, but most authorities believe it originated in France in the 16th Century. The tune is strikingly simple, being an eight-measure theme repeated three times.

The Author

A traditional carol with probably folk-song origin.

No. 40
From Greenland's Icy Mountains

Words by Reginald Heber   **Music by Lowell Mason**

The Hymn

On the abutment of a railroad bridge in Wrexham, England, is a memorial tablet erected in 1926 which reads "To the glory of God and in memory of Reginald Heber, Bishop and poet who in the old vicarage near this site in 1819, wrote the missionary hymn 'From Greenland's Icy Mountains go Ye into All the World and Preach the Gospel to every creature'." The writing of the hymn had an interesting inception. Reginald Heber's father-in-law, who was dean of the church in Wrexham, asked Heber to write a hymn which could be sung at a missionary service which was to be held the next day.

Heber went into the corner of the room and while his father-in-law conversed with a group which was in the room at the time, began his writing. After a few minutes, so the story goes, Heber read the first three stanzas of the hymn he had written. "That will do very well," said the dean to which Heber replied "It is not finished." In a few more moments he had written a fourth stanza. The next day it was sung in the missionary service and has since been sung around the world.

The Composer

Lowell Mason (1792-1872) has been called the father of American church music. He was also the first to introduce the teaching of music in the public schools. His collections of hymns and sacred music were standard in the churches of America for a century. He composed new music for many English hymns," "From Greenland's Icy Mountains" being one of them. The original copy in Mason's own handwriting hangs in the Independent Presbyterian Church in Savannah, Georgia.

The Author

Reginald Heber's (1783-1825) life was a very happy one, being born in a home of wealth and culture. This did not deter him from becoming an ardent student of the Bible which he could at an early age quote almost in toto. He entered Oxford University at seventeen. His first writings of hymns was to fill an ambition to better the hymn singing in the Anglican Church of which he was Rector. Later, he was sent to Calcutta, India, and made a Bishop. Here he preached incessantly against the caste system that was so strong in that country.

No. 41
Father in Heaven We Do Believe

Words by Parley P. Pratt   **Music by Jane Romney Crawford**

The Hymn

"Father in Heaven We do Believe" is a hymn which expresses a firm belief in the promise of the Lord and a prayer that our sins may be forgiven so that those promises may be fulfilled with each of us.

The Composer

Jane Vilate Romney Crawford, organist and member of the general board of the Primary Association appointed May 1919, was born December 31,1883 in Salt Lake City, Utah, a daughter of Heber John Romney and Kate Ada Miller.

She attended the Salt Lake City schools and was a student of the University of Utah. She took private instruction in music, art, and kindergarten work. She filled a mission for the Latter-day Saint Church in 1905-1906 to the Northern States and in company with her husband, filled a mission to England in 1911-1913. She was an officer in the Ensign Stake Primary Association, Y.L.M.I.A., and Relief Society. Jane Crawford has been an instructor of music and served as a member of the Church Music Committee and as a member of the National Music Week Committee on three different occasions.

On June 16, 1909 she was married to Alexander Clyde Crawford. On April 16th, 1956, Mrs. Crawford passed away.

The Author — Parley P. Pratt (See No. 20)

No. 42
Carry On

Words by Ruth May Fox   **Music by Alfred Durham**

The Hymn

Leonard Grant Fox, son of Ruth May Fox, gives the following account of the writing of "Carry On":

> An invitation had been sent throughout the church (LDS) for a song — words and music — which would be appropriate for the M-Men and Gleaners to sing at the conference of the Mutual Improve-

ment Association scheduled for June, 1930, the centennial year of the Church.* A number of songs were submitted, but none was quite what had been hoped for. At a meeting of the executive officers of the M.I.A. the subject was discussed with some concern as the time was getting short. The meeting closed about noon, and Sister Fox was heard to say, "I guess I'll have to see what I can do." Sister Van Noy recalls, "That same afternoon she came and said, 'Elsie, will you type this up?' It was the lyrics to 'Carry On.' Next morning she brought the song, having changed only one word, and asked me to make several copies." Sister Rae Grant Taylor remarked, "I walked through the office of Ssister Fox and she handed me a sheet of paper, saying, 'Rae, how is this for the song?' I was thrilled."

But the music was needed. Brother Alfred M. Durham was invited by Sister Fox to write the music for "Carry On." A few days later he called on Sister Fox. They found a piano where Brother Durham played his composition. For some time they went over the song together. After this interview Sister Fox remarked, "The music is lovely, just what I had in mind, something lively and catchy, a tune everyone can sing easily."

Sometime later the M.I.A. sponsored a contest for a theme-song for their organization. "Carry On" was submitted, and it was chosen as winner and gained immediate popularity.

The song was introduced to the Church at the MMen—Gleaner Session of the M.I.A. Conference, June 8, 1930, where the entire program was presented by M Men and Gleaners. One man, J. Harold Keddington, was the chorister, and another, Lorin F. Wheelwright was the organist. Early in the program the song was sung by the M Men and Gleaners, who filled the body of the Tabernacle. While singing the words in the chorus, "Holding aloft our colors," etc., they raised their programs (half green and half gold) and waved them - an impressive sight. Then, as the concluding song, the entire congregation participated in singing "Carry On."

On one occasion Sister Fox said, "One day Brother George F. Richards asked me, 'How did you get the inspiration to write that song?' and I replied, 'It came so easy I think it was inspired'."

Following a remark that "The music does much for the song," Brother Durham responded, "The music was inspired by the words, they are the body of the song, the music is the adornment."

---

*Note: The M.I.A. Conference of June 1930 was planned around the theme- "Onward with Mormon Ideals." The theme inspired the words to "Carry On."

49

Elsie Hogan Van Noy: "I like to tell people I was the first one to read and to copy 'Carry On.' I am always thrilled when I hear it. I am sure it was inspired. The entire circumstance bears out that feeling."

J. Harold Keddington: "Whenever I hear 'Carry On' I like to tell people that I directed the song the first time it was sung by a congregation."

Lorin F. Wheelwright: "It was the thrill of my life."

As a final tribute to Ruth May Fox, April 15, 1958, seventy-five of her grandchildren and great-grandchildren closed her funeral service by singing "Carry On." It was both a tribute and a promise. This chorus was also directed by J. Harold Keddington with Lorin Wheelwright as organist.

The Composer

Alfred Durham was born in Parowan, Utah, a son of Thomas and Caroline Durham. He served in many church, civic, and musical capacities but his name will be remebered longest and best for his composition "Carry On." Elder Durham served in the bishoprics of both the Logan first and the Salt Lake 17th wards and was an active member of the Bryan Ward at the time of his death. In addition he served the Church as a receptionist on Temple Square for twelve years. He also had completed three Church missions to New York, Michigan, and the Tongan Islands. He studied music at the Julliard School under Frank Damrosch and taught music in Utah schools for forty-two years. He was at one time head of the music department at Murdock Academy in Beaver, supervisor of music for Beaver and Logan city schools and taught school in Salt Lake city. Mr. Durham was interested in civic and governmental affairs serving in the Utah State Legislature for ten years, representing Beaver and Salt Lake Counties, and also served as Iron County Clerk. An active Kiwanian, he was chairman of the music committee of the Kiwanis International, and was a charter member of the Logan Kiwanis. He served as general chairman of the Cache Valley Centennial celebration. Alfred Durham loved his fellow men and had the ability to make and keep friends that few people enjoy. His family feel that they have been exceptionally blessed to have a father such a true servant of the Lord. His death occurred in 1957.

50

The Author

Ruth May Fox was born November 16, 1853, in Westbury, Wiltshire, England, to James and Mary Ann May. Her mother died when Ruth was sixteen months old. During early childhood she lived with relatives and friends. In 1856 her father went to America, leaving Ruth with a widow, who also had a daughter. In October of that year he sent for them, and he and the widow married upon their arrival in America.

They lived in Philadelphia for nearly two years, and in July 1867 they started for Zion, traveling nine days by rail to reach North Platte. After buying supplies Brother May had enough money to buy only one yoke of oxen. He joined Brother Gentry who had one yoke and a wagon. Brother May would drive all the way for his share of the wagon. With the wagon filled with supplies, Ruth and her sister walked most of the way. As they entered the valley, Ruth caught a a glimpse of the city below, and asked in disappointment, "Did we come all this way for that?"

Her father became a carder in Brigham Young's factory. Ruth and her sister, Clara, also worked in the factory. Later Brother May and Brother Wilkinson bought some carding machines, and the girls worked for them, earning $10.00 a week, working from 7:30 a.m. to 6:00 p.m. with a half day off on Saturday.

Ruth May Fox

Alfred M. Durham

51

Ruth was married May 8, 1873, to Jesse W. Fox, in the Endowment House, and to them was born a family of twelve, six boys and six girls.

At seventeen, Ruth became a teacher in the Fourteenth Ward Sunday School. In 1879 she was installed as a counselor to Clara C. Cannon in the Ward Primary, with Martha Horne (later Martha Horne Tingey) as the other counselor, with whom she was associated in Church work for the next fifty years. Ruth served forty years as a member of the General Board of the Young Women's Mutual Improvement Assn., eight years of that time as President, having succeeded Martha Horne Tingey, March 28, 1929, at the age of 75. She retired in October 1937 at the age of 84.

During these years Ruth May Fox served twenty-six years as a guide on Temple Square, twelve years as a member of the Board of the Travelers' Aid, was active with the American Red Cross at the time World War I was in progress, and served in seven different homes as a volunteer nurse. In February 1934 she was honored by the Salt Lake Federation of Women's Clubs as one of seven women who had rendered distinguished community service. She died at the age of 104 years.

No. 43

Father, Thy Children to Thee Now Raise

Words and Music by Evan Stephens

The Hymn

"Father, Thy Children to Thee Now Raise" is one of the many hymn texts which Evan Stephens wrote. It is a joyous outpouring of gratefulness for our Heavenly Father's goodness.

The Composer and Author — Evan Stephens (See No. 144)

No. 44   # Glory to God On High

Words by John E. Bode   **Music by Felice de Giardini**

The Hymn

The text of this hymn is a variant from Luke 2:14, "Glory to God in the Highest, and on Earth, Peace, Goodwill toward men." The usual text sung for this hymn is "Come, Thou Almighty King" the author of which is unknown.

The Composer

Felice de Giardini was an Italian Violinist-Conductor of opera in London. In later life Giardini traveled the Continent, finally reaching Moscow in Russia, where he died in poverty. The hymn tune to "Glory to God on High" was originally called "Moscow" probably being composed while Giardini lived there. The three-measure phrases sometimes produce a rhythmical discrepancy in the minds of singers. Giardini was born in 1716 and died in 1796.

The Author

John E. Bode was born in London in 1816. He was educated in Eton and Oxford universities. In 1847 he became Rector at Westwell, Oxfordshire, and in 1860 was Rector of Castle Camps, Cambridgeshire. Many poetical works survive him. He died in 1874.

No. 45

The Glorious Gospel Light Has Shown

Words by Joel H. Johnson   Music by Leroy J. Robertson

The Hymn

Dr. Robertson says of this hymn,

> The music to this hymn was written to a text which concerns the church doctrine relative to the work and baptism for the dead. The musical treatment is in keeping with the dignity of the subject. The words should always be uppermost in the minds of those who perform this hymn. It can be sung by the congregation or the choir.

The Composer

Leroy J. Robertson was born in Fountain Green, Utah. A graduate of the New England Conservatory of Music, 1923; Brigham Young University, Provo, Utah, A.B. and M.A. degrees, 1932; The University of Southern California, Los Angeles, Ph.D. 1954. Appointed to the faculty of Brigham Young University in 1925. Appointed Professor and Chairman of the music department, University of Utah in 1948.

Member of Phi Beta Kappa; Kappa Gamma Psi. Fellow, Utah Academy of Arts, Sciences, and Letters. Member of the Executive Music Committee of the Church of Jesus Christ of Latter-day Saints. Member of the American Society of Composers, Authors, and Publishers (ASCAP). Compositions include works for symphony orchestra; concertos for violin, cello, and piano and orchestra; two string quartets; quintet for piano and string quartet; an oratorio (Book of Mormon) for chorus, soloist, organ, and orchestra; choral compositions; instrumental and vocal solos. Compositions have been performed in this country and abroad. Several of them have been given special awards including the Trilogy which won the Reichhold award of $25,000 in 1947. At the present time he is the chairman of the General Church Music Committee.

The Author — Joel H. Johnson (See No. 62)

Come, Listen to A Prophet's Voice

Words: Anonymous   **Music by Joseph J. Daynes**

The Hymn

"Come, Listen to a Prophet's Voice" is a joyous outpouring of gratitude for the restored gospel.

The Composer — Joseph J. Daynes (See No. 62)

The Author — Anonymous.

No. 47

God Be with You Till We Meet Again

Words by Jeremiah Eames Rankin   **Music by William Gould Tomer**

The Hymn

"God Be with You Till We Meet Again" grew out of Dr. Rankin's interest in the derivation of the word "good-bye" which he found to be a contraction of "God be with ye." In the three stanzas in the hymnbook the words, "God be with you" are sung seven times and "Till We Meet" is sung eighteen times.

This song is distinctly a farewell hymn of gospel song vintage. It was popularized by the great revivalists, Moody and Sankey.

The Composer

Three musician friends of Dr. Rankin collaborated in producing the tune, but W. G. Tomer is given the credit as its composer. In form it is a song of the ballad variety, having a "verse and chorus." Often the chorus is omitted.

The Author

In 1889 Jeremiah Eames Rankin became the President of Howard University Washington, D. C., a Negro Institution. He was of Scotch descent, born in New Hampshire in 1828. He was educated for the ministry. Rankin held several Congregational Pastorates in New England. He died in 1904.

No. 48

God Moves in a Mysterious Way

Words by William Cowper   **Music by William Bradbury**

The Hymn

In the histories, biographies, and memoirs of William Cowper, examined by the writer, there is nothing to indicate just when "God

Moves in a Mysterious Way" was written.* One story related that "once upon a time" when he felt his weakness coming on, he yielded to an impulse to drown himself in the River Thames; that he called a cab and asked the cabman to drive him to the river; that a heavy London fog suddenly gathered, and the cabman lost his way; that after driving aimlessly round and round for some time, the cabman refused to continue and ordered his passenger out; that Cowper stumbled to the walk and found himself in front of his own door.

When he recovered his senses, he sat down and wrote "God Moves in a Mysterious Way, His Wonders to Perform." There is some justification for the survival of this story. One writer says: He "had an intense delusion that it was the divine will for him...to drown himself, but the driver of the vehicle missed his way, and Cowper was diverted from his purpose." Then, too, Cowper's own memoirs state that he was driven to the Thames with suicidal intent but was prevented from carrying out his purpose by the appearance of a wharf porter sitting on a pile of goods.

However, there is no doubt that the hymn was written in view of his own dreadful experiences, and the hand of Providence is plainly seen in preventing the consummation of an evil design. The hymn was included in the *Olney Hymns* as already stated which were published in 1787.

The poem extols the power and omnipotence of the Almighty and his infinite skill and wisdom in working out his divine plans. It carries a message of hope to the Saints who are fearful and entreats them to be courageous against the ills that seem to beset them; it contains prophetic lines that the purposes of God will be gradually unfolded hour by hour and though experiences may be bitter, yet the fruit of righteousness will be sweet; that blind unbelief will lead us to grope in the dark and seek for the truth in vain, while if we trust in God, the Great Interpreter, all will be made plain.

It is said that "poets are prophets" and one is almost persuaded that this is true when he ponders on the analogy between this immortal hymn and a revelation given a prophet of God three-quarters of a century later. Was Cowper's hymn a "flash from the Eternal Semaphore?"

The Composer

To Latter-day Saints, the most popular tune to this hymn is the one known as the favorite of President Wilford Woodruff and scheduled as No. 48 in *Latter-day Saint Hymns*. It is extremely simple in

---

*From George D. Pyper's *Stories of Latter-day Saint Hymns*.

55

composition, but when sung by large congregations, it is very impressive. Under the name of "Harvey's Chant" it was written by William Bachelder Bradbury. For additional information See No. 166.

The Author

The life of William Cowper, who wrote the hymn, "God Moves in a Mysterious Way" is one of pathos, tenderness, doubt, disappointment and despair. He was a defeatist, dreading the unknown, afraid to live, afraid to die, yet possessing such qualities of mind and heart that endeared him to many noted friends and gave him a secure place among the English poets.

William Cowper was born on November 26, 1731, at Great Berkhamstead, Hertfordshire, England, the son of a rector of Berkhamstead, chaplain to King George II. His mother, Ann Donne, of honorable lineage, died when William was six years of age. He was a delicate child, sensitive and shy, sheltered and protected by a doting mother. At her death the boy was placed in Doctor Pitman's school near his father's place of residence. Here he was so tormented and bullied by a boy five years his senior that although his tormentor was expelled, William's experience left a feeling of terror and helplessness that affected his entire life. During one of these persecutions he found a line in the Bible that gave him temporary comfort. It was—"I fear nothing that man can do unto me." This resulted in a spiritual exaltation that saved him from total collapse. At ten he was sent to Westminster where he companioned with such students as Warren Hastings and Churchill, the poet.

At eighteen, Cowper left Westminster and attached himself to a Mr. Chapman, a London attorney. In 1754 he was called to the bar, but his "inferiority complex" and his preference for literature kept him from practicing law. During his association with Mr. Chapman, he fell in love with a cousin, Theodora Jane Cowper, but his uncle, Ashley Cowper, forbade a marriage on account of their close relationship, and young Cowper was again thrown into despair and near madness. Neither of the lovers ever married.

From necessity Cowper sought employment, and his cousin Major Cowper, who had the right of nomination, presented him as clerk of the House of Lords. All seemed favorable for a happy and lucrative position when the hand of fate again struck him. His enemies insisted upon an examination before the bar of the house to test his fitness for the clerkship. As the time approached for the examination Cowper developed a terrified state of mind. The fear of the test, together with a consciousness of an intimate deformity that had all through his life depressed him, were too much for his delicate constitution. His mind gave way, and he decided to end it all by suicide. Purchasing a bottle of laudanum, he called a coach and asked to be driven to the Thames wharf, where he determined to drink the laudanum and jump into the river; but finding a guard there the deed was prevented. Returning to his quarters, he poured the poison into a small basin and when he reached for it with intent to drink the contents, the fingers of both his hands contracted so that he could not hold the vessel. Recovering in wonder, he threw the poison out of the window. The night before the test, with a tottering brain he again attempted to kill himself with a pen knife, but the blade broke. He then tried to hang himself with a garter, but the garter broke, and he fell to the floor utterly deranged. Of course, his chance of obtaining the position in the House of Lords was now gone, and under the care of Doctor Cotton he was taken to St. Albans, a mental hospital where he remained for two years. In 1763 he was taken in charge by his friends, the Unwins, father, mother, son, and the "Mary" of his letter. Upon Mr. Unwin's death, in 1767, the family including Cowper, moved to Olney, and there Cowper formed an intimate friendship with John Newton. This friendship was a strange mixture of personalities. "In his youth, Newton had been a wild, despairing blasphemer; in his, Cowper an irresolute, despairing, would-be suicide. One was driven to Christ by the violence of his sins, the other by the violence of his sufferings."

William Cowper

The result of this friendship was the publication of *Olney Hymns* one of the 18th century's best contributions to the development of English Hymnody. It contains 348 hymns, 280 by Newton, 68 by Cowper. One of the most popular of Cowper's hymns in this collection was "God Moves in a Mysterious Way, His Wonders to Perform."

No. 49

In Humility Our Savior

Words by Mabel Jones Gabbott　　　**Music by Rowland Hugh Prichard**

The Hymn

With its present text the hymn "In Humility My Savior" is a sacramental hymn. Several other hymn texts have been used with this popular hymn tune-notably "Love Divine All Love Excelling" and the original Welsh hymn, translated being "Onward March All Conquering Jesus."

The Composer

Rowland Hugh Prichard 1811-1887 wrote this lovely hymn tune known in the Welsh as "Hybuydol," when he was rather young. It has been used in many hymn anthem arrangements and is found in most hymnals. Prichard was born near Bala, Wales. For many years he was a loom tender's assistant in the Welsh Flannel Mills. He acquired a knowledge of harmony and wrote many fine hymn tunes which were published in Welsh periodicals. He died in Holywell, Wales.

The Author

Mabel Jones Gabbott was born in Malad, Idaho. In 1937 she was called to spend two years as a missionary in the Northwest. At this time she met her husband-to-be who together with the mission President, Preston Nibley, encouraged her to use her gift of writing. In 1945, she was invited to meet with others to consider new lyrics for the hymnbook. Three of her lyrics were accepted. "In Humility My Saviour" is one of them.

No. 50

God of Our Fathers, We Come unto Thee

Words by Charles W. Penrose　　　**Music by Ebenezer Beesley**

The Hymn

"God of Our Fathers, We Come unto Thee" is a hymn of prayer and dedication. Each phrase of this hymn is beautifully written and has interesting individuality. It should be sung with special attention to the form of each phrase. The rests in the various measures of the chorus are most effective.

The Composer — Ebenezer Beesley (See No. 94)

The Author — Charles W. Penrose (See No. 145)

No. 51

Abide with Me

Words by Henry F. Lyte   **Music by William Henry Monk**

The Hymn

"Abide with Me" is counted among the greatest of Christian hymns.* In *Anglican Hymnology*, by Rev. James King, M.A., of London, by vote of representatives from 52 hymnbooks, "Abide with Me" is classed as Number 5 among the best hymns. In the *Best Church Hymns*, by Rev. Louis F. Benson, D.D., it has ninth place in a vote of 107 hymnbooks.

It is said that Dr. Lyte received his inspiration for writing "Abide with Me" from the words of the disciples (Luke 24:49) as they walked toward Emmaus and said to Jesus:

"Abide with us; for it is toward evening and the day is far spent."

There is considerable variance, however, in stories concerning the time and place of the writing of this hymn. A grand niece of the hymnologist tells that the hymn was written about a fortnight before he died at Nice; that his spirit was in Brixham though his body was in Nice. But his daughter, writing three years after his death, gives a more authentic account of the birthplace of this beautiful hymn. She says:

> There is no doubt that he wrote it at the rectory of Brixham as the sun was setting, and his eyes looked over the beloved waves of Torbay, Old Harry, and Berry Head. There is internal evidence of this in the opening lines—
>
> Abide with me; fast falls the eventide,
> The darkness deepens; Lord, with me abide.
>
> He knew that his health was failing and that death was not far off. As he watched the setting sun, he drew from its last rays the inspiration of the mystical lines—
>
> Swift to its close ebbs out life's little day,
> Earth's joys grow dim, its glories pass away.
>
> The setting and framework of the hymn is Brixham and the symbolic pageantry of the Devon sunset.

---

*From George D. Pyper's *Stories of Latter-day Saint Hymns*.

Another account published in *The Spectator*, October, 1925, states that Lyte went to see an old friend, William Augustus Le Hunte who was dying, and who kept repeating "Abide with me." After leaving the bedside the account says, "Lyte wrote the hymn and gave a copy to William's brother which was left amongst his papers. It was first printed in a publication called *Remains*, in 1850."

While "Abide with Me" is not an original LDS hymn, and was not included in the early hymnbooks of the Church, it is now popular and revered number published in *Latter-day Saint Hymns* though all the stanzas are not published in these books. How it is regarded by the Christian world, a reverence shared by the Latter-day Saints, expressed in an English newspaper, commenting on this hymn, on the anniversary of Lyte's death, it says:

> What is the secret of healing power? Its divine simplicity. Its inspired truthfulness and sincerity. Every word is a cry from the human heart. Its rhythm is magically right because it follows the passion of the soul in wave after wave. It melts the human mind. It transfigures the human intellect. In sorrow and desolation it comforts and consoles. There is not a false note in its music. That is why it is the hymn of hymns.

The Composer

As already stated, Henry F. Lyte composed a tune to be used with his hymn, but whatever the cause, it sank into oblivion. When *Hymns, Ancient and Modern* was compiled in 1861, and no tune was found for "Abide with Me," the music editor, Dr. William Henry Monk, by request, composed the tune now so well-known throughout the entire Christian world. It is said that in ten minutes Dr. Monk completed the composition.

The composer was born in London in 1823. He was a writer of many hymn tunes used in Protestant churches in England and Scotland. He died in 1889.

Lyte himself had hoped that he might not be mute and useless while lying in his grave. He had prayed—

> O Thou whose touch can lend
> Life to the dead, Thy quickening grace supply
> And grant me swan-like my last breath to spend
> In song that may not die.

And while his composition was not associated with his hymn, yet his song has not died, and Dr. Monk's appropriate tune has helped to give it immortality.

The Author

Henry Francis Lyte, who wrote the immortal hymn, "Abide with Me," was born at Ednam, near Kelso, Roxburgshire, Scotland, June 1, 1793. He was the second son of Captain Henry Lyte who was the eleventh in direct descent from his progenitor, and who presented his work "The Light of Britayne," to Queen Elizabeth at St. Paul's when she went to give thanks for the defeat of the Spanish Armada.

As a boy the subject of this sketch studied at Portora, the Royal School, at Enniskillen. Trinity College, Dublin, however was his Alma Mater. And so England, Scotland, and Ireland all share in his fame. His ancestors can be traced further back than Shakespeare's or Milton's. At twenty Lyte was the winner of three prize poems in three years. He early decided to follow the medical profession but gave up this intention and took holy orders, becoming a curate of Taghmon, near Wexford. Ill health caused him to resign, and after a visit to the continent, he went in 1837, to Marazion, Cornwall, where he married an Irish woman named Anne Maxwell, daughter of Reverend W. Maxwell, D.D., of Falkland, who wrote the twenty-fourth chapter of Boswell's *Life of Johnson*. In 1823, Lyte became "perpetual curate" of Lower Brixham, and for twenty-four years labored among the humble fisherman of Devonshire. With his wife and two children he lived in the rectory which overlooked the sea. Rose trees which he planted there still bloom.

Many interesting stories of his character have been handed down from one generation to another; how he climbed Berry Head at night to warn the fishing fleet of the weather; how he gave bottles of rare old wine to sick fishermen and their wives.

Lyte was of delicate health, and his condition finally developed into tuberculosis. As he approached the end, he decided to go to the warmer climate of southern Italy. Against the advice of his family and friends he addressed his flock and gave communion before departure. Various stories concerning the writing of "Abide with Me" are told in this sketch.

The day following his farewell address, Dr. Lyte began the journey to Italy, but could travel no farther than Nice, France. That peace for which he longed came to him there, November 20, 1847, the year the pioneers came into Salt Lake Valley. Lyte died with uplifted hands saying: "Peace, joy." His body rests in the English cemetery at Nice.

From All That Dwell below the Skies

Words by Isaac Watts　　　　　　　　　　　　　**Music by John Hatton**

The Hymn

"From All that Dwell below the Skies" is a paraphrase of Psalm 117. Seventeen other Psalm paraphrases by Watts have survived in current hymnals.

The Composer

John Hatton was born at Warrington, near Liverpool, England and is sometimes known as John of Warrington. He resided on Duke Street. History records that he was killed in a stagecoach accident. Only one tune is credited to him. It is the universally known tune "Duke Street" to which the Watts hymn has been appended in the Latter-day Saint Hymnal. The tune "Duke Street" is a perfect example of a fine hymn writing. It is so popular in Protestant churches that many different texts are used with it. His death came in 1793.

The Author — Isaac Watts (See No. 168)

Great King of Heaven, Our Hearts We Raise

Words by Carrie S. Thomas　　　　　　　　　**Music by Leroy J. Robertson**

The Hymn

This is a hymn of praise. It can be used in church services by the congregation or the choir and also for secular programs of a serious nature.

The Composer — Leroy J. Robertson (See No. 45)

The Hymn

Carrie S. Thomas was born in April 1848, at Plymouth, England, a daughter of Michael and Jane Stockdale. She was educated in English schools and was a lady of artistic temperament and literary attainments. She emigrated to Utah in 1864 and the following year was married to Richard K. Thomas. She was president of the Y.L.M.I.A. of the Seventh Ward, Salt Lake City, for a number of years and attended conventions of the National Council of Women in Cleveland, Ohio, and at Washington D.C. Mrs. Thomas also traveled in Europe, accompanied by her daughters. She was a charter member of the Utah Womens Press Club and Reaper's Club. She was the mother of twelve children, eight of whom were living at the time of her death in 1931.

God of Our Fathers Whose Almighty Hand

Words by Daniel C. Roberts   Music by G. W. Warren

The Hymn and the Composer

The only title to fame that Daniel C. Roberts had besides being a prominent and upright citizen, was from his hymn "God of Our Father Whose Almighty Hand."

Roberts wrote it in 1876 for a celebration of the "one hundredth" anniversary of the Declaration of Independence. It was sung on that occasion on July 4th, in Brandon, Vermont, a tiny village of fourteen hundred people, to the tune of the "Russian Hymn." Later, when the Hymnal of the church to which Roberts belonged was to be revised, he sent the hymn to the committee without his name attached to it. It was selected and printed in 1892, anonymously, but in 1894 it was chosen to be sung at the Adoption of the Constitution of the United States Ceremony.

At that time George William Warren, organist of the St. Thomas Church of New York City, wrote the present musical setting for it.

The original version of the tune has a two measure trumpet fanfare as an introduction. The hymn's wide use at patriotic celebrations has made it very popular in America.

After the first singing of the hymn, Mr. Roberts wrote "My little hymn had a very flattering official recognition, but that which would gladden my heart most is popular recognition which it has not received."

Little did Mr. Roberts know what the destiny of the hymn would be a decade later.

The Author

Daniel C. Roberts was born on Long Island, New York, in 1841. He served as a soldier in the Union Army in the Civil War. Later he became a Rector in several Episcopal Churches. At the same time he served as President of the New Hampshire Historical Society; President of the State Normal School in Vermont; and Chaplain of the New Hampshire National Guard. He died in 1907.

No. 55   Down by the River's Verdant Side

Words Anonymous   Music Anonymous

The Hymn

We have no clue as to the authorship of this hymn or whence

came the tune, but the following story may have a bearing on its use in early pioneer days.

Colonel Thomas L. Kane, a United States army officer, who was a personal friend of President Brigham Young, wrote a vivid decription of the farewell party for the first company of the Mormon Battalion, held at Winter Quarters on July 15th 1846:

> There was no sentimental affectation at their leaving. Light hearts, lithe figures, and light feet had it their own way from an early hour till after the sun had dipped behind the sharp skyline of the Omaha Hills. Silence was then called and a well cultivated mezzo soprano voice, belonging to a young lady with a fair face and dark eyes, gave, with quartette accompaniment, a little song the notes of which I have been unable to obtain—a version of the text, touching all earthly wanderers: "Down by the river's verdant side, low by the solitary tide Will Zion in our memory stand—our lost, our ruined native land."

No. 56   No. 57

Guide Us, O Thou Great Jehovah

Words by Robert Robinson   **Music by John Hughes**

The Hymn

The imagery of the hymn "Guide Us, O Thou Great Jehovah" is drawn wholly from the Bible. Its general setting is from the march of the Israelites from Egypt to Canaan. It was first titled "Strength to Pass through the Wilderness."

Two translations of the hymn are in common use - the one as found in the Latter-day Saint hymnal by Robinson and the other, by Peter Williams the first stanza of which follows:

> Guide Me, O Thou great Jehovah,
> Pilgrim through this barren land.
> I am weak but Thou art mighty;
> Hold me with Thy powerful hand.
> Bread of heaven,
> Feed me till I want no more.

The Composer

"Guide Us, O Thou Great Jehovah" has been sung to several tunes. It was published in the 1889 *Latter-day Saint Psalmody* with the tune of a popular ballad "In the Gloaming" by Annie Fortescue Harrison. When the Latter-day Saint hymnbook was revised in 1948, it was proposed by the General Church Music Committee that the Welsh tune "Cym Rhondda" composed by John Hughes, be used in the place of "In the Gloaming." To satisfy some members of the committee, who felt the old tune should be retained, both tunes were printed side by side in the 1950 edition of the Hymnal.

"Cym Rhondda" by Hughes (1872-1932), who was a coal miner in Wales, but had a little knowledge of harmony, was written on a piece of tarpaulin with chalk. He harmonized it with common chords. At lunch time he called a group of his fellow workers together and they sang the hymn for the first time. It was then introduced and sung at the anniversary service at Capel Rhondda, Ponlypride, Wales. This anniversary marked the beginning of World War I. where many Welsh soldiers were present at this festival. The soldiers took the tune over to France, and it was so contagious that even the Germans caught the strain of this simple but magnificent piece of music. It is not a folk tune at all, as some historians have stated it, but Hughes' original composition.

The Author

William Williams (1717-1781). Traditional By Robert Robinson. The low-lying stone building in Pantycelyn, Wales, in which William Williams was born, is still standing. Descendents continue to live there. To enter the house is like stepping back two-hundred years. Few items are changed. When William was twenty years old, he joined the dissenters movement which had spread throughout England, and for forty-three years he preached it in his native country of Wales. He was persecuted during the whole of his preaching career often being "beaten." Although a great evangelist, he was better known for his hymns—eight-hundred of which came from his gifted pen, but unfortunately most of them were never translated into English.

No. 58

Have I Done Any Good in the World Today?

Words and Music by Will L. Thompson

The Hymn

Both words and music of this thoroughgoing gospel song were written by Will Lamartine Thompson (1847-1909) of East Liverpool, Ohio. No other information seems to be available concerning this rather popular number or its composer and author.

No. 59

Great God to Thee My Evening Hymn

Words by M. M. Steel　　　　　　　　**Music by Edward P. Kimball**

The Hymn

"Great God to Thee My Evening Hymn" is a hymn which acknowledges man's helplessness on earth, coupled with a prayer to the Lord for His constant care.

The Composer — Edward P. Kimball (See No. 178)

This hymn tune ranks high in excellence in traditional hymn tune form. The architectural arching of the various phrases gives it thoroughgoing expressiveness.

The Author

Mahonri Moriancumer Steel or Steele was born May 1, 1849 in Salt Lake City, Utah, the son of John Steel and Catherine Campbell. With his parents he was a pioneer in George A. Smith's company which settled Parowan, Iron County, Utah in 1851. He was baptized in 1857 and in the Winter of 1900 moved with his parents to Toquerville, Washington County. He participated in the battle with the Navajo Indians in December, 1866 and served in the Utah militia during the Blackhawk Indian War. He was ordained an elder in 1866. In 1868 he drove a four-yoke ox-team in Daniel D. McArthur's company to the terminus of the Union Pacific Railroad, to bring emigrants to Utah. In 1869 he married Emily Bunker, daughter of Bishop Edward Bunker, a member of the Mormon Battalion. He served on a mission for the Church to Liverpool and upon his return was chosen to be a counselor in the bishopric and also later as counselor in the stake presidency of the Panguitch Stake. He was ordained a patriarch in 1898 by Apostle Francis M. Lyman.

Edward P. Kimball

No. 60   Hark, The Herald Angels Sing

Words by Charles Wesley   Music by Felix Mendelssohn

The Hymn

This hymn was written by Charles Wesley in 1738 just a year after his conversion. The original poem had ten stanzas. The last four stanzas dealt with theology which John Wesley, brother of Charles, used in his classes in theology. They gave explanations of the Garden of Eden story, pre-existence, and atonement for Adam's sin, by Christ. These stanzas are never printed now.

The Composer — Felix Mendelssohn (See No. 370)

The tune of this popular carol is a hymn tune style. It should be sung in a vigorous manner with distinct diction.

The Author — Charles Wesley (See No. 10)

No. 61   He Is Risen, He Is Risen

Words by Cecil Alexander   Music by Joachim Neander

The Hymn

The Easter hymn "He Is Risen" is one of a series of seven hymns in which the author, Mrs. Alexander, endeavored to make the Apostle's Creed understood by children.

The Composer

Joachim Neander was born in Bremen, Germany in 1650. His early life, while at school, was riotous and unseemly but on hearing Theodore Under-Egek, a Bremen pastor, speak in a service one Sunday, he was touched and became a convert to the Pietest Cult. Later he became Rector Assistant to Under-Egek. After Mr. Under-Egek died, Neander became a reactionist and virtually left the church. It is said that he lived alone in a cave during this time. However, he received great consolation in the writing of hymns. Many of his hymns were readily received by the Lutherans and are still in universal use. Neander was rated as one of the finest German hymnists.

The Author — Cecil Frances Alexander (See No. 201)

No. 62   High on the Mountaintop

Words by Joel H. Johnson   Music by Ebenezer Beesley

The Hymn

"High on the Mountaintop"* is essentially a missionary call, one to be expected from the pen of such a staunch preacher of the

---

*From George D. Pyper's *Stories of Latter-day Saint Hymns.*

gospel as Joel H. Johnson. He no doubt had in mind the promise recorded in Isaiah:

> And it shall come to pass, in the last days, that the mountain of the Lord's house shall be established in the top of the mountains, and shall be exalted above the hills; and all nations shall flow unto it.
>
> And many people shall go and say, Come ye, and let us go up to the mountain of the Lord, to the house of the God of Jacob; and he will teach us of his ways, and we will walk in his paths; for out of Zion shall go forth the law and the word of the Lord from Jerusalem. (Isaiah 2:2-3.)

Here we find the key to Johnson's lines. He follows the scripture very closely—a banner on Zion's hill waves to and warns the world. The promise has been fulfilled, the light of truth has attracted the gaze of the world; a house of the Lord has been built and many have come up to the mountain to serve the Lord and learn of his ways, in order to save themselves and work out salvation for their dead.

Circumstances that have a bearing upon this scripture are more than passing strange. Although the people of Utah made several attempts to secure Statehood under the name of Deseret they were unsuccessful, but later were admitted into the Union under the name of Utah. When we understand the meaning of the word it seems as though something more than human intelligence shaped the course of events. Here is a definition of "Utah":

> Utah is a corruption of the word Eutaw and is the name of an Indian tribe that lived in these valleys and mountains long ago . . . Retaining their traditions and folklore they tell us that their forefathers called this the Land of Eutaw, or "high up." Utah means "in the tops of the mountains."—*Levi Edgar Young, Head of the Department of History, University of Utah.*
>
> The Indian name Utah, a corruption of the word Eutaw, means "in the tops of the mountains," or, as the Indians themselves express it "high up!"—*George Earl Shankee in State Names, Flags, Etc.*

In an article on this subject, Elder Don B. Colton, former Congressman from Utah, director of the Church Missionary Home, and member of the Deseret Sunday School Union, wrote as follows:

> To me it is extremely interesting to note that in naming this Territory wherein the temples of the Lord were first built, Congress, without knowing it, selected the name which means "top of the mountains." Surely everyone familiar with the history of The Church of Jesus Christ of Latter-day Saints knows that all nations have furnished representatives who have come here because the temples were built here and because "many people" could more fully learn the ways of the Lord, and could "walk in his paths."

There is no special or dramatic incident attached to the writing of this hymn but "High on the Mountaintop" is truly a song of the restoration, a clarion call to the nations.

The Composer — Ebenezer Beesley (See No. 94)

The Author

In the Historian's Office, Salt Lake City, is filed the journal of the writer of "High on the Mountaintop," a favored hymn of President John Taylor. The journal reads like a romantic drama. It is a recital of tribulations and hallelujahs; of a man who had a burning testimony of the divinity of the restored gospel of Jesus Christ.

Joel Hills Johnson, the son of Ezekiel and Julia Hills Johnson, was born at Grafton, Massachusetts, March 23, 1802. When he was a small child, his parents migrated to Vermont, and from there Joel went with his uncle to Cincinnati, then a very small village. From there his father took him to Pomfret, New York, where he lived until he was 21 years of age. He had little opportunity for education, but was very religious, dutiful to his parents, and studied the scriptures by firelight. On November 22, 1826, he married Anna P. Johnson. About this time he invented a shingle cutter which was used in the United States.

In 1830, he returned to Ohio where he met elders of the Church of Jesus Christ of Latter-day Saints, read the Book of Mormon, believed, was baptized June 1, 1830, ordained an elder and appointed to preside over the Amherst branch of about one hundred Saints. He met the Prophet in 1831. In 1832 he was called on a mission to New York; in 1833 he moved to Kirtland built a sawmill and furnished lumber to finish the temple; in 1835 he missionaried through Ohio and the South. He preached in all the towns around Kirtland and baptized many, receiving a blessing from the First Presidency of the Church for his labors in missions and his help in building the house of the Lord.

He was present at the calling and ordination of the first twelve apostles, attended the dedication of the Kirtland Temple, and was a witness to some manifestations mentioned in the life of Joseph Smith. He helped to organize Kirtland Camp and traveled as far as Springfield, Illinois, where he organized a branch of forty members; then he was called to Carthage, Illinois, and was the first elder who preached there; and here he organized a branch. Sidney Rigdon and Bishop Partridge called on him on their way from Missouri to Commerce (Nauvoo) to seek a location for the Saints. In 1840 he moved to Crooked Creek and was seven miles from Carthage when the Prophet and Patriarch were martyred.

He received his endowments at Nauvoo, May, 1846; was driven out by a mob of one hundred, leaving several thousand dollars' worth of property to the vandals. He moved to Winter Quarters, and left there July 5th; arrived in Salt Lake Valley October 11, 1848, and settled at the mouth of Mill Creek Canyon, where he was made bishop and justice of the peace—not for long, however, for he was called to go south with George A. Smith, and his movements in Southern Utah are recorded in his journal in faithful detail. He filled many offices of trust, including membership in the Territorial Legislature of 1849 and 1850.

Joel H. Johnson had a natural gift of poetry, and had education been possible for him, his name would no doubt be among the foremost of Zion's poets. His journal contains 736 hymns and songs. A pamphlet entitled "Voices from the Mountains," containing both prose and poetry by Brother Johnson, was published in 1881; and a book of poems containing 344 pages entitled "Hymns of Praise," selected from the "Songs of Joel," appeared in 1882. On the manuscript copy appear these penciled words:

> Were all my thoughts in one combined,
> Were thunder's voice with lightning speed
> My gift to speak to all mankind,
> All ears should tingle then, indeed.

Joel H. Johnson

"High on the Mountaintop" bears the date February 19, 1853. In a brief sketch of his life pinned to his journal, Brother Johnson writes:

"After being baptized in 1831 I never lived but a short time in any one place on account of mob violence. And since I have been in Utah I have made eleven new places. Was never called on a mission without responding to the call and never asked to speak in public on the principles of religion when I excused myself. I have written nearly or quite one thousand spiritual hymns and sacred songs, now in manuscript entitled 'Zion's Songster, or the Songs of Joel," a few of which have been published in the Church works."

Brother Johnson died September 24, 1883, at Johnson, Utah.

No. 63   Holy Temples on Mount Zion

Words by Archibald F. Bennett   **Music by Alexander Schreiner**

The Hymn

Elder Archibald F. Bennett gives the following account of the writing of the hymn "Holy Temples on Mount Zion":

> When the 1950 edition of the Latter-day Saint Hymnal was being planned, I received a request from Alexander Schreiner of the Church Music Committee, to prepare the words of a hymn on temple work with the object of its being included in the new hymnbook then in the course of preparation. He stated that the committee had informed Elder Mark E. Petersen that they needed some more hymns on temple work and that Brother Petersen had suggested that I write these words.
>
> In accordance with that assignment I prepared the words for the hymn "Holy Temples on Mount Zion," No. 63, and also that of another on the gathering of Israel. The words of this second poem were later in *The Improvement Era.*

Temples are the Holy of Holies to Latter-day Saints. Only the faithful attend there, seeking blessings and divine inspiration. The idea of a temple which is more than a mere church meeting place is unique to the Church of Jesus Christ of Latter-day Saints. Therefore this hymn of poetic praise, alluding to purity of hearts, exaltation, eternal and celestial bonds, redemption and freedom for spiritual prisoners, dead, but desiring entrance through baptism into Christ's fold.

The melody has a character of exultation, of joyful, vital energy. The melody begins with a rising (motive) design, suitable to the ideas of high temple spires, of the upward reach. The third and contrasting line expresses the quieter sentiment of serenity and prayer and is followed by the upward motive of sacred service.

71

The Composer — Alexander Schreiner (See No. 24)

The Author

Archibald Flower Bennett was born March 17, 1896, at Dingle, Bear Lake Co., Idaho, a son of William David Bennett and Emma Neat. He was baptized in May, 1904, by Zebulon W. Jacobs. With his parents he went to Alberta, Canada, in the summer of 1899, the family residing at Magrath until 1907, when they moved to Taber. There young Archibald was ordained to offices in the Aaronic Priesthood and was ordained an elder November 30, 1914, by Bryant R. McMullin. He graduated from the Taber High School in 1914, and from the Calgary Normal School in 1915. He then taught school until his enlistment in the Canadian Mounted Rifles, March 26, 1916. With them he went overseas, transferring in England to the Fort Garry Horse, with which unit he was in active service in France from December 1916 to April, 1919. He received his discharge in Winnipeg, Canada, June 2, 1919. For one year he taught in the Taber High School and for two years in the Knight Academy in Raymond, Alberta. He served for a time as stake superintendent of the MIA in the Taylor Stake.

On December 21, 1921, he married Ann Ella Milner, (daughter of Benjamin Franklin Milner and Sarah Ellen Kinsman), in the Salt Lake Temple. To them have been born two sons and three daughters.

In July, 1922, Brother Bennett and his family moved to Salt Lake City, where he attended the University of Utah, graduating with a B.A. degree in 1925, and receiving his Master's degree in 1926. During this period he was regularly employed evenings in the registry division of the Salt Lake Post Office. On October 9, 1927, he was ordained a seventy by Melvin J. Ballard. Having been actively engaged in genealogical research for a number of years, he was appointed secretary of the Genealogical Society of Utah, September 1, 1928.

In August 1940, Brother Bennett was sustained a member of the Sunday School General Board.

He has prepared and published twenty-three texts on geneaology.

He is a recognized authority on genealogical research.

No. 64

Hope of Israel

Words by J. L. Townsend   Music by William Clayson

The Hymn

One could sermonize at length on the apt title of the song "Hope of Israel." The perpetuation and growth of the church membership

72

is in large measure dependent on the continuing faith of the youth. "Onward, Onward, Youth of Zion" is a militant command to the "Children of the Promised Day" to rise in might "With the Sword of Truth and Right."

The Composer

A warm note of praise is due the pioneer composers of the Church for the musical legacies given to the people.* Among those deserving mention is William Clayson, who composed six of the music settings for Joseph L. Townsend's hymns. Like many of the early hymn writers and composers, he was an Englishman by birth, having first seen the light of day at Wilby, Northamptonshire, England. He worked on a farm when only ten years of age, and there received an injury which resulted in lameness for life. At the same tender age he learned the first rudiments of music by practicing on a ten-penny whistle. At sixteen he received instruction on the flute and became an efficient performer. He embraced the gospel and was baptized on May 26, 1835, by Elder Mark Lindsay. In 1859, he was ordained an elder and presided over the Irchester Branch. Two years later he was released and sailed for America on the packet ship *Manchester*, arriving in Salt Lake City in September, 1861. He settled in Payson where he married Susan Moulton, his English betrothed, and lived there the remainder of his life. He studied thorough bass and harmony from the works of Dr. Lowell Mason and others.

In 1877, Elders Clayson and Townsend became associated in the Payson Sunday School and there collaborated, Brother Clayson composing the music for his friend's hymns, as before mentioned. These have been printed in many languages, and on account of their simple harmonies have been sung at home and fireside in many countries of the world.

William Clayson was an enthusiastic worker in the Church, an ardent civic patriot, and much beloved by all. He passed to his reward July 28, 1887.

The Author

A large number of our most popular Sunday School songs, many of them sung in our regular religious services, were written by Joseph L. Townsend and set to music by a number of our composers.

One writer has said that "there is no better viewpoint to study the development of the reactions of Christian belief than that offered by hymnody"; and another, writing specifically of Mormon music,

---

*From George D. Pyper's *Stories of Latter-day Saint Hymns*.

73

already quoted in this volume says, "Mormon history reads more like a romance than a reality, and the hymnbook presents almost every phase and important event of that history as embedded in contemporaneous hymns and songs." It may be added that there is probably no phase of Mormon history or theology that has not been developed in songs and hymns. This tendency is nowhere more strikingly shown than in the songs of Joseph L. Townsend, for they cover the subjects of love, fealty, valor, rewards, reverence, restoration, the Lord's bounty, adoration of the Savior, and other themes.

Born in Canton, Bradford County, Pennsylvania, August 9, 1849, Joseph Longking Townsend spent his boyhood days on a farm. His education at the West Side High School of Cleveland, Ohio, Girard, Kansas, Kidder and University of Missouri, included algebra, physics, rhetoric, drawing, architectural and mechanical drawing, Latin, Greek, and landscape gardening. At twenty-one he was the initial student at the Agricultural College of Missouri, was offered a professorship there, but on account of illness was prevented from accepting the position. A change for the benefit of his health brought him to Salt Lake City on August 8, 1872, and six months later he joined the Church. He taught penmanship at Morgan's Commercial College; became principal of the high school of Payson, and there married Miss Alta Hancock by whom he was blessed with eleven children.

Brother Townsend conducted a drug and mercantile business at Payson for fifteen years, then served two years as teacher of Penmanship at what was then called the Brigham Young Academy, at Provo, and later accepted a position as manual training teacher in the Salt Lake City High School. He was a devoted Latter-day Saint and fulfiilled a mission to the Southern States. He was the author of many beautiful poems, and his songs will keep him in reverence for all time.

Brother Townsend, at the solicitation of the writer, very kindly furnished the information concerning the origin of a few of his songs, — the motive for writing them.

"Let Love Abound" was produced to counteract too many frivolous and critical groups in our villages.

"Nearer, Dear Savior, to Thee," Brother Townsend calls his heart song.

"Beautiful Words of Love" was the response to the good sentiments expressed and the beautiful songs sung at a conference of the Latter-day Saints.

Actual work in a large Sunday School suggested the need of

better order while partaking of the Sacrament. "I Do Remember Thee" and "Reverently and Meekly Now" were written for the express purpose of quieting the nervous disorders of many pupils. Edwin F. Parry and Ebenezer Beesley were happily inspired to write suitable musical settings for the words. These songs helped to create a reverential feeling and had much to do in creating the beautiful atmosphere now universally maintained.

"O What Songs of the Heart" is an inspiration intended to throw a brighter light on some of our doleful funerals.

"That the Lord Will Provide" was suggested by an old hymn from England entitled "Though Troubles Assail and Dangers Affright"—setting the same theme in modern thought.

"What Prize Shall be Your Reward?" was formed as an appeal to those of our faith who are not accepting their privileges.

"Kind Words Are Sweet Tones of the Heart," one of the most popular and appealing of Brother Townsend's songs, was composed while he was laboring in the superintendency of a very large Sunday School. He heard a number of fault-finding remarks among the people. It occurred to him how much finer it would be if he could hear kind words spoken oftener. With this thought in mind he wrote the song which has been translated into many languages. Some have called it his best sermon. It is said that is stopped the gossiping tongues of the people and produced a kindlier feeling in the town where he lived.

"The Iron Rod"—the word of God—is based upon the dream or vision of Nephi recorded in chapter two of the *Book of Mormon* which was studied by 100,000 Sunday School and Mutual Improvement members the year this volume went to press.

When Brother Townsend was asked by the writer to give the origin of "When Jesus Shall Come in His Glory," he hesitated because of its sacred import to him. However, he left it to the writer's judgment. It is so lovely that it is reproduced here in his own language:

"Since I became a member of our Church, in January, 1873, I have been instructed in my faith with many gifts of the Holy Spirit.

"It was after a wondrous vision of the advent of our Savior that I wrote the lines describing the events in the order therein presented. and among these have been many remarkable dreams and visions.

"The vision placed me on a wide open prairie with no buildings or improvements in view. The time seemed to be early summer, for the abundant flowers were in bloom. With me was a group of Church officers, all in the usual apparel of present fashions, and without

75

banners, flags, or other insignia. Yet we were all aware of the great events soon to be displayed.

"A solemnity prevailed that hushed all conversation, and our group of brethren was intently gazing at the great masses of brilliant clouds approaching from the eastern horizon. When this wondrous pageant reached the zenith, our group of brethren saw angels and Saints within this glorious sheen of vapor, while it settled down till just above us.

"Then, one whom we recognized by his glorious and majestic appearance, descended and joined our group who were all officers of the Holy Priesthood.

"The long-expected King and Savior greeted us. He called by name and embraced and gave a holy kiss to the brow of each brother, while he gave to each the boon of the Comforter, the assurance of celestial glory.

"This was our reward of approval. My brethren were filled with an ecstasy of joy, and from the Heavenly Host above came the songs of joy that announced again, 'On earth peace, goodwill toward men.'

William Clayson

"The wondrous vision closed. Awakened in the mortal sphere again I felt the superb thrills of happiness that few men have ever attained. As a lesson in life's progress it has ever been retained in memory; as a comforter it has blest and sustained me for over half a century."

Joseph L. Townsend has rendered a distinct service to his Church and people by his gospel messages given in song. He died at the age of 92 in Payson, Utah, April 1st 1942.

No. 65
How Beautiful Thy Temples, Lord

Words by Frank I. Kooyman   Music by Tracy Y. Cannon

The Hymn

Brother Kooyman tells his own story about the writing of this hymn:

> When in 1945 the Church Music Committee sent out a call to songwriters for additional sacred songs to be included in a contemplated new hymnbook, this hymn was one of the several written in response to that appeal. From the laboratory of his old-world experience the author could bring forth nothing pertaining to the work for the dead. It was a brand-new principle to him, appealing strongly to the devotional side of his nature. A spiritual experience of his paternal grandfather which he heard from his mother's lips after he embraced the restored gospel also impressed him deeply. The grandfather, at one time, in vision—as father Lehi calls an inspired dream-experience (1 Nephi 8:2)—found himself in the spirit-world in front of what seemed to be the gates of heaven. Many were entering, and sincere grandfather (who had conscientiously lived according to the light granted him) was about to enter also when somebody held him back, placing a hand on his shoulder: "No, Kooyman, you cannot go in yet; something has to be done first." Greatly surprised, he woke up and for the balance of his earthly life wondered what it was that "had to be done first." The Rev. Polman, his dominie, too, was puzzled. "Why, my good friend, you are one of the best sheep of my flock," he exclaimed, "if you cannot go to the green pastures of heaven, what will become of the rest of us!"

The Composer — Tracy Y. Cannon (See No. 1)

Brother Cannon gives one terse statement about the composing of this hymn tune. "I was assigned to write music for these words written by Frank I. Kooyman for the 1948 edition of 'Hymns, Church of Jesus Christ of Latter-day Saints'."

The Author — Frank I. Kooyman (See No. 99)

No. 66

How Firm A Foundation

Kirkham

The Hymn

This soul-satisfying hymn has won a place in the heart of every devout worshiper of the Lord.* Since 1773, it has been included in almost every hymnbook. It has cheered the drooping spirits of millions of depressed and downcast people. It has engendered faith in God and his promises and strengthened many a faltering footstep.

The scriptural basis for the hymn is found in Isaiah 43:1,2, and in the Epistle of Paul to the Hebrews wherein he writes "And be content with such things as ye have, for He hath said 'I will never leave thee, nor forsake thee'."

"How Firm a Foundation" was the favorite hymn of many noted Americans. It was loved by the wife of President Andrew Jackson, and "Old Hickory" had it sung at his deathbed. It was also rendered at the funerals of General Robert E. Lee, Theodore Roosevelt, and Woodrow Wilson.

The following dramatic story concerning this hymn was published in the *Sunday School Times* of December 17, 1901:

"General Curtis Guild, Jr., tells how this hymn, wedded to the Christmas tune 'Adeste Fideles' was sung on a famous Christmas morning. The Seventh Army Corps was encamped on the hills above Havana, Cuba, on Christmas eve of 1898—a beautiful tropic night. Suddenly a sentinel from the camp of the Forty-ninth, Iowa, called 'Number 10—twelve o'clock, and all's well." A strong voice raised the chorus and many voices joined in until the whole regiment was singing. Then the Sixth-Missouri added its voices, and the Fourth-Virginia, and all the rest till then, on the long ridge above the city, where Spanish tyranny once went forth to enslave the new world, a whole army corps was singing.—

Fear not, I am with thee, O be not dismayed,
For I am thy God, and will still give thee aid;
I'll strengthen thee, help thee, and cause thee to stand,
Upheld by my righteous, omnipotent hand.

More than a hundred years ago, Emma Smith, called by divine revelation, and led by inspiration from the same Holy Source, com-

---

*From George D. Pyper's *Stories of Latter-day Saint Hymns.*

78

piled the spiritual hymns of the Church of Jesus Christ of Latter-day Saints. The collection of ninety hymns included many of the most popular Christian hymns, among the foremost being "How Firm a Foundation." Many a Mormon heart has been warmed by its consoling promises. One of the most pathetic incidents, very different from that which occurred during the Civil War, is related by Amanda Smith, whose husband and son were killed and another son seriously wounded at the Haun's Mill Massacre, a dark chapter in Church history. The following story is told by Mrs. Smith in Edward W. Tullidge's *Women of Mormondom*.

All the Mormons in the neighborhood had fled out of the state, excepting a few families of the bereaved women and children who had gathered at the house of Brother David Evans, two miles from the scene of the massacre. To this house Alma had been carried after that fatal night.

In our utter desolation, what could we women do but pray. Prayer was our only source of comfort; our Heavenly Father our only Helper. None but he could save and deliver us.

One day a mobber came from the mill with the captain's fiat:

"The captain says if you women don't stop your d—d praying he will send a posse and kill every d—d one of you!"

And he might as well have done it, as to stop us poor women praying in that hour of our great calamity.

Our prayers were hushed in terror. We dared not let our voices be heard in the house in supplication. I could pray in my bed or in silence, but I could not live thus long. This godless silence was more intolerable than had been that night of the massacre.

I could bear it no longer. I pined to hear once more my own voice in petition to my Heavenly Father.

I stole down into a corn-field, and crawled into a "stout of corn." It was as the temple of the Lord to me at that moment. I prayed aloud and most fervently.

When I emerged from the corn, a voice spoke to me. It was a voice as plain as I ever heard one. It was no silent, strong impression of the spirit, but a *voice*, repeating a verse of the Saints' hymn:

"The soul that on Jesus hath leaned for repose,
I will not, I cannot desert to his foes;
That soul, though all hell should endeavor to shake,
I'll never, no never, no never forsake."

From that moment I had no more fear. I felt that nothing could hurt me. Soon after this the mob sent us word that unless we were all out of the state by a certain day we should be killed.

The day came, and at evening came fifty armed men to execute the sentence. I met them at the door. They demanded of me why I was not gone? I bade them enter and see their own work. They crowded into my room, and I showed them my wounded boy. They came, party after party, until all had seen my excuse. Then they quarreled among themselves and came near fighting.

At last they went away, all but two. These I thought were detailed to kill us. Then the two returned.

"Madam," said one "have you any meat in the house?"

"No," was my reply.

"Could you dress a fat hog if one were laid at your door?"

"I think we could!" was my answer . . . .

And then they went and caught a fat hog from a herd which had belonged to a now exiled brother, killed it, and dragged it to my door, and departed.

These men, who had come to murder us, left on the threshold of our door a meat offering to atone for their repented intention. . . .

The Lord had kept his word. The soul that on Jesus had leaned for succor had not been forsaken even in this terrible hour of massacre.

The origin of "How Firm a Foundation" was for many years enshrouded in doubt. In early publications of hymnbooks it was credited to "Kirkham" and "K—." Later, in some publications, it was credited to George Keith. That Keith was a publisher of books, who initialed his surname "K," lent plausibility to the belief of some that he wrote it. Where the credit to "Kirkham" originated is not known.

More recently, Reverend H. L. Hasting, of Boston, and Dr. John Julian, editor of *Dictionary of Hymnology*, making separate researches, concluded that the hymn was written by Robert Kean, a preceptor for Dr. John Rippon, who was pastor of a Baptist Church in London from 1773 to 1836, and who first published the hymn credited to "K—" in his selection of *Hymns from the Best Authors*. A few slight changes have been made in the original words.

The Tune

The tune to which "How Firm a Foundation" is usually sung by the Christian churches is "Adeste Fideles" ("O Come, All Ye Faithful") now called the "Portuguese Hymn." The composition was first heard in the Portuguese Chapel, London, and given the name of "Portuguese Hymn" by the Duke of Leeds.

H. Augustus Smith in *Lyric Religion* says the tune was probably of English origin. Vincent Novello, organist of the chapel, gave John Reading, organist of Winchester Chapel from 1675 to 1681, the credit for the composition.

In an article published in the *American Etude* of January 1937, Mrs. W. Henry Herndon says:

Its origin is not definitely known. By some it is ascribed to a little known composer, Portugallo (Portugal): by others it has been credited to the author of the words; while still others believe it to be a folk tune without regular authorship. In the Southern States it is almost universally sung to a tune known as "Foundation." . . . In many books of the Southland it will be found in the "buckwheat notes" invented by an ancester of Charles Wakefield Cadman. . . . This is undoubtedly the tune beloved by the knightly general, Robert E. Lee.

Neither the "Portuguese Hymn" nor "Foundation" is the one most loved and sung by the Latter-day Saints as published in their hymnbooks. The composer of the Mormon tune is unknown, but whoever the author and composer were they have bequeathed to the world a legacy that has enriched the spiritual lives of millions of Christian people. The hymn has buoyed up the faith of hundreds of thousands of Latter-day Saints, comforted them in times of trouble, made good the glorious promises so beautifully poetized, and sanctified to them their deepest distress.

"How Firm a Foundation" should be memorized by every Latter-day Saint. And when synchronized with holy scripture, such as the following, it becomes, indeed, a rod and a staff, to hold one in God's "sovereign, eternal, unchangeable love:"

When thou passest through the waters, I will be with thee; and through the rivers, they shall not overflow thee; when thou walkest through the fire, thou shalt not be burned, neither shall the flame kindle upon thee. (Isaiah 43:2.)

No. 67
How Gentle God's Command
Words by Philip Doddridge   **Music by Hans George Naegeli**
                                    Arr. by Lowell Mason
The Hymn

This hymn "How Gentle God's Commands" is based upon Psalm 55:22. "Cast thy burden upon the Lord and he shall sustain thee."

The Composer

"How Gentle God's Commands" is an arrangement of a composition of Johann or Hans Naegeli (1773-1836), a Swiss composer. He was a pioneer music teacher in Switzerland. Lowell Mason, an early American composer, followed the teachings of Naegeli. The undulating flowing melody of this tune is beautifullly in harmony with the text, although the two were not associated when the composition was written.

The Author

Phillip Doddridge was born in London in 1702. He was educated for the ministry but became a non-conformist. He preached in an independent congregation in Northampton and received wide attention. His hymns were, in the main, based on scriptural texts. He died in 1751.

No. 68
How Great the Wisdom and the Love

Words by Eliza R. Snow   **Music by Thomas McIntyre**

The Hymn

Of the twenty-two poems written by Eliza R. Snow, published in the Latter-day Saint Hymnal, "How Great the Wisdom and the Love" is probably sung oftener in the congregations of the Saints than any other hymn.* In the Sunday Schools and regular Sacrament meetings it is a general favorite.

This sacred hymn is based upon the Lord's Supper as related in Matthew 26:26-30, as follows:

> And as they were eating, Jesus took bread, and blessed it, and brake it, and gave it to the disciples and said, Take, eat; this is my body.
> And he took the cup, and gave thanks, and gave it to them, saying, Drink ye all of it.
> For this is my blood of the new testament which is shed for many for the remission of sins.
> But I say unto you, I will not drink henceforth of this fruit of the vine, until that day when I drink it new with you in my Father's kingdom.
> And when they had sung an hymn, they went out into the Mount of Olives.

In a revelation given to the Prophet Joseph Smith, April, 1930, on church government, the Lord says:

> It is expedient that the Church meet together often to partake of bread and wine (water) in the remembrance of the Lord Jesus.

As far as we can ascertain there was no particular incident, other than the scripture, that inspired the writing of this hymn— just the Christ-centered spirit of a gifted poetess. It was no doubt penned following an uplifting communion service—a sacred love

---

*From George D. Pyper's *Stories of Latter-day Saint Hymns.*

feast. The song centers in the sacrificial offering of Christ on the altar of humanity. But it gives its message in terms of Mormon theology. We have, then, (1) the pre-earth scene, in which our Savior was set apart, (a) to redeem man from the effects of the "fall," and (b) to set a pattern of life here below; (2) the essential work Jesus performed on earth, the shedding of his blood; (3) the manner in which he did this work, by "obedience;" (4) the opening up of the way in which we are to go, if we are to become like him; (5) a statement of how complete is his plan of salvation, in which love, justice, and mercy meet; and (6) an appeal to us to "remember him" when we partake of the Lord's Supper. Thus we complete the circle of thought from Christ in the ante-mortal world to Christ in our lives.

The Composer

Thomas McIntyre, the composer of the beautiful tune to "How Great the Wisdom and the Love," was a native of Edinburgh, Scotland, first seeing the light of day in that historic city on the 4th day of November, 1833. He was the son of Malcolm and Jane McIntyre, but Thomas knew little of them. His mother died when he was a child and his father left the children with friends. He was cared for by a minister named McPherson, who gave him his early training in both religion and common schooling. At an early age he studied the Tonic Sol Fa system and put it to good use when he was converted to

Thomas McIntyre

83

the truths of the Church of Jesus Christ of Latter-day Saints and appointed as chorister of the Edinburgh church choir. This position he efficiently filled for over three years. Then, in 1859, he immigrated to Utah and endured the experience of pulling a handcart over one thousand miles to Salt Lake City. It took three months to make that journey. His first home was in the Twelfth Ward. In 1860 he married Miss Emma Cook, daughter of Joseph and Elizabeth Cook, of Braintree, England. Thirteen children were the fruit of this union. He settled in the 21st Ward, and for twenty-five years was actively engaged in the Sunday School work of that ward officiating for ten years as first assistant superintendent. Being an experienced cornetist, he used his instrument in furthering the musical interest of his people. In 1886 he was appointed by the Deseret Sunday School Union as conductor of a musical festival in the great Tabernacle, in which 12,000 Sunday School children took part; also of another festival July 25th, 1888; was teacher in the 18th Ward seminary and Latter-day Saints College for two years.

The extent of Brother McIntyre's musical activities is indicated by his membership in Ballou's and Croxall's bands and the Salt Lake Theatre and Careless' orchestras. Also he joined the Tabernacle Choir when James Smithies was conductor, and when according to his own story, there were only three tenors—S. Barron, Alexander C. Pyper, and himself. (Alexander C. Pyper was the father of the writer of these song sketches.) Brother McIntyre continued as an active member of the Tabernacle Choir for years under directors Charles J. Thomas, George Careless, and Ebenezer Beesley. He died February 9, 1914. One son, Joseph McIntyre, became a nationally known pianist.

Although Brother McIntyre wrote many compositions, the one joined to Eliza R. Snow's "How Great the Wisdom and the Love" is the only one that has found a place in the Latter-day Saint hymnals; but its sweetness and simplicity will no doubt insure it a lasting place among our hymns.

The Author — Eliza R. Snow (See No. 139)

No. 69

How Long, O Lord, Most Holy And True

Words by John A. Widtsoe   **Music by B. Cecil Gates**
The Hymn

The hymn "How Long, O Lord, Most Holy and True" is academically a well-written hymn. The music is in chorale style. It is definitely a choir hymn and should be placed in the choir section of the hymnbook.

The Composer

B. Cecil Gates was born in the Hawaiian Islands in 1887, the son of Jacob F. Gates and Susa Young Gates.

The life of B. Cecil was one of high aspirations and brilliant promise of success. But a sudden physical disability forbade the culmination of his fondest hopes. He began the study of music at the age of thirteen years. He attended music conservatories in Boston and Berlin. His teachers included Scharwenka, Heffley, Dennie, and Robitschek.

In 1913 he was appointed director of music at the Latter-day Saints University. In 1919 he organized the McCune School of Music and Art. From 1924 to 1929 he served as head of the music department of the Utah State University at Logan. He was the director of the Lucy Gates grand opera company. He also served as the director of the Salt Lake Oratorio Society, the Young Men's Mutual Improvement Association, and as a member of the General Church Music Committee. He was a successful composer, among his most notable compositions are: "The Festival Overture" which he dedicated to the Salt Lake Philharmonic Orchestra, "Resurrection Morning" an Easter cantata, and "My Redeemer Lives" an excerpt from the oratorio "The Restoration." But his name will be perpetuated by his setting for the "Lord's Prayer."

He carried on by sheer will power during his long illness. He died August 31, 1941.

The Author

Like Nephi of old, Dr. John Andreas Widtsoe felt that he had been highly favored of the Lord in all his days. Born on the tiny island of Froyen, Norway, January 31, 1872, he moved to Logan, Utah, when he was twelve years of age—halfway around the world from the place of his birth. The Lord had favored the mother of John and his brother Osborne by bringing through his missionaries the gospel message of hope to her—and to her sons.

Like Nephi, also, Dr. Widtsoe could say that he had seen many afflictions in his day—but he had triumphed over them and turned them to his advantage. When Dr. Widtsoe was a child of six, his father died, leaving the widow and her two sons to make their way. Wealth they did not have, but they knew the value of work. Difficulty also confronted them when they moved to a land where their native Norwegian had to be supplemented by the more difficult English. But to Dr. Widtsoe his adopted tongue became the means of expressing his original thoughts in strong, succinct language. Thirty books and innumerable articles and manuals bear testimony to the fact that he mastered what might to others have seemed a handicap.

Poverty in the new land was always waiting for the Widtsoes, but pride and self-reliance were strong enough to defeat this affliction. Of course, "grits" became the substitute for more appetizing food during one long period of privation. Through this and similar experiences Dr. Widtsoe learned the value and the wise use of money as well as the value of wholesome food.

To him as to his mother and brother the blessings far outweighed the afflictions—and his testimony has rung out to this generation that the Lord is anxious to bless his people, if they will but follow after his teachings.

Education was important to Anna Gaarden Widtsoe, as it had been to her husband; and her children, no matter at what sacrifice to herself, must have the opportunity that would come with a college education. Dr. Widtsoe worked summers and after school to provide as much of the needed money as possible. Scholarships, fellowships, also, assisted the young student—but with it all went the diligent, happy service of a mother who wished the best for her sons, even in 1894 he was graduated from Harvard University, with highest honors, mortgaging the home to insure the desired training.

With his marriage to Leah Eudora Dunford on June 1, 1898, he received one more impetus for educational achievement. With her in the succeeding fall he went to Georg Augustus University, Goettingen, Germany, on a Parker fellowship from Harvard University— and on money that he had borrowed. Two years later he returned with the prized scientific degree Ph. D. and with a still greater prize, his and his wife's first child, a daughter, whom they named in honor of his mother Anna Gaarden Widtsoe.

"The desert places shall blossom as the rose" had long been in the mind of Dr. Widtsoe. He knew that the Lord had promised it, and man could help fulfil the prophecy. He turned his attention to the life-giving irrigation projects that have made the great arid plains bear bountiful harvests. His last great project, aside from his calling as an apostle of the Lord, was in the interest of reclaiming the barren regions of our great neighbor to the north, Canada.

His service to the state of Utah is well known and deeply appreciated. He developed the experiment station of the U.S.U. on a recognized basis, secured the appointment of probably the first agricultural agent in the United States and sent a qualified woman as home demonstrator into an outlying area. For almost nine years he served as president of the Utah State University and then received the call to become president of the University of Utah, a position he held for five years. He became president during a most difficult period, but with his usual genial, sincere recognition of the problems he reached conclusions and initiated programs that quickly won the support of the board of regents, the faculty, and students.

Naturally, the foremost incentive in his life was his Church activity; it was what gave purpose and direction to all of his multitudinous activities. From the time of his baptism in 1884 throughout his life he accepted the calls that came to him—serving as secretary of the deacons' quorum and of his priests' quorum, and later as stake secretary for the elders' quorums. For ten years (1895-1905) he was a member of the Cache Stake Sunday School board, and one of his assignments as an apostle had been as an adviser to the Deseret Sunday School Union. Even during his years of study in Germany he served as a missionary. From 1906 to 1936 he served as a member of the Y.M.M.I.A. general board, and in 1907, having become a seventy, he was set apart successively as president in two quorums of the seventies. From March 17, 1921, Dr. Widtsoe has served as a member of the Council of the Twelve Apostles, during which time he has presided over the European Mission of the Church, organizing the Czechoslovak Mission. He has rendered yeoman service in the genealogical society, the Church board of education, the Church welfare committee, in addition to the pressing weekly assignments at stake quarterly conferences throughout the United States, Canada, and Mexico. He was called to the editorship of *The Improvement Era* in 1935, which position he held with many others until his death in 1952.

No. 70

Come Thou Fount of Every Blessing

Words by Robert Robinson   **Music by John Wyeth**

The Hymn

"Come Thou Fount of Every Blessing" is a personal hymn of gratitude for the Lord's gracious mercy. It is also a prayer that the Lord "Bind the heart" of the supplicant to him. This hymn has a warming melodic line.

The Composer

John Wyeth was born in Cambridge, Mass. in 1770. He became a printer and later a publisher. He traveled extensively and finally settled in Philadelphia where he died. While the hymn tune of "Come Thou Fount of Every Blessing" has been ascribed to John Wyeth in the Latter-day Saint Hymnal, there is a possibility that he was the publisher of the hymn rather than the composer. This hymn was first published in his collection "A Repository of Sacred Music" in 1810. Most of the hymns of this compilation were written by Wyeth and it is very likely that "Come Thou Fount" was one of them. He died in 1858.

The Author

Robert Robinson, (1735-1790) was called "a man of genius;" "as unstable as water," who was given to changing his faith and church frequently.

After many misdeeds, he, with several companions went to a Methodist service. Of this event he writes; "It was, I confess, to pity the folly of the preacher, the infatuation of the hearers, and to abhor the doctrine that I went pitying the poor deluded Methodists, but came away envying their happiness." After his conversion, he became a great preacher but was unorthodox as far as any particular church tenets were concerned. "Come Thou Fount of Every Blessing" was his best-known hymn. He died as he had always wished "soft, suddenly, and alone."

No. 71

I Have Work Enough to Do

Words by Josephine Pollard   **Music by William J. Kirkpatrick**

The Hymn

The tune for this hymn is in the gospel song idiom. The refrain of earlier editions was left off in the 1950 printing. Because of boyhood associations with this song in its entirety, this writer senses that the elimination of the chorus gives a feeling of incompleteness.

The Composer

W. James Kirkpatrick was born at Duncannon, Pennsylvania in 1838. He was educated at common schools and studied music while learning his trade of carpenter at Philadelphia. At that time he associated with the Methodist Episcopal church. In 1858, he assisted A. S. Jenks in collecting camp-meeting songs for "Devotional Melodies" and thereafter, in the intervals of his commercial engagements, poured out a stream of compilations issuing some forty-seven volumes in conjunction with J. R. Sweeny and over forty more after the latter's death. Many times his own compositions were included among these collections which had immense success.

The story is told that Kirkpatrick died at four a.m. one morning in 1921 while writing a hymn about heaven.

The Author

Nothing is known of Josephine Pollard at the present writing.

There Is a Land Whose Sunny Vales

Words and Music by O. P. Huish

The Hymn

"There Is a Land" is a Utah song with a college campus flavor. Its atmosphere is rather remote from that of a hymn.

The Author and Composer — Orson P. Huish (See No. 85)

No. 73

Improve the Shining Moments

Words and Music by R. B. Baird

The Hymn

"Improve the Shining Moments" contains a most valuable exhortation on making the most of "time." It is not a hymn but is a song that is not out of place in a hymn collection because of its commanding subject matter.

Robert Bell Baird was born in Glasgow, Scotland in 1855. He had thirteen brothers and sisters. With part of his family he emigrated to America and settled in Willard, Utah, about the year 1863.

Robert B. Baird

In 1876 he joined The Church of Jesus Christ of Latter-day Saints and was baptized on the sixth day of September. He married Anne Gwenthlyn Davis of Willard October 27th 1876. They were the parents of eleven children.

Elder Baird evidently received his musical education from Evan Stephens with whom he was associated for a number of years. In 1884 he was appointed leader of the Willard ward choir. He also taught music in the public schools of Willard and the surrounding communities. Our best information surmises that his compositions for which he will always be honorably remembered, were written during the time he was teaching in the public schools. Three are published in the Latter-day Saint Hymnal Nos. 73, 200, 190.

Later in his life he became associated with the Oregon Shortline railroad. Elder Baird also served as a Willard city councilman.

He died on the 28th of May 1916 and was buried in the Willard Cemetery.

No. 74

In a World Where Sorrow

Words by Lanta Wilson Smith   Music by E. O. Excell

The Hymn

The hymn "In a World Where Sorrow" is a typical revival song. Its popularity is due to its rhythmical form and sentimental text.

The Composer

Edwin O. Excell, born in 1851, was a composer of gospel songs. He was also a publisher toward the turn of the century. Many well-known gospel songs saw the "light of day" through his publications. He was a native of Uniontown, Pennsylvania. At twenty years of age he moved to the Pacific Coast and worked as a brick mason studying piano in his spare hours. Excell was an excellent singer.

One day Sam Jones, the evangelist, heard him sing and engaged him as chorister. They worked together for twenty years.

At the time of his death in 1921 he was selling one-hundred thousand hymnbooks annually. He was a kindly man and a true Christian.

The Author

Lanta Wilson Smith wrote the gospel song "In a World Where Sorrow" which was set to music by E. O. Excell and published in his collection *Jubilant Praise*.

It May Not Be on the Mountain's Height

Words by Mary Brown   **Music by Carrie E. Rounsefell**

The Hymn

Most hymns make their greatest impact with the first line, but this hymn by Mary Brown is an outstanding exception in that the last line "I'll go where you want me to go" is the challenging line. As a hymn of dedication it is as forthright as "Do what is right, let the consequence follow."

The Composer

The tune was originated by Carrie E. Rounsefell of Boston, Massachusetts. She used to do evangelistic work, and accompanied her singing with an old-fashioned zither. One day an old friend handed her the words of "I'll go where you want me to go," and immediately a tune came to her. She struck one chord on her zither and sang the song.

Later, another friend of hers wrote the tune down for her, and she had it published in a somewhat modified form. It has become a favorite at consecration meetings. She was born in 1894.

The Author

Nothing has come into the hands of this writer of the biography of Mary Brown, author of this popular gospel song.

God of Our Fathers, Known of Old

Words by Rudyard Kipling   **Music by Isaac B. Woodbury**

The Hymn

The sixtieth anniversary of Queen Victoria's reign was celebrated in momentous style in 1897. Dignitaries came to London from all over the world. The culmination of the events attendant to the celebration, was a huge naval and military parade.

Rudyard Kipling, England's greatest poet at the time, was asked by the London *Times* to write something to commemorate the great event. He had difficulty finding a suitable theme. Finally as he viewed the parade, and with stunning impact "Lest We Forget" flashed into his mind. This phrase gradually evolved into the imperishable "Recessional." Someone has said that now in the light of the addition of air power and atomic missiles to the military might, a new "Recessional" of impelling deterent force, should be written for all nations, "Lest We Forget."

The Composer

Isaac B. Woodbury, (1819-1858), was a self-taught musician. He was born in Beverly, Massachusetts, but made his greatest contributions to music after he moved to New York City. Here he edited two collections of music *The Dulcimer* and the *Liber Musicus* and in addition, he published several instruction books. "God of Our Fathers" was a composition he published in the *Dulcimer* under the title *Selena*. A second musical setting of this distinguished poem is also in the Latter-day Saint Hymnal (No. 77). It is from the pen of the Latter-day Saint composer, Leroy J. Robertson. See No. 45.

The Author

Rudyard Kipling, 1865-1936, was born in India. His fascinating novel, *Kim*, together with *Plain Tales from the Hills*, describe in a delightfully readable manner, the people of his birthplace. He traveled extensively and wrote of his wonderful experiences. In England he published the *Barrack Room Ballads*. In America, he published *Captains Courageous*. He married an American woman from Vermont. After his retirement in 1907, he received the Nobel Prize for literature.

No. 78 Beautiful Zion Built Above

Words by George Gill   Music by J. G. Fones

The Author

This familiar hymn was written by an Englishman, George Gill, who was born in Devonshire in 1820. The hymn was written while he was laboring as a missionary on the island of Mangaia, Cook Islands. Later he returned to England and became a pastor in a small church. He died in 1880.

The Composer

Joseph G. Fones was born in England June 18, 1828. He was a retiring, unassuming person possessing a lovable character. He was a coal miner in his native land. A miraculous healing, wherein Mormon elders administered to him after he had been crushed by a great lump of coal, led to his conversion to the Mormon Church. Elder Fones was a self-taught musician.

Soon after his conversion he organized a choir at Barrow in Furness, England. When they sang they drew large crowds.

A little later when he came to America and to Utah he settled in Union, Salt Lake County. The people of Union Ward in Salt Lake County had assisted his emigration in order that he could organize a choir for them. This he did with great success. He was sent to Levan, Utah, by the church authorities to organize a choir and a band. He stayed in Levan for four years and then was sent to several other Southern Utah towns as an appointed ambassador of church music.

Joseph G. Fones had little chance for an education since he went into the coal mines as a young boy. However he had a love for learning and his musical talents were early recognized. After he came to Utah he composed several fine hymns and anthems for the choirs of the church, including the Tabernacle Choir. Three are found in the 1950 edition of the Latter-day Saint Hymnal. They are:

"Beautiful Zion Built Above" No. 78.

"For Our Devotion, Father" No. 107.

"I'll Praise My Maker While I've Breath" No. 254.

Death came to him in 1906.

No. 79

I Need Thee Every Hour

Words by Annie S. Hawkes   **Music by Robert Lowry**

The Hymn

Mrs. Hawkes says that the hymn, "I Need Thee Every Hour" welled out of her heart as she was doing her ordinary housework. The popularity that the hymn attained was a constant astonishment to her until she felt its comforting influence at the death of her husband. Its fervent prayer for divine companionship was a great source of peace to her in her time of sorrow. It is a fine example of the personal hymn: "*I* need thee every hour," "O bless *me* now *my* Savior."

The Composer

Dr. Robert Lowry (1826-1899) was a musician-pastor. He wrote many hymn tunes but attained his greatest prominence as the composer of "I Need Thee Every Hour." He added the chorus part of the hymn to Mrs. Hawkes' verses to make it conform to the gospel song form. One author says that this chorus "I Need Thee, O I Need Thee, Every Hour I Need Thee" is one of the most poignant passages ever written into a sacred song.

The Author

Mrs. Annie Sherwood Hawkes was born in Hoosich, New York, in 1835.

Her very first attempts at writing poems were published in newspapers when she was only fourteen years of age. In 1859 she moved to Brooklyn where she met Dr. Lowry, pastor of a Baptist church. His encouragement launched her on a career of hymn writing. He wrote the music to several of her hymns, including "I Need Thee Every Hour." Mrs. Hawkes died in 1918.

I Stand All Amazed

Words and Music by Charles H. Gabriel

The Hymn

The first printing of this hymn in the Latter-day Saints Church Sunday School book was an arrangement, probably the original, wherein in the verse part of the song the men sang the melody of the duet with the altos. In the 1950 edition of the Latter-day Saint hymnal, the melody is given to the sopranos. The change canceled out a musical effect which was very pleasing and unusual in hymn writing.

The Composer and Author

George B. Stebbins said that Charles H. Gabriel was the "most gifted and brilliant writer of gospel hymns for forty years."

Gabriel was born in the late eighteen-fifties on a farm in Iowa. He began writing hymns when only a boy. At seventeen he went to California on twenty-five dollars which his mother gave him from her scanty earnings working in a store. In 1892 he came back east to Chicago with a wife, a baby, a plug hat, a cane, and sixteen dollars.

Gabriel found work helping to prepare an Epworth League Songbook. Thirty-five other song compilations are credited to him.

No. 81

Israel, Israel, God Is Calling

Words by Richard Smyth   Music by Charles C. Converse

The Hymn

The original words of the song "Israel, Israel" were "What a Friend We Have in Jesus" written by Joseph Scriven in 1855. Although a gospel song it has found its way into some of the most sophisticated hymnals of the world.

The Composer

The composer of "Israel, Israel, God Is Calling" wrote the tune under the pseudonym of "Karl Redan" and published it in a Sunday School collection called *Silver Wings*, in 1870. This tune was used in the earlier days of the Latter-day Saint Church with several other hymns which were in the same meter, notably "O My Father" and "What Was Witnessed in the Heavens."

Charles Converse was born in Warren, Massachusetts, in 1832. He studied music in Leipzig, Germany. Upon returning home he entered the Albany, New York law school, graduating in 1861. Composing music was a hobby with him but a very prolific one. Songs, oratorios, string quartets, and two symphonies came from his pen, all of which were accredited to "Redan." He died in 1918.

The Author

Richard Smyth was born in Dublin, Ireland, on Christmas day 1838. He was known in Pioneer days in Salt Lake City as "Smyth the Hatter." He was converted and joined the Latter-day Saint Church in his native land and served as a missionary in the then Liverpool branch before emigrating to the United States in 1863, crossing the plains to Utah.

Richard Smyth served on two missions to Ireland, his native land. On one of his missions he met a man who had determined from his research that baptism by immersion was proper. All the churches in the community in which he lived practiced baptism by sprinkling. Feeling he had no other recourse he baptised himself by immersion.

When Elder Smyth was guided miraculously to him and preached the gospel which teaches baptism by immersion, the man and his entire family were converted and joined the Church of the Latter-day Saints.

While Salt Lake was his home he spent some time in Cache and Sanpete counties. In 1890 Elder Smyth formed a corporation with George Goddard under the firm name of Goddard & Company, a

Richard Smyth

95

hatter and cleaning establishment. When the firm was later dissolved, Richard Smyth continued his work as a hatter in his home.

He was a poet and a writer of more than ordinary ability, and many of his early efforts appeared in the *Millennial Star* and the *Juvenile Instructor*. His hymn "Israel, Israel, God Is Calling" was a great favorite with the Saints throughout Great Britain in the early days. Richard Smyth died July, 1914 in Salt Lake City.

A small girl in the Smyth home was told that her great-grandfather wrote the hymn "Israel, Israel, God Is Calling." She determined to learn all of the verses. One Sunday at the Sacrament meeting the song was sung. The excited youngster could not rest until she had informed everyone on the row that her great-grandfather wrote that hymn. Then she joined in the singing without a book and sang with all the exuberance at her command.

Think of the number of people now living who could point with pride just as the little Smyth girl, to the fact that their grandfather or great-grandfather or mother or even their great-great-great-grandfather or mother wrote a particular hymn which is published in the Latter-day Saint Hymnal.

No. 82

It Came upon the Midnight Clear

Words by Edwin H. Sears   **Music by Richard S. Willis**

The Hymn

"It Came upon the Midnight Clear" is a popular Christmas carol in America. It can be found in almost every publication of Christmas carols. It is also one of the first American carols to receive recognition by English publishers.

The Composer

The tune was composed and arranged from a book of *Church Chorals and Choir Studies* by Richard Storrs Willis (1819-1900). It was first published in 1850.

The Author

Edwin Hamilton Sears (1810-1876) was a humble clergyman of Mayland, Massachusetts. He received his religious education at the Union College of the Harvard Divinity School. He published several volumes of religious writings.

For twelve years he edited the *Monthly Religious Magazine* Two Christmas hymns will perpetuate his name. They are "Calm on the

Listening Ear of Night" and "It Came Upon the Midnight Clear."
Reverend Sears was a Unitarian but in one of his letters he emphatically stated, "I believe and preach the divinity of Christ."

No. 83

Jehovah, Lord of Heaven and Earth

Anonymous   **Music by Oliver Holden**

The Hymn

The anonymous author of "Jehovah, Lord of Heaven and Earth" makes a poetic plea to the Lord that his word may "spread from pole to pole" until "songs of joy salute the skies" "from men of every tongue."

The Composer

Oliver Holden (1765-1844) was born in Shirley, Massachusetts. He followed the avocations of carpenter, minister, and musician as well as serving a term in the Marine Corps. He helped rebuild the town of Charleston, Massachusetts, after its burning by the·British. Mr. Holden was rich in real estate holdings, kept a music store, and taught music. He gained the honor of being elected a member of Congress. From 1818 to 1833, he served as preacher in a Puritan Church which he built himself unaided. Nine different hymn collections were recipients of his many hymn compositions. His organ is now in the rooms of the Bostonian Society in the Old State House of Boston.

The tune to which "Jehovah, Lord of Heaven and Earth" is sung in the Latter-day Saint assemblies is one of the oldest American hymn tunes in use today. Several musical characteristics of this hymn tune make it intriguing on a first hearing. Its forthright beat note rhythm in the beginning, the horn fifth in the fifth measure, the double duet in measures five and six, the half note measures-seven and twelve, and the rhythm of the thirteenth measure, challenge attention and give a lasting impression.

The Author — Anonymous.

No. 84

Jesus, Lover of My Soul

Words by Charles Wesley   **Music by Simeon B. Marsh**

The Hymn and the Author

Written in 1739, this hymn has been declared by some to be the greatest of the sixty-five hundred hymns of Charles Wesley. Many lines of the hymn were undoubtedly inspired by unusual experiences which Wesley had. One was deliverance from a most terrible storm while on an unseaworthy vessel. (See the first stanza of the hymn.) Another was his recovery from a usually fatal combination of diseases. The third was a night-long vigil of preaching and praying in a prison with ten condemned men. The great hymn is a reflection of these events. During the past century, few hymns have been as extensively used as this one. Its popularity increases with its age. However, there is on record seventeen proposed changes in the first stanza. The word "lover" in the first line, the word "bosom" in the second line, "dearer" in the third line, and the word "still" in the fourth, have all been made subjects of controversy. One editor has written the following version which indicates most of the proposed alterations:

> Jesus, refuge of the soul,
> To thy sheltering arms we fly
> While the raging billows roll
> While the tempest's roar is high.

Many versions appear in the different hymnbooks but the editors of the Latter-day Saint Hymnal adopted the original lines unaltered.

The Composer

Simeon Buckley Marsh was born in Sherburne, New York, in 1798. At the age of twenty years he organized a singing school and for thirty years taught music in and around Albany, New York. A letter in the Library of Congress reads: "Music is my element, and a great enjoyment and aid in my religious life. I anticipate a place in the Heavenly Choir before long, with my beloved contemporaries, Hastings and Mason (two early American musicians). Oh, what a prospect!"

While riding on horseback from one singing school to another, he composed the music which later was adapted to the words of "Jesus, Lover of My Soul."

This musical setting is somewhat more sophisticated than that by Mr. Holbrook (See No. 259) but has never had the wide acceptance as has the latter. The harmonization given this tune in the Latter-day Saint Hymnal is very well-adapted to four part performance and is heard to advantage in this arrangement. Mr. Marsh died in 1875.

No. 85 Jesus, My Savior True, Guide Me to Thee

Words and Music by O. P. Huish

The Hymn

"Jesus My Savior True" with its quasi-sentimental musical setting is most appealing. It is a beautiful example of earnest supplication. The arrangement for Male Chorus (No. 311) is very effective. It was used on the 1935 European tour by the Salt Lake Tabernacle Choir.

The Composer and Author

This article contributed by Ada A. Huish, Payson, Utah, states:

Orson Pratt Huish was born September 9, 1851 in England to James W. and Helen Niblet Huish. At the age of nine he came to America with his mother and family. His father having preceded them had settled in St. Louis, Missouri. His early life was spent in farming and cattle raising.

He established a general store at Moab, Utah, one in Eugene, Oregon, and one in Albuquerque, New Mexico.

Orson Huish also studied commercial photography. Later he established a modern pharmacy called the Huish Drug, with his son David as pharmacist.

He is best known for his musical compositions. He had written about three-hundred songs, most of them have not been published. There are three in the Latter-day Saint Hymnbook-"Guide Me to Thee," "Utah, the Queen of the West," 'Come unto Jesus."

About 1925 he wrote "Each Day a Mother's Day." This was published and was very popular in Payson, Utah, his home town. The first mother's day after its publication a copy was presented to every mother in his ward during Sabbath School services.

He wrote words and music for the Payson High School's "The Silver and the Green." Just a few years before his demise Mr. J. L. Townsend asked him to write a funeral hymn and "Blessed Are the Dead" was written.

I think this was one of his last compositions. He had hundreds of musical articles to his credit; many have been published; and he has been given awards for his achievements and highly honored by musical authorities. He died December 4, 1932.

The Huish Band

In 1880 the Huish Band was organized at the home of James W. and Helen Huish, with the following seven of their eight children as members: Edward A., Joseph W., Orson Pratt, Frank, James W., Jr., Frederick A., and Florette. The oldest brother was their leader. He had some musical training in England before coming to Payson, Utah. The sister, Florette, was probably the first girl to play the drums in a Utah band. She also possessed a delightful voice and sang with the band.

When the band traveled they gave three nights of entertainment in each town. The orchestra played for dancing with special acts and singing at intermission, on the first night. The second brought forth the vaudeville performers, and the third evening the dramatic cast presented its score. It was the first of its kind of entertainment for some of the towns. The band traveled to towns south of Payson to the end of Southern Utah. Produce and hard work were often received in exchange for tickets of admission. At one time the Huish Band played in Salt Lake City, Utah, to honor a Senator from West Virginia. They proudly marched up Main Street and back on State Street, and Held's Band gave them praise and recognition.

No history of music in Utah would be complete without recognizing the pioneering efforts of such organizations as the Huish Band.

No. 86

Jesus of Nazareth, Savior and King

Words and Music by Hugh W. Dougall

The Hymn

This hymn explains the purpose of Christ's mission on earth and his gift of eternal life to us.

The Composer and Author

Hugh Dougall was born in Salt Lake City in 1872, a son of William Bernard and Maria Young Dougall, daughter of President Brigham Young.

Orson Pratt Huish

Hugh W. Dougall

He was a missionary to the Southern States 1894-1896. He studied music in Berlin, Germany; Paris, France; London, England; and in New York City. He has been an opera and concert singer throughout the years. He also taught singing at Carnegie Hall, New York City, for two years. He has been a teacher in Salt Lake City for forty-five years with much success. The "Bridge Builder" is one of twenty songs that he has composed. It has been used extensively by the Mutual Improvement Associations of the Church.

Hugh Dougall was both author and composer of the hymn "Jesus of Nazareth, Savior and King" although this credit was not given to him in the 1950 edition of the *Latter-day Saint Hymns.*

No. 87
O What Songs of the Heart
Words by Joseph L. Townsend   Music by William Clayson
The Hymn

"O What Songs of the Heart" is a hymn which expresses the Latter-day Saint philosophy of life after death, wherein families will be again united.

The Composer — William Clayson (See No. 64)
The Author — Joseph L. Townsend (See No. 64)

No. 88
Jesus Once of Humble Birth
Words by Parley P. Pratt   Music the English Chorister
The Hymn

"Jesus Once of Humble Birth" is used most often as a sacramental hymn. Elder Pratt says of his hymns, "My hymns sprang into existence one after another as occasion called them forth, at times, and in places, and under circustances widely varying." Parley P. Pratt published a hymnbook while he was on a mission in Manchester, England. It was made up of about fifty of his original hymns, the tunes of which he selected from English sources. Many were published with no identification of the composer. Such a one is "Jesus Once of Humble Birth."

The Composer — Anonymous

The dynamic markings found in the earlier editions of the hymnal are omitted in the 1950 edition. It is my opinion after hearing it sung by congregations both ways, that the loud and soft variations enhance the interest in this hymn.

The Author — Parley P. Pratt, See No. 20.

Joy to the World

Words by Isaac Watts   **Music by George Frederick Handel**

The Hymn

"Joy to the World" has universal acceptance as a Christmas Carol throughout Christendom, since its publication by Isaac Watts in his *Psalms of David* in 1719. It has been translated into many languages, including Latin. Periodically lines have been changed to suit the tastes of certain people or the creeds of certain denominations. There are many people now who prefer to sing "Let Heaven and Nature Sing," an early version, as the fourth line of the first stanza, instead of the line printed in the Latter-day Saint Hymnal, "Let Saints and angels sing."

The Composer

Although doubt is expressed by some historians, it is usually held that the great George Fredrick Handel composer of *The Messiah*, composed "Joy to the World." It is reminiscent of certain phrases in the Messiah, notably the first four notes of the chorus "Lift up Your Heads." It is interesting to note also that the first phrase of this carol is set to the complete descending major scale. The version used in the Latter-day Saint Hymnal is from Lowell Mason's publication of 1829, presumably an arrangement by Mr. Mason.

Handel was born in Halle, Saxony, February 23, 1685. Johann Sebastian Bach was born one month later in Eisenbach, but these two musical giants never met although they lived and worked in the same country. Both made their imprints on the musical world with such force that even today they stand as models: each in his own style. Bach wrote in the classic tongue while Handel wrote in the vernacular. Bach became the idol of the students; Handel the idol of the people.

Handel's musical work is made up of three parts. At a very early age he was placed under the tutorship of Zachau, a musician of rare teaching ability.

With him, he learned to sing, to play the organ, the violin, the oboe, the clavier, and he was given a substantial start in harmony, counterpoint, fugue, and composition which he began at the age of eleven years. Later Handel met Mattheson who did much to assist him to musical maturity. Strange to say, Handel almost lost his life at the hand of Mattheson when they fought a duel over a trivial matter of leadership in an opera. Handel was saved when Mattheson's sword was broken as the point struck a button on his coat. The two duelists immediately embraced and remained friends ever afterward.

The second period of Handel's life was devoted mainly to the writing and producing of operas. His sojourn in Italy fostered this type of composition. His life in England, where he became a citizen, was marked by the writing of oratorios. Handel will always be remembered best as the composer of the "Messiah."

Handel's genius was hailed by his contemporaries as well as the musically great who followed him. He died in 1759.

The Author — Isaac Watts (See No. 168)

No. 90

Know This That Every Soul Is Free

Words by William C. Gregg   **Music by Evan Stephens**

The Hymn

The doctrine of the "free agency" of man was never more clearly reiterated than in the poem "Know This that Every Soul Is Free to Choose His Life and What He'll Be."

The Composer — Evan Stephens (See No. 144)

No information has come to hand concerning the life of William C. Gregg, but his oft-quoted poem "Know this that every man is free" stands as a monument to his memory for its deep-seated truth.

No. 91

Let Each Man Learn to Know Himself

The anonymous hymn "Let Each Man Learn to Know Himself" is a versified sermon on the evil of judging one's neighbor. The music of the number is in simple song form. It cannot be classified as a hymn, but the words contain a forceful lesson for daily conduct. It was published in the *Millennial Star* of 1862 Volume XXIX page 464. In some way the name of Philip De La Mare became associated with it. Members of the De La Mare family who live in Tooele, Utah, however, contend that he could not have been the author of the poem because he had no literary ability of which they were ever aware.

No. 92

Gently Raise the Sacred Strain

Words by William W. Phelps   **Music by Thomas C. Griggs**

The Hymn

This hymn, used by the Salt Lake Tabernacle Choir as a theme song for its nationwide broadcast, was included in the collection made by Emma Smith in 1835 under divine authority.* There is no dramatic

---

*From George D. Pyper's *Stories of Latter-day Saint Hymns*

story known concerning the origin of the hymn. It was no doubt written while Brother Phelps was under the spell of the Sabbath and the solemn Sacrament. It expresses gratitude for the return of the day of rest and its attendant blessings, thoughts on eternal life, the great reward, and the day of Sacrament in remembrance of the Lord, a day for gifts of broken hearts and willing sacrifices—a type of blessed things to come, when the Saints will be gathered in eternity, to praise God in sweet accord. It sings of repentance and forgiveness, and enjoins all to fast and pray, as God ordains, and to praise him for his goodness and his love.

The Composer

The composer of "Gently Raise the Sacred Strain" was Thomas C. Griggs, an English convert to the Church of Jesus Christ of Latter-day Saints. He was born in the town of Dover, County of Kent. Shortly after his baptism, May 17, 1856, he and his mother immigrated to America, arriving in Boston, July 11, 1857. It was here he first became interested in music, joining a brass band in that city. At the close of the Civil War, mother and son crossed the plains in Captain Joseph Horne's Company, arriving in Salt Lake City, September 13, 1861. He played in John Eardley's and Mark Croxall's bands. During the early sixties he was employed by Walker Brothers in their branch house at Camp Floyd. There he joined a class in vocal

Thomas C. Griggs

104

training and became leader of the choir at that place. He dated his career as a choir leader from that time. Returning to Salt Lake City he joined the Tabernacle Choir and sang under five of the leaders— C. J. Thomas, Robert Sands, Ebenezer Beesley, George Careless, and Evan Stephens. In April, 1880, while on a mission to Great Britain, he was named as conductor of the Tabernacle Choir, with Ebenezer Beesley as his assistant, who conducted during Brother Griggs' absence. Upon his return, Brother Griggs graciously suggested that Brother Beesley continue as conductor with himself as assistant and that was done. For ten years previous to his mission and two years upon his return, he directed the Fifteenth Ward Choir, then one of the best in Salt Lake City.

From 1874 to 1891, Elder Griggs was superintendent of the Fifteenth Ward Sunday School and from 1891 to 1901 superintendent of the Salt Lake Stake. In 1889, he was sustained as a member of the Deseret Sunday School Union Board which position he held until his death. He and Brother Beesley compiled the first *Deseret Sunday School Song Book* and assisted in the compilation of the *Latter-day Saints Psalmody.* In May, 1900, he was named business manager for the Union, a position he also held until his death. He was an indefatigable worker and did much to improve music in the Church. He died August 12, 1903.

The Author — William W. Phelps (See No. 213)

No. 93   Let Earth's Inhabitants Rejoice

Words by William Clegg   **Music by Leroy J. Robertson**

The Hymn

The music of "Let Earth's Inhabitants Rejoice" reflects in a joyous but noble manner, the message of the words which describe the glories of the millennial day when peace shall reign upon the earth. The hymn's straightforward style makes it useful for any service or on any occasion where this subject is treated.

The Composer — Leroy J. Robertson (See No. 45)

The Author

William Clegg was born in Hull County of Yorkshire, England, May 2, 1823. Opportunities for an education were limited and young Clegg went to work at the age of fourteen as an apprentice at file cutting where he labored for seven years. Four years thereafter he worked at the trade of tempering files.

In 1847 he married Sarah Elizabeth Oates. They had twelve children. In 1850 William joined the Latter-day Saint Church and

105

labored as a local missionary in England.

One night he dreamed of receiving a letter from a former English missionary, Jack Stewart, with a draft in it for his transportation to America. A few days later the letter came. In 1863 the family sailed to America. It was a rough voyage, lasting fifty-three days. After arriving in New York they were transported to Omaha in cattle cars. This journey was indeed arduous because the Civil War was raging at the time and often the railroad tracks were torn up. From Omaha they journeyed to Utah by ox-team. A baby girl was born to them on the way. They finally settled in Springville, Utah.

William Clegg was a studious person, especially of the scriptures. He learned Hebrew and could compare translations. He was an intimate friend of John Hafen, the artist. Hafen painted a picture of him which was hung in the gallery in Springville. His literary works were numerous. On his deathbed he requested his daughters to sing "I Know that My Redeemer Lives." William Clegg died March 30, 1903 at the age of eighty.

No. 94

Let Us Oft Speak Kind Words

Words by Joseph L. Townsend   **Music by Ebenezer Beesley**

The Hymn

"Let Us Oft Speak Kind Words to Each Other" is not a hymn in form but its admonition is so pertinent to Christian conduct that it is very appropriate in a hymn collection. For a statement from its author concerning the writing of the hymn see No. 64

The Composer

Listed eminently among the pioneer composers of the Latter-day Saints is the name of Ebenezer Beesley.* Many popular and praiseworthy compositions came from his tuneful pen and will be treated in other articles. He is mentioned here párticularly because of his lovely musical setting to Joseph L. Townsend's friendly and peacemaking lines, "Kind Words Are Sweet Tones of the Heart." Brother Beesley certainly caught the spirit of the song and fitted to it a melody that has reached the hearts and stirred the emotions of many Latter-day Saints.

Ebenezer Beesley was born December 14, 1840, at Bicester, Oxfordshire, England. As a child he developed great musical talent, showing that tendency even at two years of age. The meeting of the Wesleyan Choir at the home of his parents at the time aided in the development of the boy's natural gift. At the age of six some influen-

---

*From George D. Pyper's *Stories of Latter-day Saint Hymns.*

tial ladies offered to have him trained as a choir boy at St. George's Chapel, Windsor. He being their only living child, his parents refused to part with him. That refusal, which we believe was inspired, changed the whole course of the lives of that family. The parents soon after joined the Church of Jesus Christ of Latter-day Saints. Ebenezer was baptized September 22, 1849, and emigrated to Utah in 1859.

Brother Beesley, after living in Tooele for a short period, moved to Salt Lake City, locating in the Nineteenth Ward. Leading the singing in the Sunday School, revising and preparing music for the *Juvenile Instructor,* directing the ward choir, studying the violin under Professors C. J. Thomas and George Careless, composing Sunday School music, compiling songbooks for Sunday Schools and Mutual Improvement Associations, later directing the production of the *Latter-day Saints' Psalmody,* were some of his busy activities until August, 1880, when he was appointed director of the Salt Lake Tabernacle Choir. For more than nine years he directed the destinies of that great organization. He was a member of George Careless' Salt Lake Theatre orchestra and directed it in the conductor's absence. At the conclusion of his period with the Tabernacle Choir, Brother Beesley taught again at Tooele, then at Lehi, after which he returned to Salt Lake City, where he died March 21, 1906.

The Author — Joseph L. Townsend (See No. 64)

No. 95

I Know That My Redeemer Lives

Words by Samuel Medley   Music by Lewis D. Edwards

The Hymn

In searching various books on hymnology, very little is found concerning Medley's hymn.* One by Wesley of the same title is more often mentioned. It begins:

> I know that my Redeemer lives
> And ever prays for me, etc.

However, Samuel Medley's hymn is the one used by the Latter-day Saints, and while it is not of Latter-day Saint origin, Emma Smith certainly had the inspiration of her divine calling when she selected it as one of the ninety hymns compiled in the first Mormon hymn-book. It fits in perfectly with Latter-day Saint philosophy.

The late Edward P. Kimball, commenting on this song, wrote:

---

*From George D. Pyper's *Stories of Latter-day Saint Hymns.*

There is in this hymn a commingling of joy, faith, assurance, solace, comfort, reverence, aspiration, and a soul-satisfying conviction of heavenly bliss.

Doubt is a close kin to despair; belief and hope are bright rays of encouragement beckoning us to carry on and be of good cheer in spite of impending disaster. Faith and knowledge of the right kind fortify with an armor of righteousness which knows no defeat.

When doubt, discouragement, or any foe of the Spirit of God manifests itself, pray and then sing or even play this truly inspired song and a new light to cheer and bless will kindle your soul.

The style of this song is necessarily grand through its simplicity, but it takes a cultivated mind to appreciate the beauty of sheer simplicity, and of course the best type of worship is truly simple; hence this song, recognizing the sublime truth of the Redeemer's mission, is one of the most impressive hymns in our possession.

Medley's tendency to repeat certain key words in the refrains of his songs is highly accentuated in this hymn. The repetition of "He Lives" is emotionally effective.

To hear this loved song rendered by an assembly of devoted Latter-day Saints is a spiritual baptism. It becomes a mass-testimony of many of the truths of the restored gospel of Jesus Christ. It runs the gamut of religious experience. It testifies that Christ rose from the dead and visualizes the reality of the resurrection. It declares that he is our ever-living head, ready to plead for us and feed our hungry souls in times of need, to guide and strengthen us when faint, to silence our fears and calm our troubled hearts. With increasing intensity it acclaims Christ as our kind, wise, heavenly friend, our Prophet, Priest, and King, whose love is all-embracing and never-ending, and through whose redeeming power we shall conquer death and be safely guided to our heavenly home. The last stanza is a glorification of the name of our Savior and ends in high ecstasy with the complete assurance: *I know that my Redeemer lives.*

The Composer

Professor Lewis D. Edwards, the composer of the present popular setting of "I Know That My Redeemer Lives," was the son of David T. and Esther Edwards and was born in Aberdare, South Wales, in 1858. Coming to America, he spent some of his young years in Pennsylvania, singing in church choirs. Traveling west he was converted to the Mormon faith, baptized at Ogden, Utah, March 31, 1878, and moved to Willard, Utah, the next day. There he met Evan Stephens, under whose tuition he soon learned to play the organ. There, also, began a lifelong friendship between these two men. He progressed rapidly in the study of harmony and composition. In 1879, while teacher of the Willard Primary class, he composed many songs for Latter-day Saint children and became bandmaster. In 1880, he succeeded Professor Stephens as leader of the Willard choir and directed the singing in the Sunday School. He also conducted singing classes at Harrisville, Brigham City, Farmington, and Centerville. He taught part of a term begun by Professor Stephens at Ogden and was teacher of music in the Ogden City Schools. He wrote and produced an opera called *The Two Orphans*.

In 1891, Professor Edwards moved to Preston, Idaho and taught in the Oneida Stake Academy until August, 1900. In 1892, he conducted the "Sage Brush Glee Club" and "Choral Union" of Logan. In 1898, the Preston Choir under his leadership sang at the Eisteddfod at Salt Lake City and won two prizes.

He composed many Sunday School songs. His anthem, "Our Father in Heaven," was sung daily at the dedication of the Salt Lake Temple. He won a prize for his anthem, "Who Can Stand against the Works of the Lord?" Other medals were awarded at Cleveland, Ohio, Lafayette, Indiana, at Williamsport, and at the Salt Lake Eisteddfod in 1898. For a short time he was director of music in the Salt Lake City Schools. He died at La Grande, Oregon, March 4, 1921.

The first tune to this song that we have any record of was written by George Careless and went through all the editions of the *Latter-day Saint Psalmody* under the name of "Redeemer." In December,

Lewis D. Edwards

1886, a tune by Edwin F. Parry was published in the *Juvenile Instructor*; but with all the marvelous composing ability of George Careless and the melodic genius of Edwin F. Parry they did not fully catch the spirit of this song as did the Welshman, Lewis D. Edwards, who wrote the present popular tune. The date of the writing is unknown, but it was published in *Deseret Sunday School Songs* in 1909 and now in *Latter-day Saint Hymns*.

If Samuel Medley had been here to direct, he could not have suggested a tune more appropriate than this one, for Edwards caught Medley's style by giving accent to the key words which the hymnist loved to repeat in his refrains. As far as the Latter-day Saints are concerned, Edwards has linked his name with Medley's for all time.

The Author

Samuel Medley, the author of "I Know That My Redeemer Lives," was born at Chestnut, Herefordshire, England, June 23, 1738. His father being the keeper of a school, Samuel received a good education. Put to work as an apprentice to a London oilman and not liking the work assigned him, he rebelled and joined the British Royal Navy as a midshipman. Though properly trained in Christian virtues, he became dissipated and reckless. In a battle with a French fleet, in 1759, he was so badly wounded that he was unable to continue in actual service. He had a great dread of the amputation of a limb. Under this strain some fraction of his religious training returned, and in penance he prayed all night. In the morning he was advised by an astonished surgeon that his limb could be saved. He was filled with joy and thanksgiving, but not until he had heard a powerful sermon by Dr. Watts did his awakened conscience lead him into religious paths. He joined the Baptist Church, established a school in London, and soon started to preach. In 1767 he was appointed pastor of a Baptist Church at Wartford, Herefordshire, and began a labor of exalted Christian love which continued for twenty-seven years. He became very popular, won the confidence of his people, and thousands came to hear him.

Samuel Medley wrote many hymns including "I Know That My Redeemer Lives." These were first published in magazines and periodicals and afterwards—in 1789—compiled and printed in book form. Two other volumes appeared, the last a posthumous one—being published the year after his death which occurred July 17, 1799.

A *Memoir* of Medley was published by his son in 1800, which is said to be authentic. In 1833, another memoir, by his daughter, Sarah, showed a hatred for her brother, for his not displaying the love and forbearance so manifest in her father's life and hymns.

Hear Thou Our Hymn, O Lord

Words and Music by Frank W. Asper

The Hymn

Both words and music of this short four line hymn were written by Frank W. Asper.

The Composer and Author

Frank W. Asper comes of pioneer stock. Four of his ancestors fought in the American Revolution. In 1861 his father crossed the plains in a covered wagon, with a melodeon as one of his prized possessions. His first teacher was Annie Maeser, daughter of the educator Karl G. Maeser, and at the age of seven, after some study with Ebenezer Beesley, former conductor of the Tabernacle Choir, he was his teacher's accompanist. His first pipe-organ solo in public was played in the Assembly Hall at the age of twelve. After three years' study in Europe, Frank Asper studied in Boston for five years, and was instructor at the New England Conservatory after graduating there with honors. Besides study at Stern's Conservatory in Berlin, he also studied at Boston University, University of Utah, and Chicago Musical College. He numbers among his teachers such men as Jonas, Buonamici, and Chadwick. In April 1924, he was appointed organist at the Tabernacle and has served there continuously since that time. He began playing the national broadcasts soon after the beginning in 1929. He organized the Utah chapter of the American Guild of Organists, has been the head several years, and is now Regional Chairman of Wyoming, Idaho, and Utah. He is also a Fellow in that organization. In 1938 he was awarded the honorary degree, Doctor of Music, from Bates College. He has many published compositions for organ to his credit and was contributor and co-author of the recent LDS Hymnal. He has concertized extensively in Europe, Canada, Mexico, as well as in the United States. He has played for the present kings of Denmark, Sweden, and Norway. He was born in 1892.

No. 97

Lo! On the Water's Brink We Stand

Words Anonymous   **Music by Leroy J. Robertson**

The Hymn

Dr. Robertson says that his hymn is written for baptismal services. It can be sung by a quartette of well-balanced voices, a chorus or by the congregation.

The Composer — Leroy J. Robertson (See No. 45)

The Author — Anonymous

No. 98

Let Us All Press On

Words and Music by Evan Stephens

The Hymn

"Let Us All Press On" is a song of exhortation. Both the words and the music were written and composed by Evan Stephens.

Evan Stephens made liberal use of the vigor of long and short note combinations in many of his compositions. His poetic ability and his enthusiasm for the Latter-day Saint Church brought from his pen a great number of hymns and anthems of lasting worth to the Saints of the latter days.

The Composer and Author — Evan Stephens (See No. 144)

No. 99

In Memory of the Crucified

Words by Frank I. Kooyman   **Music by Alexander Schreiner**

The Hymn

According to the composer of this hymn, it is a sacramental hymn, directing us to the emblems, and thoughts which should be in our meditations at that time. Calm, not rousing to action, but rather inviting to contemplation of divine qualities. This hymn melody is written in the style of the old German chorale.

It is unusually sacred in its expression, being clearly directed to our Heavenly Father with these words: "May thy sweet Spirit here abide, that all may feel its glowing power." And the purpose of this hymn is clear, also: "to prepare our minds and hearts for the partaking, worthily, of the emblems of the Sacrament."

Elder Kooyman's old-world religious experience: the limited administration of the Lord's Supper there—only a few times a year—may have had a tendency to make him more appreciative of its constant use in the restored Church. Be that as it may, he feels that with the coming of the true gospel, old-new Evangel into his life, there also came a better understanding, a fundamental change in his valuation of the Sacrament.

The Composer — Alexander Schreiner (See No. 24)

The Author

Frank I. Kooyman was born in Terschelling, north of Holland on November 12, 1880.

112

Frank I. Kooyman, a member of the LDS Church Historian's Office staff, is a native of Terschelling, one of the Frisian islands located north of Holland's mainland. In his 17th year he moved to Amsterdam, accepted the restored gospel there in his 19th year. In 1902 he started on a full-time mission for the Church in the land of his birth and served over three years.

In Amsterdam he was employed for five years in the District Court Record Office - in Salt Lake City for twenty years as book-keeper-cashier of a wholesale firm.

At the completion of his mission, in 1905, he moved to Utah and kept active in the Church. Successively he served as a president in four quorums of seventy, worked in several Sunday Schools (in one as superintendent) and for over four years, concurrently with his other Church activities, had charge of the Hollanders' LDS organization. After his second mission to his native country, he served another four years as president of the Hollanders' Church congregations.

In 1929 was called to preside over the Netherlands Mission; in this capacity served nearly four and a half years. His wife (Elisabeth) and three of their seven children accompanied him. With his wife he visited most of the missions in Europe in that period.

Articles by him, defending and explaining the latter-day message, appeared in many magazines and newspapers, allaying much prejudice.

While in the mission field and between his two mission terms, he translated fifty or more Church songs into the Dutch, which appeared in five editions of *Heilige Lofzangen* or Sacred Hymns.

In 1951-1956 he assisted with the retranslation into Dutch of the Book of Mormon, Doctrine and Covenants, and the Pearl of Great Price - also with the translation of the temple ceremonies into Dutch, used now in the Swiss edifice.

He translated, while in the Netherlands, Edward H. Anderson's *Brief History of the Church*, Parley P. Pratt's *Voice of Warning*, and Dr. John A. Widtsoe's *Rational Theology*.

In 1947-1957 assisted with arranging and proofreading of the new Church songbook, *Hymns*, edition of 1948 and some following printings.

His wife, Elisabeth, passed on in 1937. Four years later he married Frances E. Ludwig, his present companion.

Fourscore years of age now, he keeps active in Church affairs.

Lord Accept into Thy Kingdom

Words by Mabel Jones Gabbott   **Music by Alexander Schreiner**

The Hymn

This is a hymn, according to its author, intended to be sung at baptismal occasions. It is clearly doctrine of the latter-day dispensation of the gospel. It speaks of baptism not only for the living but also is applicable by proxy for the dead.

The melody is expressive of happy feelings which are engendered naturally when new members are "born" into the Church and fold of Christ.

The Composer — Alexander Schreiner (See No. 24)

The Author — Mabel Jones Gabbott (See No. 49)

No. 101
Lord Accept Our True Devotion

Words by R. Aldridge   **Music by Joseph J. Daynes**

The Hymn

"Lord Accept our True Devotion" has in it the elements of popularity and longevity. The repetitive phrases "Never Leave Us," "Ever Guard us" and Ever praising" create an indelible impression on all who sing or hear this hymn.

The Composer — Joseph J. Daynes (See No. 232)

The Author

No information has come to light from sources available to your author concerning R. Aldridge.

No. 102
Though in the Outward Church Below

Words Anonymous   **Music by W. A. Mozart**

The Hymn

"Though in the Outward Church Below" is a hymn text based on the parable of Jesus "The Wheat and the Tares" Matthew 13th chapter verses 24-30.

The Composer

This famous tune is taken from an opera by Mozart (1756-1791),

The Magic Flute. It is not known who made the arrangement found in the Latter-day Saint Hymnal.

The Author — Anonymous

No. 103

The Lord Is My Light

Words by James Nicholson   **Music by John R. Sweeney**

The Hymn

"The Lord Is My Light" is based on the twenty-seventh Psalm of David. It is a striking declaration of faith, hope, and trust. It should be sung with forthright assurance and with a tempo that pushes forward.

The Composer

John R. Sweeney (1837-1897) was a gospel song writer and compiler. The third and sixth measures of the chorus of "The Lord is My Light" hint of coloratura style. Song styles which are foreign to the traditional hymn pattern are sometimes found in many of the hymns of lesser musical worthiness.

The Author

Nothing is at hand concerning the life and works of Reverend Nicholson.

No. 104

The Lord Is My Shepherd

23rd Psalm   **Music by Thomas Koschat**

The Hymn

"The Lord Is My Shepherd" is one of many versifications of the great twenty-third Psalm of David. This psalm is one of the most beloved passages in the entire scriptures. It has been set to music over and over again.

The Composer

Thomas Koschat's fine bass voice was responsible for his turning to music as life's vocation. He was born in 1845 but later went from his home near Klagenfurt to Vienna to study science. Incidentally he joined the Court Opera chorus. Soon he was made the leader. As he became more and more engrossed in music, he turned to composition. He wrote over a hundred quartettes for male voices. He also wrote

115

three operas. The music to "The Lord Is My Shepherd" is unusual as a hymn, in that the melody of the first three phrases is in the alto voice part. The original words used in Koschat's time for this tune are: "Forsaken, forsaken am I, etc." He died in 1914.

No. 105
Lord, Dismiss Us with Thy Blessing

Words by John Fawcett   **Music by Jean Jacques Rousseau**

The Hymn

This hymn is purely one for dismissal. It is a prayer that God's Spirit will always be with us. In the original second stanza some doctrine was expressed with which modern editors did not agree and as a result it has been largely rewritten by them.

The Composer

Jean Jaques Rousseau (1712-1778) was an untaught musician, who gained much prominence in France through a series of controversial articles about music and musical notation. He wrote an opera *Le Devin der Village* which caused additional furor of controversy in spite of the fact that it had a successful initial production. A folk song incorporated in the opera was the music from which "Lord, Dismiss Us with Thy Blessing" was taken. It was first used in England about 1825. Later, it found its way into American hymnals.

The Author

John Fawcett's life was a gradual ascent from poverty to prominence. He was born in 1739 and early in life he determined to be a clergyman. Just out of his teens and married, he received a call to go to Wainsgate, England, to be the pastor of the Baptist Church. As there was no parsonage for some years the Fawcett family "boarded around." Finally a call to become the Pastor of Carter's Lane Baptist Church in London. A two-wheeled cart was packed with the family belongings on the day set for the departure, but the farewell of the village parishioners was so touching that Parson Fawcett suddenly ordered the cart to be unpacked, and the family returned to their home. Mr. Fawcett remained in Wainsgate as pastor for fifty-four years.

The Sunday following his intended departure, he presented the church with a new song "Blessed Be the Tie that Binds" and a little later he wrote for his evening services "Lord, Dismiss Us with Thy Blessing." His death in 1817 was greatly mourned in that little community.

Master, the Tempest Is Raging

Words by M. A. Baker   Music by H. R. Palmer

The Hymn

"Master, the Tempest Is Raging" is a versification of the scriptures found in Matthew, eighth chapter, verses twenty-four to twenty-six: "And, behold, there arose a great tempest in the sea, insomuch that the ship was covered with waves: but he was asleep. And his disciples came to him, and awoke him, saying, Lord, save us: we perish. And he saith unto them, Why are ye fearful? Then he arose, and rebuked the winds and the sea; and there was a great calm."

The Composer

This song is one of the few in the hymnbook which are marked dynamically, and this feature has much to do with its popularity in Latter-day Saint assemblies. H. R. Palmer (1834-1907) was a New Yorker by birth. He showed much musical talent as a youth, and at seventeen, he became a church organist. His musical education was gained in New York and Europe. His professional work included director of the Rushford Academy, organizer, and conductor of the Church Choral Union of New York City, and conductor at large. The Choral Union had at times as many as four thousand singers. A Doctor of Music degree was conferred upon him by the Chicago University in 1881. His publications are many: his sacred songs alone numbering hundreds. Among his best-known hymns and songs are: "Just for Today," "Galilee, Blue Galilee," and "Peace Be Still."

The Author

Mary Ann Baker almost became an unbeliever when her father and mother and brother were all stricken with an uncurable disease. But an unusual incident restored her faith. It was in 1874 when the Reverend H. R. Palmer asked her to write some songs on Sunday School lessons. The theme was "Christ Stilling the Tempest." She hesitated to try, remembering how St. Anatolius, fourteen-hundred years before, had written a most beautiful poem on this incident:

> Fierce was the wild billow, dark was the night;
> Oars labored heavily, foam glimmered white:
> Trembled the mariners, peril was nigh,
> Then saith the God of Gods, peace, it is I.

Summoning her courage however, and remembering her own distress, she wrote, "Master, the Tempest Is Raging."

Dr. Palmer composed the tune. It came to light in 1881 when it was first published and attained great popularity.

When James A. Garfield, President of the United States, was stricken with his last illness, the song was sung at his bedside, and after he died it was sung in many parts of the nation at memorial services held in his honor.

No. 107

For Our Devotion, Father

Words by Henry W. Naisbitt   **Music by J. G. Fones**

The Hymn

The hymn "For Our Devotion" should be placed in the "choir" section of the Latter-day Saint Hymnal. Its musical form requires that all four voice parts be equally sustained to bring out the effects intended by the composer.

The Composer — Joseph G. Fones (See No. 78)

The Author — Henry W. Naisbitt (See No. 278)

No. 108

Jesus Mighty King Of Zion

Words by Fellows   **Music by Tracy Y. Cannon**

The Hymn

The words of this hymn written by a man or woman the last name of whom is the only identification, speak poetically of the Latter-day Saint belief in baptism by immersion.

The Composer — Tracy Y. Cannon (See No. 1)

Tracy Y. Cannon gives us the year in which he composed this hymn as 1948. He wrote it especially for the 1948 edition of "Hymns" Church of Jesus Christ of Latter-day Saints.

The Author

No information has been found concerning author Fellows.

No. 109

Precious Savior, Dear Redeemer

Words and Music by H. R. Palmer

The Hymn

The Hymn "Precious Savior, Dear Redeemer, May each soul in Thee Abide" is a fervent prayer.

The Composer and Author — H. R. Palmer (See No. 106)

Choose the Right

Words by Joseph L. Townsend   Music by Henry A. Tuckett

The Hymn

"Choose the Right" is a hymn of exhortation whose moral is obvious. It is written in gospel song form with verse and chorus.

The Composer

Henry A. Tuckett was a candy maker in Salt Lake City who made music a hobby. Your writer remembers, when he was a small boy, attending a children's music class taught by Henry A. Tuckett. The class culminated with a concert, featuring Brother Tuckett's own compositions.

The Author— Joseph L. Townsend (See No. 64)

No. 111

MIA, We Hail Thee

Words by Ruth May Fox   Music by W. O. Robinson

The Hymn

The song "MIA, We Hail Thee" is exclusively a song for the young people's organizations of the Church of Jesus Christ of Latter-day Saints.

The Composer — William O. Robinson (See No. 134)

The Author — Ruth May Fox (See No. 42)

No. 112

Lead, Kindly Light

Words by John Henry Newman   Music by John Dykes

The Hymn

Never was a hymn more the result of an event or circumstance than "Lead, Kindly Light." Its author was returning from Palermo, Italy to France on an orange boat. In the Straits of Bonifacis, between Corsica and Sardinia, the sea became calm and remained so for a week, making progress impossible. A gray fog shut out the view of the land. On all sides were dangerous cliffs and islets which could not be seen. The captain of the boat lost his bearings. Was ever a setting more perfect to bring forth the lines of "Lead, Kindly Light, amid the encircling Gloom." Newman titled the hymn "The Pillar of the Cloud" but when it was first published in 1836, it was given the caption "Faith." Now it is known by its first line, "Lead, Kindly Light."

The Composer

John B. Dykes (1823-1876) showed great musical ability as a child. When he was ten years old, he began to play the organ in his grandfather's church. He received his main training in St. Catherine's College in Cambridge, England. Upon graduation, he was ordained a deacon and became organist at Malton, Yorkshire, England. During his lifetime, he held many responsible church positions. His hymns exhibited much skill in part-writing. "Lead, Kindly Light" is somewhat intricate in this respect and is therefore more difficult for congregational singing. Dykes died January 22, 1876, and was buried in St. Oswald's Churchyard in Sussex, England. He composed over three-hundred hymns.

The Author

John Henry Newman (1801-1890) was a rebellious, strong-willed boy at home, giving his father and mother much concern. His early inclinations led him, in later life, to hold himself in high esteem. He rested in the thought that "There are only two supreme and luminously self-evident beings, myself and my Creator." When a young man, Newman espoused the cause of the Anglican Church. His preachings were among the most distinguished of his generation. In 1843 some of his writings on Apostalic Succession were repudiated by the bishops of the church. This action caused Newman to leave the church and join the Roman Catholic Church. He received immediate recognition as a Catholic by the Pope, and in 1880, after receiving several other high offices, he was made a Cardinal. Many books have been written about Cardinal Newman but his name will go down in history most of all as the author of "Lead, Kindly Light."

No. 113
The Lord My Pasture Will Prepare

Words by Joseph Addison   Music by Dimitri Bortniansky

The Hymn

"The Lord My Pasture Will Prepare" represents dignified verse, Trust and confidence in the Lord are given poetic grace in the lovely lines of this hymn.

The Composer

Bortniansky (1751-1825) was responsible for standardizing and elevating Russian Church Music to an honored place in religious song. As a young man, he studied music in St. Petersburg, Venice, Rome and Naples. He wrote two operas which were produced with success, but it was not until he was appointed choir master in the Royal Church of the Empress, that he made his mark. Here, he worked his reforms and became a prodigious composer of church music. Tschaikovsky edited a complete edition of Bortniansky's sacred works, requiring ten large volumes. The music for "The Lord My Pasture Will Prepare" was one of his many hymn tunes.

The Author

Joseph Addison (1672-1719) was the co-author of an English paper called the *Spectator*. It was here that he published his famous critical essays justifying them in these words: "The great and only end of these speculations is to banish vice and ignorance out of the Territories of Great Britain." Addison was elected to Parliament as a result of his writing a poem called *The Campaign* which was in praise of the Duke of Marlborough's victory at the battle of Blenheim. Addison's uprightness and talent won respect for him in all political circles and among the distinguished of England. He wrote four hymns which were published in the *Spectator;* "The Lord My Pasture Will Prepare," was one of them.

No. 114

More Holiness Give Me

Words and Music by Philip Paul Bliss

The Hymn

"More Holiness Give Me" is a petition to the Lord for more holiness, more patience, more faith, and more adherence to all other Christian virtues. It is a thoroughgoing gospel song and is very popular. The flow of the melody in the twelve-eight meter form is in great measure responsible for its universal acceptance.

The Composer and Author — Philip Paul Bliss (See No. 301)

No. 115

America

Words by Samuel F. Smith   **Music by Henry Carey**

The Hymn

The famous American patriotic hymn "America" was written by Samuel Francis Smith (1808-1895). While translating a collection of German songs and hymns, Reverend Smith became intrigued with one of the tunes which was unfamiliar to him. Not knowing that the British had already adopted the tune for "God Save the King," but recognizing the patriotic quality of the German version, Smith said;

> I instantly felt the impulse to write a patriotic hymn of my own, adapted to the tune. Picking up a scrap of waste paper which lay near me, I wrote at once, probably within half an hour, the hymn "America" as is now known everywhere.

121

The imagery of the hymn is not that of America as a whole, but only that part east of the Alleghenies northward where the author lived. Woods and templed hills, for example, certainly does not portray the plains of the middle states or the mountains of the west. But the universal passion for "sweet freedom, sweet land of liberty," and God's mighty protection forever with which the hymn is imbued, makes it a vital, living essence of patriotism. This hymn was first sung at the Park Street Church in Boston, July , 1832, by a children's choir trained by Lowell Mason from which place it spread throughout America.

The Composer

The origin of the air is not definitely known but it is sung as a patriotic song in several different European countries notably in Denmark, Germany, and England. "God Save Our Gracious King" is sung in England by demands of custom, at the beginning or the close, and sometimes both, of every festal occasion. Fragments of the tune appear in the works of certain master composers, but in 1740, it was published complete although anonymously in *Thesaurus Musicus*. The melodic line is logically put together, each phrase is an outgrowth of the preceding one. The climax is fitting in the next to the last measure on the highest tone of the tune. It is both singable and listenable. The common attribution designating Henry Carey as composer, has been proved false.

The Author

Reverend Samuel Francis Smith, was born in Boston in 1808. He died in 1895. He graduated from Harvard University in 1829. His classmate, the great Oliver Wendell Holmes, wrote for a class reunion, a witty stanza which is a subtle eulogy of Reverend Smith:

> And there's a nice youngster of excellent pith-
> Fate tried to conceal him by naming him Smith;
> But he shouted a song for the brave and the free,
> Just read on his medal, "My Country," of Thee.

After preparing for the ministry, Smith became pastor of the Baptist Church in Waterville, Maine. Later he served as professor of languages in Newton Center, Massachusetts. The house in which he lived for fifteen years, is still in existence.

His interest in the Baptist missionary work took him to many of the missions of the world. He was also the editor of the Baptist hymnal *The Psalmist* (1843). Reverend Smith's life was spent editing, preaching, teaching, translating, managing, and writing. In fact, he died suddenly at the age of eighty-seven, entering a train on his way to fill a speaking engagement.

122

Nay, Speak No Ill

Words Anonymous   **Music Anonymous**

The Hymn

Nothing is at hand as to who the author of this hymn is, or who composed the music.

The ever timely admonition of its message, however, will make it a permanent favorite in the Latter-day Saint hymnal. It is interesting to note that many hymns of great worth, have come to us anonymously.

Nearer, Dear Savior, to Thee

Words by Joseph L. Townsend   **Music by William Clayson**

The Hymn

This hymn is one of prayer for companionship with our Father in heaven.

The Composer — William Clayson (See No. 64)

The Author — Joseph Townsend (See No. 64)

Now Let Us Rejoice

Words by W. W. Phelps   **Music Anonymous**

The Hymn

More perhaps than any other hymn in our collection, "Now Let Us Rejoice" reminds us of the lily—not the one that "grows in the field" and that Jesus bids us to "consider" but rather the one that springs out of the slime of the open miasmatic pool.*

This is the most beautiful of flowers, the most delicate, the most artistic in its shape and coloring. Yet it is produced out of the most unpromising of materials; it grows where one would never look for beauty and grace and loveliness. Somehow it manages to suck up only the makings of perfection from the mud, to transform this on the way up its long, slender stem, and then to exhibit its wonder to the eye of the passer-by. "Gilding the lily" is a phrase that expresses the utter futility of human power to improve upon this delicate artistry.

It was something like that in the writing of this beautiful hymn.

When William W. Phelps wrote this poem, he was living in what was known at "Zion," located in Jackson County, Missouri. The

---

*From George D. Pyper's *Stories of Latter-day Saint Hymns.*

place had about twelve hundred Latter-day Saints. They had built homes, some of which were of burnt brick and two stories in height, great acres were put under cultivation, a school was established, a press set up (*The Evening and Morning Star*), and everything pointed to the building of a commonwealth that would realize the dream of those who lived there. Phelps was editor of the *Star*.

But the song was not written then.

Presently, in 1833, a mob, plentifully armed and numbering between four and five hundred, came upon the settlement at Independence. They tore down the two-story brick building in which the press was housed and in the lower part of which Phelps lived; they destroyed the press, burned the books and papers, drove Mrs. Phelps and her baby out upon the street; they closed the Gilbert and Whitney store, and tarred and feathered Bishop Partridge and another man named Allen; and they served warning on all the Saints living in the country not to do any more work or build or buy or sell in their settlements. Later, when the chill of November came, all the Saints were ejected from the county, and were not allowed to take with them any clothing or food. And later, more than two hundred houses in which they had lived were destroyed.

"Now Let Us Rejoice" came out of this situation. Defeat, frustration, homelessness, suffering, privation, hunger, even—these produced a hymn that still gives hope and sustenance to hundreds of thousands who live in better times.

It was not fanaticism that brought it forth; it was faith; not a sense of permanent, but only of temporary frustration. Few hymns express better the feeling of joy, of promise, of the future look. It was the lily coming out of the ooze.

The Composer

No composers are listed for the tunes by which "Now Let Us Rejoice" was sung in the beginning. One in four-quarter measure is found in an early hymnbook by J. C. Little and G. B. Gardner. It does not fit the words as does the three-quarter measure of the present tune.*

Mormon Hymnals page 267, a quotation by Samuel P. Bayard says of this tune "Possibly a waltz, sounds maddeningly familiar and is maddeningly untraceable."

The Author — W. W. Phelps (See No. 213)

---

*See supplement.

Lord, We Ask Thee Ere We Part

Words by George Manwaring   **Music by Ebenezer Beesley**

The Hymn

This hymn is a closing hymn of prayer. It is well written, dignified and enticingly singable.

The Composer — Ebenezer Beesley (See No. 94)

The Author — George Manwaring (See No. 136)

No. 120

Now Thank We All Our God

Words by Martin Rinkart   **Music by Johann Cruger**

The Hymn

"Now Thank We All Our God" was originally, a "short grace
before meals." The first stanzas which are found in the Latter-day
Saints Hymnal are based on the apocryphal book of Ecclesiastius, a
volume of writings not admitted to the Old Testament, but which was
used in the early Christian Church between two hundred A.D. and
four hundred A.D. for supplementary reading. This hymn with its
triumphant tone, is often sung on occasions of national rejoicing; for
example on the completion of the Cologne Cathedral in 1880, in
1897 for the Diamond Jubilee of Queen Victoria, the ending of the
Boer War in 1902, and lastly in an arrangement by Mendelssohn,
for a festival commemorating the invention of printing.

The Composer

Johann Cruger (1598-1662) was one of the most distinguished
musicians of his time. After a thorough schooling in Guben, his
birthplace, and the Jesuit College at Olmitz, he settled in Berlin. He
was a prolific hymn writer and some twenty of his creations have
survived the test of time. He was editor and contributor to several of
the hymn publications of the day.

The Author

Translation by Catherine Winkworth.

Martin Rinkhart's life (1586-1649) was one of astounding
suffering and tragedy. After he graduated from the Leipzig University,
he rose rapidly from schoolmaster to cantor, then to deacon, then
pastor and finally to arch-deacon of Eilenburg. His life was contemporaneous with the Thirty Years War. Eilenburg became a city of refuge for the fugitives from the war, but soon it was overcrowded and
unsanitary. Famine stalked the land and disease followed. Rinkhart

125

soon found himself alone to take care of the dead, all other officials and priests having either died or fled. He records that he read forty to fifty burial services a day. In all, 4,480, including his wife! Eight-thousand persons were buried en masse, interment being without funeral services of any kind. The strain proved too great for Rinkart, and he at last succumbed to the hardship. With all, Rinkart was a prolific writer, being the author of sixty-six hymns. Some received acceptance in Germany, but one, "Now Thank We All Our God," has had universal acceptance.

Catherine Winkworth (1827-1876), a devoted translator of German hymns, made the English translation of the hymn as it is used to-day.

No. 121

Jesus, Savior, Pilot Me

Words by Edward Hopper   **Music by J. E. Gould**

The Hymn

Two items are involved in the writing of "Jesus, Savior, Pilot Me." One, Reverend Hopper, the author, was well acquainted with seamen and the sea, and second-the gospel story of Christ calming the storm on Galilee, furnished content for the hymn.

The Composer

John Edgar Gould's lilting tune to "Jesus, Savior, Pilot Me" with its repetitious phrases is rather charming. This fact has added much to preserve the hymn in popular favor. Gould was born in 1822 and died in 1875.

The Author

Dr. Edward Hopper (1816-1875) was a native of New York City. He was educated for the ministry in the Union Theological Seminary. His most important assignment was that of pastor in a mission church for seamen. Most of his poems and hymns were written anonymously, including "Jesus, Savior, Pilot Me." He acknowledged it to be his, however, when he read it in 1880 at an anniversary service for the Seamen's Friend Society. Reverend Hopper died of a heart attack while writing a poem he entitled "Heaven."

No. 122

Now the Day Is Over

Words by Sabine Baring-Gould   **Music by Joseph Barnby**

The Hymn

This hymn is an evening prayer based on a passage of scripture in Proverbs 3:24. "When thou liest down, thou shalt not be afraid:

yea, thou shalt lie down, and thy sleep shall be sweet." Originally there were eight stanzas in the hymn. Only two are found in the Latter-day Saint Hymnal, numbers one and three. The main impact of the hymn is found in these two stanzas. When the Tabernacle Choir toured in Europe in 1955, every concert was concluded by singing this hymn of benediction.

The Composer

Sabine Baring-Gould wrote both words and music for the first publication of this hymn, but later Joseph Barnby (1831-1896), an English organist, conductor, and composer made a setting of the hymn and published it in a volume that he called *Original Tunes to Popular Hymns.* (1869.) This setting is now the more popular. Barnby was a child prodigy and at sixteen entered the Royal Academy of Music in London. When his musical education was completed, he organized choral societies. It is said by one author that he introduced more new and great music to the English people than any other musician. He composed two hundred and fifty hymns but "Now the Day Is Over" is the one for which he is best known. His beautiful lullaby "Sweet and Low" is also a great favorite.

The Author

Sabine Baring-Gould (1834-1924) was a prodigious literary author. He wrote eighty-five books on widely varied subjects. He has more titles in the British Museum than any other writer of his time, but he never used a secretary. He got his work done by this motto; "The secret is simply that I stick to a task once I begin it." He tells of conducting night school with the students situated on two floors of a building. "The Hymns" says he, "were performed somewhat laggingly as the singing had to bump down the stairs into the kitchen. and one strain of the tune after another came up irregularly through the chinks in the floor—the notes from the stairs also jostled." Mr. Gould lived to be ninety years old working to educate people religiously all the while.

No. 123

O God Our Help In Ages Past

Words by Isaac Watts   Music by William Croft

The Hymn

"O God Our Help in Ages Past" was a favorite hymn of the late Elder Charles Callis of the Council of the Twelve Apostles of the Latter-day Saint Church. The genius of the great hymnist Watts is amply displayed in the various lines of the hymn. His text is based on the Ninetieth Psalm.

The Composer

William Croft (1677-1727) was born in Nether Eatington, England, and was educated in music at the Royal Chapel. At thirty years of age he was given the responsibility of being organist at Westminster Abbey. Later he received a Doctorate of Music from Oxford and was made composer to Queen Anne's court, where he composed many hymns, anthems, and instrumental music. "O God Our Help" is a hymn of noble mien. Bach and Handel used the melody of this hymn in some of their compositions.

The Author — Isaac Watts (See No. 168)

No. 124

Nearer, My God, to Thee

Words by Sarah Flower Adams   **Music by Lowell Mason**

The Hymn

"Nearer My God to Thee" became popular when Lowell Mason set it to music in 1856 and published it in a collection known as the Sabbath hymn and tune book. It was given a performance in 1900 in Philadelphia by fifteen hundred trained singers before the Christian Endeavor Union, at which the President of the organization arose and said, "I wonder if we shall ever listen to such singing again?"

As the *Titanic* was sinking, the doomed passengers sang "Nearer My God to Thee." Those who were fortunate enough to get into life boats, heard the song.

On his deathbed, William McKinley murmured the words, "Nearer, My God, to Thee."

The Composer — Lowell Mason (See No. 40)

Lowell Mason's music was the first respectable church music in America. His indefatigable efforts to improve music in the churches of America cannot be overestimated.

The Author

Sarah Flowers Adams (1805-1848) was the daughter of the editor of the *Cambridge Intelligencer* in England. She became interested in literature at an early age and wrote many poems during her short lifetime of forty-three years. Although a Unitarian, denying thereby the doctrine of the Trinity, Sarah Adams' hymns have been adopted by all Christians.

O God, the Eternal Father

Words by W. W. Phelps   **Music by Felix Mendelssohn**

The Hymn

The noted Latter-day Saint poet W. W. Phelps has created in this hymn a lovely sacramental number by making an amplified paraphrase of the blessings used in the Latter-day Saint sacramental services on the bread and the water. Several phrases are quoted identically as they appear in the two great sacramental prayers. These prayers constitute a solemn renewal of covenants and obligations to our Father in heaven.

The Composer — Felix Mendelssohn (See No. 370)

The tune for "O God, the Eternal Father" was taken from a four-part song by Mendelssohn, entitled "Farewell to the Forest." The original words describe in poetic terms the solace and peace found in the soft whispers of the forest. The changes made in the final phrase of music, when it was incorporated in the 1950 edition of the Latter-day Saints hymnal, in this writer's opinion, eliminated one of the most charming effects of the entire composition.

The Author — William W. Phelps (See No. 213)

No. 126   America the Beautiful

Words by Katherine Lee Bates   **Music by Samuel A. Ward**

The Hymn

"America the Beautiful" is a hymn of faith: faith in God; faith in America; faith in brotherhood; and faith in humanity. Its powerful, prayerful appeal that America be all that is good and great and noble, has brought it to the status of one of our most beloved national songs. There are many telling lines in this impressive hymn. In verse one "And crown thy good with brotherhood." In verse two "a thoroughfare of freedom"; in verse three, Miss Bates reflects her New England ancestry in the words "liberating strife" and again the positive plea that "All success be nobleness." The fourth stanza uses the word "alabaster" in the line "Thine alabaster cities gleam." This is explained by a quote from the author wherein she tells that in 1893 she went to the Columbian Exposition in Chicago where the White City made such a strong appeal to her patriotic feeling that it was in no small degree responsible for the last stanza of the hymn. The first line of "America the Beautiful" was written at once on viewing from the fifteen-thousand foot summit of Pikes Peak at sunrise, the majestic mountains of Colorado and the "wind waved gold of the vast wheat fields of Kansas."

The Composer

The hymn-tune "Materna," which was adapted to "America the Beautiful" was written by Samuel A. Ward in 1882. Ward was born in Newark, New Jersey, December 28, 1848. As a young man, he established a retail music store and pursued the practice of music on an amateur basis, organizing and directing the Newark Orphan's Club. He composed a number of songs and piano pieces. After his death in 1903, the children of Newark erected a brass plaque to his memory. Many composers have felt that the Ward tune is inadequate and have written other settings. At one time a substantial prize was offered for a better setting of the hymn, but in spite of the fact that some six hundred compositions were submitted, the money was never awarded to anyone. This hymn, with the tune "Materna" has so entrenched itself now, because of its wide publication in the song and hymnbooks of the day, it is extremely doubtful if any other setting will ever become popular. Many built up hymn-anthem arrangements, based on the "Materna" tune, are now appearing and its use is increasing as the years go by.

The Author

Katherine Lee Bates was born in Falmouth, Massachusetts, in 1859. She graduated from Wellesley College in 1880 and in 1885 came back to the school as professor of English literature. She traveled widely including such countries as Egypt, Syria, and Italy. She wrote many poems, stories, and articles about her travels as well as editing many of the English classics.

The writing of "America the Beautiful" immortalized her name. Katherine Bates wrote "America the Beautiful" in the summer of 1893. She kept it in her notebook for more than two years. In 1895, she allowed it to be printed in a denominational paper, and in 1904 it was revised and published in a collection of famous songs with a musical setting by Silas G. Pratt. Later it was adapted to the hymn-tune "Materna" of Samuel A. Ward. Miss Bates died in 1929.

No. 127

O'er the Gloomy Hills of Darkness

Words by Williams   **Music by H. H. Peterson**

The Hymn

"O'er the Gloomy Hills of Darkness" is a prayer that the gospel soon shall spread until it encompasses the whole earth and that its message will be heard by every tribe and people.

The text of this hymn is based on the following quotation from

Philippians chapter two, verses ten and eleven; "That at the name of Jesus every knee should bow and every tongue should confess that Jesus Christ is Lord."

The Composer

Hans Henry Petersen was born December 25, 1835 in a small village near Slagelse, Denmark. His father was a mason by trade and although very industrious was unable to provide for his large family. So when Hans was eight years of age he was placed with a farmer where he could earn his living while attending school. At the age of fourteen, Hans was told by his teacher that, because of scholarly aptness, the common district schools could not demand his attendance any longer; hence, after taking a preparatory course conducted by the parson of the Lutheran Church, he was confirmed according to custom of the Luthern Church.

Having tired of the drudgery of working as a chore boy, Hans apprenticed himself to a weaver and later obtained work in a grist mill. It was while working here that he first became interested in the Latter-day Saint faith. He attended meeting, in company with his father, and became convinced of the truthfulness of the gospel. On the 19th of June, 1853, he and his father were baptized by Elder Erick Ludvig, his mother having preceded them by a few days.

In response to call from the authorities, Hans began missionary labors in 1857 in the country surrounding his home and soon after was appointed president of the Svenstrup Branch of the Saints. At the age of twenty three he was chosen to preside over the Saints in the Copenhagen district.

Until he organized a choir and began taking instructions in voice, Hans did not recognize his talents along the musical lines. In this connection he wrote: "Previous to my commencement of the study of this beautiful art, the same had been a sealed book to me. I had not, until now, ever thought music possessed any charms."

During his presidency over the Copenhagen Branch about two hundred and twenty five souls entered the Church for baptism. By this time the desire to emigrate to America had become paramount in his mind. Then, too, he had fallen in love with a young girl from Helsingor who had joined the Church against the wishes of her parents and had consequently been disowned by them. Being without funds, Hans Petersen was forced to borrow the money with which to emigrate his father, mother, five brothers and sisters and his bride-to-be, Julia Maria Larsen. On the 19th of April, 1862, on board the ship anchored in the river Elbe, he and Julia were married by Elder O. N. Liljenquist, who was in charge of the company of Saints.

131

Three other companies landed at New York harbor at about the same time and all were to sent to Florence, Nebraska. At Florence they were encamped for six weeks, pending the arrival of Church ox teams from Utah. Upon the arrival of the teams, the Saints were organized into companies of about four hundred each and, since his company consisted of one hundred English and three hundred Scandinavian converts, and it being necessary to have someone in charge who could speak both languages, Hans Petersen was chosen to fill this position. The latter part of July his company commenced its tedious journey across the plains. The monotony of the journey was broken only by the occasional meeting of a mail coach or a group of Indians.

The company reached its destination the early part of October and part settled in Manti. Work was not plentiful in Manti, so Hans decided to move his growing family to Salt Lake City. While there he organized the first Scandinavian choir in Utah. In 1868 he located in Hyrum where he continued his trade as mason. Here he held many civic positions such as City Recorder, Justice of the Peace, City Marshall, School Trustee, Assistant Superintendent of Sunday School and director of the ward choir. He occupied the last position for nearly forty years, at the same time organizing and conducting the first stake choir in the Hyrum Stake. While thus engaged he composed the music for forty hymns and wrote the text for twenty, among them "Secret Prayer," "When the Mists Have Cleared Away." "The Everlasting Friend," and "My Future Home."

His daughter, Walborg, also a musician of note, writes of him: "He worked all day at his trade, brick laying, rock laying and plastering. He would sit up to the early morning hours composing and writing music by a light made of melted beef tallow with a rag in it. His faithful wife, Julia Maria, stood firmly by him and encouraged him in all his work. Nearly all the hymns and anthems which he taught his choir were arranged in the various parts and written by himself.

Independent in thought and conviction, an earnest student of and firmly rooted in the Latter-day Saint gospel, with unbounded faith in his Heavenly Father, admiring the beautiful in poetry, music and art, no wonder that he became the author of such beautiful songs. "Secret Prayer" was written at a time when many men and women of the Church were sorely tried and put to the test because of having espoused a principle the practice of which is now forbidden. He loved his work better than life itself and thousands are and will be singing his inspired efforts as a momument to his memory.

Hans Henry Petersen passed away at Hyrum, Utah December 18, 1909.

—*Audrey Petersen Boyd.*

The Author

It is obvious that only the surname "Williams" is a very indefinite clue to the identity of any particular member of this great clan.

Onward, Christian Soldiers

Words by Sabine Baring-Gould   Music by Arthur S. Sullivan

The Hymn

Whether sung or played "Onward Christian Soldiers" always stirs people to a high pitch of emotion. Although written for children and first sung by children, its content is advanced beyond the understanding of a child, yet all children love to sing it. The controversy between poet and composer is always a live issue with many hymns as to whose part of the hymn is more responsible for its acceptance or popularity. The poet in all sincerity declares that without the inspiration of his words the composer would have been helpless to write music of any value, to which the composer vehemently replies "without the inspiration of my music, your poem would have never been heard of. "Onward, Christian Soldiers" is a splendid example of the point in question.

In recounting this song's inception, Sabine Baring-Gould, the author, said that he wanted to take a group of children from one village to another for a school festival and to do so in an orderly way, he conceived the idea of having them sing as they marched along.

To satisfy his whim, he sat up one night and in great haste (fifteen minutes), wrote "Onward, Christian Soldiers." He had the children sing it next day to a theme from Haydn's D Major Symphony.

Later, H. J. Gauntlett wrote an original musical setting for the poem which was published in a well-known hymnal, but it was not until the great Arthur Sullivan, in 1872, wrote the stirring march tune that we sing today, that this hymn attained its full glory of popularity.

The Composer

Arthur Sullivan was born in London in 1842, the son of a military band master. He was surrounded by a musical atmosphere and very early learned to play all of the instruments of the band. He attended the Royal Chapel Conservatory where he won the Mendelssohn Scholarship. This entitled him to membership in the Royal Academy of Music. From here he went to Leipzig. His incidental music to Shakespeare's *Tempest* composed in Liepzig, was first performed in Crystal Palace, London. His reputation as a composer was· at once established by this performance. Although he wrote extensively in other fields of music, notably that of religious music, his immortality became a realization with his comic operas. *Pinafore, The Gondoliers,* and *The Mikado,* are as popular today as they ever were.

Arthur Sullivan standardized the comic opera in England and for that matter throughout the English speaking world. He received many honors including a Doctorate of Music, from both Cambridge and Oxford Universities, Chevalier of the Legion of Honor, and finally, Knighthood at the hands of Queen Victoria. He died in 1900.

The Author — Sabine Baring Gould (See No. 122)

No. 129

O Come, All Ye Faithful

Words and Music by John Francis Wade

The Hymn

"O Come, All Ye Faithful" is a Latin hymn of the early eighteenth century. It is said of it that more than forty translations have been made. The English translation used in the Latter-day Saint Hymnal which a Reverend Oakley of Margaret Street Chapel, London, made in 1841, is a Christmas hymn of glorification. It is quite certain that originally John Francis Wade wrote this hymn in 1744. A manuscript discovered by an English Vicar in 1946 bears out this conclusion. One edition was published in Lisbon, Portugal in 1750 from which the name "Portuguese Hymn" was derived.

The Composer

It is recorded in the manuscript that Wade composed the tune as well at the words, at least the first part. Vincent Novello, an organist in London in 1797, ascribed the tune to John Reading, an organist at Westminster Cathedral, 1665-1681. But no matter what its origin, it is one of the most popular Christmas hymns today.

The Author

John Francis Wade, author of the hymn, was an Englishman but moved to Douai, France, when a young boy. His business was that of copyist of music for Catholic Institutions.

No. 130

O Thou Rock of Our Salvation

Words by Joseph L. Townsend   **Music by William Clayson**

The Hymn

The Lord and also his Son Jesus Christ are spoken of in the Bible a number of times as being the rock. Second Samuel 22:47 "and exalted be the God of the Rock of My Salvation" and in First Cor. 10:4 "that Rock was Christ." The text of this hymn is built around the rock as a symbol of strength.

The Composer — William Clayson (See No. 64)

The Author — Joseph L. Townsend (See No. 64)

No. 131

The Star Spangled Banner

Words by Francis Scott Key   Music by John Stafford Smith

The Hymn

One contemporary historian, in a 1958 Associated Press article, declares that the "Star Spangled Banner" would never have been written if Dr. Beanes had not lost his spectacles. In the War of 1812, the British captured Dr. Beanes, a British refugee. They hustled him off to prison in a British ship in Baltimore harbor, so fast that he did not have time to pick up his spectacles.

Francis Scott Kay, a zealous American patriot, was delegated to attempt a release of the venerable doctor. He obtained the release but the British detained the pair overnight on the ship, during which time the British shelled Fort McHenry. In the early morning of September 14, 1814, the dim-eyed Dr. William Beanes kept asking "Can you see the flag?" "Can you see the flag?" When Mr. Key finally did see the flag, he began writing the first words of the "Star Spangled Banner" on an envelope, finishing it within the hour. It was first printed on a handbill with a note saying that it was to be sung "with gusto and for fun" to the tune of "Anachreon in Heaven," an old drinking song which had been used with the words "Adams and Liberty" during the Revolutionary War. In less than an hour after it was placed in the hands of a printer, it was all over town and hailed with enthusiasm. Key was acquainted with the tune of "Anachreon in Heaven," having previously written other words for it. John Stafford Smith, an English organist, wrote the tune originally as a club song for the Anachreontic Society, an association of musicians, in London. The words of the first stanza written by Ralph Tomlinson in 1778 follows:

> To Anacreon in Heaven, where he sat in full glee
> A few sons of harmony sent a petition
> That he their inspirer and patron would be.
> When their answer arrived from the jolly old Grecian
> Voice, fiddle; and flute
> No longer be mute
> I'll lend ye my name, and inspire ye to boot
> And besides, I'll instruct you, like me, to entwine
> The myrtle of Venus with Bacchus's vine.

135

"The Star Spangled Banner" was not officially adopted as the American National Anthem until March 3, 1931 — the bill making it so, being signed at that time by President Herbert Hoover. The man really responsible for the act was "believe it or not, Ripley," who published in his newspaper column in 1929, the fact that "The Star Spangled Banner" was taken for granted by all Americans as being our National Anthem, but had never been officially adopted by Congress.

In 1956 Representative Joel Broyhill of Virginia, was asked by a group of high school students, for the official version of the song. His investigation of the matter disclosed the fact that there wasn't one, although 271 versions had been copyright by the Library of Congress. The original manuscript was sold in 1933 for $24,000. Besides being sung on patriotic occasions of state or military routine, "The Star Spangled Banner" is sung or played at patriotic holiday celebrations, in churches, at the beginning or end of concerts, at the beginning of sport events, such as baseball, football, races, prize-fighting, and wrestling, and the daily opening or closing of radio and television stations.

The Composer

John Stafford Smith (1750-1836) was an English organist, composer, and tenor singer. He studied organ under his father and in 1802 became the organist in Chapel Royal, which post he held until his death. He composed numerous anthems, chants, songs, and glees, and edited much important English music of the Twelfth Century. A large part of his priceless library was lost after his death.

The Author

Francis Scott Key (1779-1843) was an American lawyer. He was district attorney for three successive terms in Washington, D. C. On September 13, 1814 during the War of 1812, he was delegated to negotiate a release for a prominent American physician, Dr. William Beanes, who had been captured and was being held by the British Navy in the Chesapeake Bay. He secured the release, but he was held aboard the Flagship of the fleet overnight during which time the fort was shelled.

No. 132

Now We'll Sing with One Accord

Words by W. W. Phelps   **Music by Joseph J. Daynes**

The Hymn

The hymn text in "Now We'll Sing with One Accord" is concerned mostly with the great work of the modern day Prophet Joseph

136

Smith—that of bringing forth the restored gospel, receiving the priesthood and the translating of the Book of Mormon.

The Composer — Joseph J. Daynes (See No. 232)
The Author — William W. Phelps (See No. 213)

No. 133
O Happy Home! O Blest Abode

Words by Mary Ann Morton   Music by Leroy J. Robertson

The Hymn

The words of the hymn "O Happy Home" reveal that in the next life souls are enlightened from the skies and blest with Jesus' mind. It should be sung with the joy that the words inspire. It is practical for either congregational or choir singing.

The Composer — Leroy J. Robertson (See No. 45)
The Author

Nothing is known of the life of Mary Ann Morton.

No. 134
O Hark a Glorious Sound Is Heard

Words by W. O. Robinson   Music by Frank W. Asper

The Hymn

This is a hymn of exhortation: "Arise and sing ye sons of Men, All Praise and Honor give, Jehovah reigns! Lord God of Hosts All Hail Thee, King most high."

The Composer — Frank W. Asper (See No. 96)

The Author

W. O. Robinson was born in Farmington, Utah in 1876, and attended schools there and at the Latter-day Saints College. He received an honorary degree-B.D. at the Brigham Young College, Logan, Utah. He went on a mission to Colorado and worked under the direction of Apostle John W. Taylor. In 1899, he married Lucy Aneta Clark. They are the parents of seven children. He studied music under Evan Stephens, John J. McClellan, Heber Goddard, Dudley Buck, and attended the American Conservatory of Music, Chicago.

W. O. Robinson was appointed head of the Department of Music at the Brigham Young College, Logan, in 1902, and remained there as head of Music, Speech, Drama, until 1922. In 1922-23, he held the position of Recreational Director for the National Recreation Association.

He was appointed field Secretary of the General Boards of MIA

W. O. Robinson

in 1924, supervising social and recreational activities and a member of the planning and production committee for the Centennial Festival *Message of the Ages* in 1930, also for the revival in 1947. Arranged Mendelssohn's *Elijah* and *St. Paul* in dramatic form and produced them in connection with J. Spencer Cornwall, the Tabernacle Choir, and the MIA. The college song "Hail, B.Y., Hail" was the inspiration for "MIA, We Hail Thee." The line "MIA, We Hail Thee!" was quoted to Sister Ruth May Fox, President of the YWMIA General Board and a poet of great ability. She was asked if she would write a song under that title. About this same time Robinson wrote the words "O Hark a Glorious Sound Is Heard," which is set to music by Frank Asper.

No. 135

O Holy Words of Truth and Love

Words by Joseph L. Townsend   **Music by Edwin F. Parry**

The Hymn

The lilting character of the music of this hymn, together with its pervading theme of "Beautiful Words of Love" are responsible for its popularity with Latter-day Saints.

The Composer

Edwin F. Parry was born in Salt Lake City June 11, 1850. He was the son of John Parry the first leader of the famous Mormon Tabarnacle Choir. John Parry died when Edwin was only eight years of age. Edwin's mother was left to struggle for a living with her four small children. Edwin was an exemplary boy and was chosen to hold several important positions in the organizations of the church. At the age of 13 he began the work of learning the printing trade and followed this work for many years. In 1896 he was called on a mission to Great Britain. Being talented in the literary field, he wrote extensively on religious subjects which were published in the *Millennial Star* of which he was assistant editor. He was also trained somewhat in music having inherited his father's talent in that line. He died in 1935.

The Author — Joseph L. Townsend (See No. 64)

No. 136

Oh, How Lovely Was the Morning

Words by George Manwaring   **Music by A. C. Smyth**

The Hymn

Joseph Smith's First Prayer" is based upon the greatest event that has occurred in these latter days.* It was inspired by the Prophet's own account of the vision of the Father and the Son; and his story is the best background that can be offered as to the origin of this hymn. He says:

> I was one day reading the Epistle of James, first chapter and fifth verse, which reads: "If any of you lack wisdom, let him ask of God, that giveth to all men liberally and upbraideth not; and it shall be given him."
>
> Never did any passage of scripture come with more power to the heart of man than this did at this time to mine. I reflected on it again and again, knowing that if any person needed wisdom from God, I did; for how to act I did not know, and unless I could get more wisdom than I then had, I would never know; for the teachers of religion of the different sects understood the same passage of scripture so differently as to destroy all confidence in settling the question by an appeal to the Bible.
>
> At length I came to the conclusion that I must either remain in darkness and confusion, or else I must do as James directs, that is, ask of God. I at length came to the determination to "ask of God," concluding that if he gave wisdom to them that lacked wisdom, and would give liberally, and not upbraid, I might venture.
>
> So, in accordance with this, my determination to ask of God, I retired to the woods to make the attempt. It was on the morning of a beautiful, clear day, early in the spring of eighteen hundred and

---

*The Peal of Great Price: Extracts from the Writings of Joseph Smith Ch. 2:11-17.

twenty. It was the first time in my life that I had made such an attempt for amidst all my anxieties I had never as yet made the attempt to pray vocally.

After I had retired to the place where I had previously designed to go, having looked around me, and finding myself alone, I kneeled down and began to offer up the desires of my heart to God. I had scarcely done so, when immediately I was seized upon by some power which entirely overcame me, and had such an astonishing influence over me as to bind my tongue so that I could not speak. Thick darkness gathered around me and it seemed to me for a time as if I were doomed to sudden destruction.

But exerting all my powers to call upon God to deliver me out of the power of this enemy which had seized upon me, and at the very moment when I was ready to sink into despair and abandon myself to destruction—not to an imaginary ruin, but to the power of some actual being from the unseen world, who had such marvelous power as I had never before felt in my being—just at this moment of great alarm, I saw a pillar of light exactly over my head, above the brightness of the sun, which descended gradually until it fell upon me.

It no sooner appeared than I found myself delivered from the enemy which held me bound. When the light rested upon me I saw two Personages, whose brightness and glory defy all description, standing above me in the air. One of them spake unto me, calling me by name, and said, pointing to the other —"This is my Beloved Son, Hear Him!"

Joseph was instructed of the Lord and in answer to the question, which of the sects was right, he says:

I was answered that I must join none of them, for they were all wrong; and the personage who addressed me said that all their creeds were an abomination in his sight; that those professors were all corrupt; that "they draw near to me with their lips, but their hearts are far from me; they teach for doctrines the commandments of men, having a form of godliness, but they deny the power thereof."

He again forbade me to join with any of them; and many other things did he say unto me, which I cannot write at this time.

Visual impression, however, increased the desire of George Manwaring to write the song, for he records that he was immediately inspired by a painting entitled "The First Vision" executed by an artist named C. C. Christensen.

It is surprising that none of the first song writers wrote intimately of the first vision. Parley P. Pratt's "An Angel from on High" and "Hark, Ye Mortals" referred to Cumorah and the Book of Mormon. William W. Phelps penned many songs of the Restoration. Evan Stephens' hymn "The Voice of God Is Heard Again" climaxed the great pageant of 1930; but it was reserved for young George Manwaring to translate into song "Joseph Smith's First Prayer." It was first sung in public in the Fourteenth Ward Assembly Hall, Salt Lake City, by a young girl named Sarah Ann Kirkman who became the wife of Patriarch Joseph Keddington, whose family is noted for its wonderful musical ability.

George Manwaring's simple lines versify three of the greatest truths of the Mormon faith: First, the power and efficacy of prayer, and the validity of the promise made in the epistle of James (1:5) that "if any of you lack wisdom let him ask of God, that giveth to all men liberally and upbraideth not and it shall be given him." Second: The reality of the power of evil, which is in the world and which almost overcame the Prophet while he was on his knees in the Sacred Grove. Third: The revealing of the personality of God, the Father, and the Son; for Joseph beheld their persons and heard their voices. It was a great and glorious latter-day theophany—a manifestation ushering in the Dispensation of the Fulness of Times. This vision is the greatest of which we have any record in sacred literature. On no other occasion, so far as we know, did both the Father and the Son appear at one time to any man. That is one of the reasons why Joseph Smith was the greatest seer that ever lived.

The Composer

Adam Craik Smyth, who wrote the music to "Joseph Smith's First Prayer" was born February 29, 1840, at Manchester, Lancashire, England. Like William Fowler who wrote "We Thank Thee, O God, for a Prophet," Adam C. Smyth was a pupil of Sir Isaac Pitman, the originator of the shorthand system, and held a diploma awarded by Sir Isaac. He immigrated to Utah early in 1864, reaching Salt Lake City in October. Strange to say, he had never heard of the Latter-day Saints until he reached the valley. Then he became interested in the gospel. He moved to Mendon, Cache County, where he was baptized. From Mendon he returned to Salt Lake City and for several years engaged in school teaching and the profession of music. Among his pupils were John D. Spencer, H. G. Whitney, B. H. Goddard, Charles B. and George F. Felt, and other well-known and popular youths of that day. Mr. Spencer, often mentioned Adam Smyth as a most interesting character.

Mr. Smyth later moved to Fountain Green, then to Manti, where he directed the local choir and became a recorder in the Manti Temple, a position which he held until his death January 12, 1909.

Professor Smyth did not confine his activities to Church and Sunday School music, for he organized a Juvenile Opera Company, and on July 21st and 23rd, 1879, produced, in the Salt Lake Theatre, Gilbert and Sullivan's *Pinafore*, repeating it December 16th, 18th, and 20th. Later, April 2nd to 7th, 1880, Smyth's company, reorganized, offered *The Grand Dutchess* and gave a revival of *Pinafore*. Again, May 2nd and 3rd, 1881, this enterprising musician produced *The Pirates of Penzance*.* He died in 1909.

The Author

Sketch by Mrs. L. A. Stevenson

George Manwaring was born in Sandback, Cheshire, England, on the 19th of March, 1854, the son of Henry and Sarah Barber Manwaring (Spelled *Mainwaring* in that country.) He had three brothers and two sisters. The family immigrated to America in 1871, after having joined the Church of Jesus Christ of Latter-day Saints. They settled in Salt Lake City and later permanently in Springville, Utah.

As a young man in England, George was apprenticed to a draper, and his artistic nature expressed itself in soft lines and lovely colors.

George Manwaring loved to sing, and on coming to Salt Lake City he joined the Fourteenth Ward Choir, where he met Electa Stevenson, daughter of the late Edward Stevenson and Emily Williams Stevenson. These two young people had interests in common which led to mutual affection, and they were married in the Endowment House on October 26, 1874. Seven children were born to them. One son, Harold Manwaring, gave his life in France during the great World war.

Soon after coming to Utah he was employed by Z.C.M.I., and is said to have decorated the first window in that institution. He later became a bookkeeper in Teasdel's Dry Goods Store and afterward a salesman for Calder's Music Company. Here he was in the atmosphere he loved most. He learned to play very well and would often sit down at the organ and sing to his own accompaniment, both at home and in public gatherings.

He edited *The Home Circle* for a short period and also became interested in art, studying for a while with the late John Hafen.

While George Manwaring's ancestors were at one time wealthy and owned estates in England under a lordship. George himself had few advantages. He was self-taught, but not uneducated, and had high ideals. As stated before, he had an artistic temperament and a love for nature, and one of the happy memories of his life in England was of gathering dainty yellow primroses which grew in the meadows.

---

*Professor Smyth lived six-nine years, but as he was born on February 29th he was able to enjoy only seventeen birthdays. Perhaps it was this fact that attracted him to *The Pirates of Penzance* which centered in the amusing paradox contained in the opera, that while the tenor hero had lived twenty-one years, counting by birthdays he was a little boy of five.

142

Adam Craik Smyth

George Manwaring

After joining the Church and coming to Utah he began to write, expressed his feelings and emotion in poems, many of which have been set to music. The best known is "Joseph Smith's First Prayer."

George Manwaring married, a second time, a young woman named Martha Whitaker. To them were born three sons. He was but 35 years of age when he died. Weakened in body he succumbed to pneumonia on the 7th of July, 1889.

To those who sing his sweetly simple songs these words of the poet Aldrich have a deeper meaning:

> They do not die who leave their thoughts
> Imprinted on some deathless page.
> Themselves may pass, the spell they wrought
> Endures on earth from age to age.*

No. 137

O Give Me Back My Prophet Dear

Words by John Taylor   **Music by George Careless**

The Hymn

President John Taylor author of "O Give Me Back My Prophet Dear" was with the Prophet Joseph Smith when the Prophet was

---

*From George D. Pyper's *Stories of Latter-day Saint Hymns.*

143

martyred. This hymn is a reflective outpouring of his feelings concerning the tragic event.

The Composer — George Careless (See No. 269)
The Author — John Taylor (See No. 269)

No. 138

O My Father

Words by Eliza R. Snow   **Music by Lowell Mason**

The Author

"O My Father" is set to the tune known as "Harwell" by Lowell Mason. President Heber J. Grant was very fond of this tune. It was sung with this setting at his funeral by the Tabernacle Choir. Of late years it is seldom used.

The Composer — Lowell Mason (See No. 40)
The Author — Eliza R. Snow (See No. 139)

No. 139

O My Father

Words by Eliza R. Snow   **Music by James McGranahan**

The Hymn

"O My Father" is considered one of the greatest of all Latter-day Saint hymns, because of its unusual doctrinal content, especially that contained in the third stanza which projects a new thought into religious philosophy; namely, that we have a Heavenly Mother in the courts on high.*

The hymn was written during a period of exciting conditions that finally had their tragic ending in the death of the Prophet and Patriarch. According to Orson F. Whitney, Eliza's marriage to the Prophet took place June 29, 1842. "O My Father" was written in 1843. So the poetess wrote it while she was the Prophet's wife. She was also a governess in his family. This close companionship gave her abundant opportunity to discuss with the Prophet many great and important things "pertaining to the kingdom of God."

It was during this period that Zina D. Huntington (afterwards Zina D. Young) was grieved over an unusual circumstance. Her mother, who had died some time before, had been buried in a temporary grave and it became necessary to remove the body to a permanent resting place. When the remains were exhumed, it was discovered that they were partially petrified. It seemed to Zina as if the very

---

*From George D. Pyper's *Stories of Latter-day Saint Hymns.*

foundation of the doctrine of the resurrection crumbled. To the question "Shall I know my mother when I meet her in the world beyond?" the Prophet responded emphatically, "Yes, you will know your mother there," A firm believer in Joseph's divine mission, Zina D. Huntington was comforted by the promise. From the discussions on the rsurrection and the relationship of man to Deity no doubt came the inspiration to Eliza R. Snow for the writing of "O My Father." The poem was written in the home of Stephen Markham and was penned on a wooden chest, the only table available in her meagerly furnished room.

The hymn is in four stanzas and is an epitome of the great drama of eternal life as revealed by the restored gospel of Jesus Christ.

The Prologue: The first stanza proclaims the literal Fatherhood of God; that we were nurtured by his side in our ante-mortal existence, connoting the truth that we were instructed in the great plan, obedience to which would enable us to regain his presence "and again behold his face."

The Play: Stanza II shifts the scene to earth-life, where we are placed in a school to see whether we will do the things required of us and prove our right to the promised restoration to God's presence. Our recollection of ante-mortal life is withheld in order that we may walk by faith; yet, not to be left wholly in the dark, a "secret something," a key that opens the door to knowledge, is given us, and through it (Stanza III) is revealed the new and glorious doctrine of a Mother in heaven.

The Epilogue: Back again into the Eternal Presence our thoughts are projected. Through obedience, and through having completed all we have been commanded to do, with the "mutual approbation" of our heavenly Parents, we claim the promise made in our ante-mortal state.

Truly "O My Father" is the drama of eternal life: not merely a hymn, but a prophecy and a revelation.

Edward W. Tullidge, in his *Women of Mormondom*, says of the hymn:

> A divine drama set to song. And as it is but a choral dramatization, in the simple hymn form, of the celestial themes revealed through Joseph Smith, it will strikingly illustrate the vast system of Mormon theology, which links the heavens and the earth.

Levi Edgar Young, in *The Improvement Era*, Volume 17, p. 751, June, 1914, says:

Standing out in reverent meaning, and a poem in very spirit is "O My Father." . . . This hymn is the embodiment of Hebraism, of some God-like thought. . . . Its beauty is in its lessons that all men are divine and by their will are in tune with their Maker. It will forever as a soul-inspiring song; it will ever be known as a philosophic lesson, for it gives something of the meaning of instinct and intuition, the great problems of the modern philosopher.

Orson F. Whitney, in the *History of Utah*, Vol 4, says:

If all her other writings, prose and verse, were swept into oblivion, this poem alone, the sweetest and sublimest of all the songs of Zion, would perpetuate her fame and render her name immortal. But she believed, with Lord Byron, that a poet should do something more than make verses, and she put that belief into practice, laboring incessantly for the promulgation of her religious faith and for the teaching and counseling of the women of her people.

"O My Father," according to fan letters received by the Tabernacle Choir, ranks second as the most popular and most beloved hymn of the Latter-day Saints. "Come, Come, Ye Saints" came first.

The Composer — James McGranahan (See No. 267)

Arr. By Evan Stephens (See No. 144)

The Author

Many biographical stories of Eliza Roxey Snow Smith have been published. From thirty-five of these the factual data contained in this brief sketch are gleaned.

This remarkable woman, one of the most noted among the women of Mormondom, was born January 21, 1804, in Becket, Berkshire County, Massachusetts. She was the second daughter of Oliver and Rosetta L. Pittibone Snow. Her grandfather was a revolutionary soldier. In 1806 the family, consisting of the parents and two daughters, moved to Mantua, Portage County, Ohio; there five other children were born.

Though Baptists, the Snows were friends to people of all denominations, and their door was open to all of exemplary habits. The children were cultured and trained in all of the Christian virtues. Eliza was especially gifted as a writer of poetry. At the early age of twenty-two she gained considerable local fame by writing, at the request of a number of newspapers, a requiem for John Adams and Thomas Jefferson, both of whom passed away on the same day—the day of days to Americans—July 4, 1826. Her poems brought her into close acquaintance with many notable scholars and theologians, among whom were Alexander Campbell, organizer of the Campbellite

Church, and his fellow-worker. Sidney Rigdon, who later became associated with the Latter-day Saints.

Eliza's mother and sister having joined the Church, she herself, after a thorough investigation, became converted and was baptized April 5, 1835. Late in the same year she left her home and moved to Kirtland where she taught a select school for girls, and for a while was governess in the Prophet's family. There her facile pen was kept busy. Under the inspired teaching of the latter-day Prophet, she advanced in the knowledge and understanding of the gospel and her whole life became devoted to its spread. Her poems now breathed the inspiration of the new-found truth, catching the glorified vision of her prophet-teacher.

Eliza's father, after her conversion, soon brought the mother, brothers, and sisters to Kirtland. In 1836 they moved to Far West. From Far West the family moved to Adam-Ondi-Ahman, from which place they were driven and suffered the persecutions incident to those gloomy days. Back to Far West the family moved, then in 1839 to Quincy, Illinois, and next to La Harpe. Later, the family settled in Commerce, afterwards named Nauvoo.

In Nauvoo, Eliza again taught school and wrote much. It was here that she wrote, "O My Father," the hymn that has placed her name among the Latter-day Saint immortals.

When the first Relief Society was organized, March 17, 1842, Eliza R. Snow was its secretary. On June 29, 1842, she was sealed to Joseph Smith for time and eternity in the celestial law of marriage. On June 27, 1844, the Prophet and his brother Hyrum were martyred.

Grief-stricken, but undaunted, Eliza became more devoted than ever to her husband's cause. She was in the exodus of February 28, 1846, wrote comforting songs for the people, and drove an ox team part of the way to Winter Quarters. Her father and mother both died at Walnut Grove, Illinois. She began the pioneer journey in June, arriving in Salt Lake Valley in October, 1847. There she was given a home by Brigham Young, to whom she was married in 1849, and lived in the Lion House until the time of her death.

From the time of her arrival in Salt Lake Valley until the time of her demise the life of this gifted woman was a busy one. She had charge of the women's work in the Endowment House. In 1866 she was set apart to preside over the Relief Societies of the wards and stakes of Zion, and labored in that capacity for twenty-one years. On October 20, 1872, Eliza began a nine months' journey to the Holy Land, visiting Liverpool, London, Belgium, France, Genoa, Venice, Rome, Naples, Corfu, Alexandria, Jaffa, Jerusalem, Athens, Constantinople, and Vienna. This trip included a pilgrimage to the Mount of Olives where the land had been dedicated for the return of the Jews. In 1875 a volume was published by her containing *Correspondence of Palestine Tourists.*

After her return, Eliza, besides engaging in numerous other activities, assisted sister Aurelia Spencer Rogers in organizing the first Primary Association. On July 17, 1880, she was set apart by President John Taylor as President of the Relief Societies in all the world. Zina D. H. Young and Elizabeth Ann Whitney were her counselors and Sarah M. Kimball her secretary. Temple work at St. George followed. On July 17, 1882, the Deseret Hospital was established with Eliza R. Snow as president.

In 1856 her first volume of poems was published; twenty years later the second volume appeared. A hymnbook and tune book she also published. First and Second Speakers, collections of poems and readings for Primary Associations, are credited to her genius.

On December 5, 1887, in her eighty-fourth year, death claimed this exceptional woman. Funeral services were held in the Assembly Hall, Salt Lake City, and interment was in President Brigham Young's private cemetery.

Eliza R. Snow

"O My Father" has been set to music by many Latter-day Saint composers, among whom may be named John Tullidge, A. C. Smyth, Ebenezer Beesley, Charles J. Thomas, George Careless, Frank W. Merrill, Edwin F. Parry, Edward P. Kimball, Tracy Y. Cannon, and Evan Stephens. President Heber J. Grant, in an article on "Our Favorite Hymns" published in *The Improvement Era*, Volume 17, Part 2, p. 777, says: "It was first sung to the tune of 'Gentle Annie' by Stephen Foster to which melody President Young often had it sung." For years it was almost universally sung to the tune of "Harwell" by Lowell Mason from the *American Tune Book*. This is President Grant's favorite. In 1893 it was sung at a funeral in Logan by Robert C. Easton to the tune of "My Redeemer," by James McGranahan, and created such a favorable impression that Frank W. Merrill published an adaption which was used by Brother Easton at the dedicatory exercises of the Salt Lake Temple, and also at the Chicago World's Fair on the occasion of the Salt Lake Tabernacle Choir's trip there in 1893. It had also been used effectively to the solo and duet from the first act of *Martha*. That arrangement was sung by this writer at the funeral of the son of President Heber J. Grant. However, "My Redeemer" seems still to be its favorite setting. Its arrangement by Evan Stephens is the one published in *Latter-day Saint Hymns*, No. 139.

No. 140

Land of the Mountains High

Words and Music by Evan Stephens

The Hymn

This hymn was written by Evan Stephens to commemorate Utah's entry as a state into the Union in 1896. Because of the irregular rhythm and snatchy melodic lines, it is not a good community song. It is best done by selected singers.

The Composer and Author — Evan Stephens (See No. 144)

No. 141

Lead Me into Life Eternal

Words by John A. Widtsoe   **Music by Alexander Schreiner**

The Hymn

This hymn is a revision of an earlier version "Father, Lead Me out of Darkness," No. 380 in the LDS hymnbook of 1927. Here Dr. Widtsoe wrote poetically as if an investigator of the gospel were singing. In this present new version the members of the Church sing of their prayer to be lead into life eternal by the gospel's holy call.

The melody is in congregational hymn style, as are the chorals of centuries ago. Such music was once written in half notes, now nearly always in quarters.

The Composer — Alexander Schreiner (See No. 24)

The Author — John A. Widtsoe (See No. 69)

No. 142
Lord, We Come before Thee Now

Words by Hammond   **Music by Harry A. Dean**

The Hymn

The hymn "Lord, We Come before Thee Now" is one of several which were submitted to the Church Music Committee just prior to the publication and compilation of our present hymnal. Of those submitted, two were chosen for inclusion in the hymnbook, the other being No. 231, "Before Thee Lord." Naturally it is popular in the territory in Southern Utah where Harry Dean lives.

The Author

No information is at hand concerning the author of this hymn.

The Composer

Harry Dean was born September 17, 1892, Salt Lake City, Utah. He was the son of Joseph H. and Sarah Arnold Dean. He was raised on a farm in Colorado until 1914 when he went on a mission for the

Harry A. Dean

150

Latter-day Saint Church in Samoa, 1914-17, where he assisted with the translation of songs of Zion into the Samoan language.

Veteran in U.S. Army during World War I.

Graduate of the Latter-day Saint McCune School of Music the first year that diplomas were given, signed by Anthony H. Lund and B. Cecil Gates.

Studied violin with Romania Hyde and Willard Weihe, piano with Lida Edmonds, instrumentation with Clarence J. Hawkins, music theory and conducting with B. Cecil Gates.

Graduated from the Brigham Young University in 1933 and secured his Master's degree two years later.

Taught music in Junior College for thirty-seven years: Gila College, Ricks College, Snow College.

Musical activities include teaching music theory, orchestra, and chorus. He has directed the *Messiah* for twenty-six consecutive years at Snow College. He has also directed the *Elijah* along with many operettas and musical dramas. In 1958 he was advanced to the status of Professor Emeritus. Harry Dean is an active member in the Latter-day Saint Church especially in the music work, having written and directed programs for celebrations of all kinds.

At present, he is Music Supervisor, Division I, comprising nine stakes in Central Utah for the MIA.

No. 143

O Say, What Is Truth?

Words by John Jaques   **Music by Ellen Knowles Melling**

The Author

Among the hymns written by John Jaques is one which has taken its place as a classic among the writings of Mormon hymnists.* It is entitled "O Say, What is Truth?" The music of the hymn was composed by Ellen Knowles Melling, a Scottish convert of Elder Jaques. Jaques, the son of Thomas and Mary Ann Heighington Jaques, was born January 7, 1827, at Market Bosworth, Leicestershire, England. In his youth he was a lover of truth, had a religious trend and a latent talent for writing. He searched for the truth with sincerity and earnestness, and in this quest contacted the elders of the Church of Jesus Christ of Latter-day Saints—the so-called *Mormon* missionaries—and became converted to their doctrines. He was bap-

---

*From George D. Pyper's *Stories of Latter-day Saint Hymns.*

tized in the fall of 1845. As an elder he became an active missionary affiliated with the branch at Stratford-upon-Avon, the home of the immortal Shakespeare.

After his marriage Mr. Jacques immigrated with his family to America and joined the Saints in their new found Zion. He crossed the ocean in the packet ship *Horizon,* which arrived in Boston, Massachusetts, June 30, 1856. He crossed the plains with the Martin Handcart company, in which many lives were lost in fierce snowstorms in the Rockies. Elder Jacques' eldest daughter was among those who perished before aid came. The little band of survivors reached Salt Lake City, November 30, 1856. "Thereafter for a half century, John Jaques labored incessantly in that which he firmly believed was the cause of human redemption. In poetry and prose he reflected the light of truth for the benefit of his fellows."

Elder Jaques was called upon to return to England as a missionary from 1869 to 1871. His appointments frequently took him to Stratford-upon-Avon. On one occasion he sat there in an attractive nook, lost in reverie, perhaps feeling the influence of the great Shakespeare himself, pondering the words of Pilate, when he asked the Master, "What is Truth?"

That question, he thought, has come down through the ages. Truth is a tiny word. Yet within it is encompassed the very foundation of the universe. In a figurative sense, those five letters stand as the supporting pillars of the bridge of experience, across which only mankind may enter into the fulness of earthly existence and reach the portals of that higher intelligence which leads in our belief, to eternal life and happiness. Truth, the key to knowledge, its quest the noblest desire of man, underlies all our progress— our civilization. In a religious sense, it is the everlasting way to everlasting life. It offers an explanation to the deep riddle of our being—the past, the present, and the hereafter. And thus meditating upon the faith he had espoused, his surrounding brought to mind the lines of Shakespeare, "It is all as true as it is strange, nay, it is ten times ten times true, for truth is truth to the end of reckoning." It was no doubt such thoughts as these that inspired him to write "O Say, What is Truth?" which has a high place in Latter-day Saint hymnody.

After Elder Jaques' return from his mission, he was employed in the office of the *Deseret News,* then in the Church Historian's Office. From 1883 to June 1, 1900, the date of his death, he was sustained as Assistant Church Historian.

Elder Jaques was a unique personality. Before he came to America he had an experience which he never forgot and which reveals his character. One day a young man, a stranger, came up to him on the street and asked for alms. Jaques refused. The very next morning he read in the paper of a death, which he immediately suspected was the beggar. He went to the morgue, to see if his suspicion was correct. It was. There lay the youth, still in death. Jaques was deeply moved.

After that, as long as he lived, he always carried in his vest pocket several pieces of silver. It was six-penny coins in England and ten cent pieces in the United States. Never afterwards did he refuse to give a fellow a coin. It eased his conscience.

The Spirit of Truth

And I will pray the Father, and he shall give you another Comforter, that he may abide with you forever; even the Spirit of Truth . . . ye know him for he dwelleth with you; and shall be in you.

When he, the Spirit of Truth is come, he will guide you into all truth. *John 14:16, 17; 16:13; Doctrine and Covenants, 6:15; 91:4.*

For the Word of the Lord is Truth. . . . *Doctrine and Covenants 84:45.*

I am the Spirit of Truth. *Doctrine and Covenants 93:26.*

Truth is knowledge of things as they are, and as they were, and as they are to come. *Doctrine and Covenants 93:24.*

He that keepeth his commandments receiveth truth and light, until he is glorified in truth and knoweth all things. *Doctrine and Covenants 93:28.*

John Jaques

Evan Stephens

No. 144

Our Mountain Home so Dear

Words by Emmeline B. Wells   Music by Evan Stephens

The Hymn

One day "Aunt Em," in conversation with Evan Stephens, whose genius she greatly admired, told him of a love song in her possession that she would like to have set to music.* He readily accepted an invitation for an evening at her home and after the reading of the poem mentioned, Evan said," Why don't you write the words for a song for me to set to music, Sister Wells?" She promised to think about it, and that same night, while others were sleeping, "Aunt Em" wrote "Our Mountain Home, So Dear." The song, with Professor Stephens' lovely music, has an appealing charm and is very popular. He, himself, remarked when choosing the six songs for the Columbia records to be made for the Church in New York, that this was one of his favorites and that he preferred it to his own hymn bearing a similar name.

On one occasion when a quartette was singing this song at a large party given in honor of "Aunt Em's birthday, President Anthon H. Lund turned to her and said "God bless you, 'Aunt Em,' for writing that beautiful hymn." This compliment to her poetic nature, pleased "Aunt Em" greatly, for she placed much confidence in President Lund's opinions. Incidentally the other song which "Aunt Em" gave Professor Stephens to set to music, he took with him to Boston when he attended the Conservatory of Music for a term, and it won for him a prize in a competition and was much admired.

Mrs. Wells was outstanding in her interest in and development of talent in the community, especially in the youth of Zion. She recognized ability and was an ardent supporter by her influence and with her pen of all who showed the least inclination in the field of art. Of an artistic temperament herself, she drew around her a coterie of friends among whom nothing could be more delightful than an evening in her home where conversation sparkled with the wit and wisdom of men and women who loved books, pictures, statuary, and music. It was in her home where the Wasatch Literary Club was organized, a group of young men and women whose names have made history among their people, many of them holding high office in church and state while others excelled in literary and artistic lines.

When she became acquainted with Evan Stephens, two kindred spirits met, both loving music, art, and God's beautiful outdoors. As

---

*From George D. Pyper's *Stories of Latter-day Saint Hymns.*

154

a result of their common admiration for nature came this exquisite song. It tells its own story; it makes its own appeal. Read it for yourself; ponder every line and study it, for it is a literary gem.

The Composer

The name of Evan Stephens awakens such a flood of recollections as warms the soul and makes the heart beat faster, "There are moments in life," says one writer, "that we never forget, which brighten and brighten as time steals away." Such moments are often recorded by me, of an intimate association with Professor Stephens of nearly half a century. It is not my intention, however, to write here the story of his life but to tell of some of my personal contacts with him and to describe a few of his unique characteristics.

From the date of his birth in the little town of Pencader, South Wales, June 28th, 1854, until the time of his death, October 27th, 1930, Evan Stephens' life was one of unceasing activity. When he was twelve years of age, he came over the ocean with his parents in a sailing vessel and walked across the plains, arriving in Salt Lake City, October 2nd, 1866. A week later the family located in Willard, Utah, where his desire to become a musician took firm root. His lowly occupations—herd boy, farm hand, wood cutter, hod carrier, railway section hand—did not stand in the way of his ambition. His talents soon secured for him "a place in the sun." Step by step he rose from obscurity to the highest position in the realm of music within the gift of his Church. His struggles and victory under adverse conditions constitute a real life lesson for every young man.

A book might be written on his various musical activities, but the high spot of his career was, of couse, his work as director of the Tabernacle Choir. It was while the choir was at the World's Fair, Chicago, in 1893, that President Woodruff said: "A shepherd boy came down from the mountains and is here today to contest in this great competition." The choir won second prize of $1000, and a gold medal for the conductor.

In looking over the diary and scrapbook of Brother Stephens one is utterly amazed at the tremendous and dynamic energy of the man. I doubt if a tab of his life would register one moment of idle time. For his work among children alone a debt of gratitude is due him.

He left many unpublished manuscripts. I asked him once which of all his compositions he liked best. He answered: "Like most fond parents, I find it impossible to answer this seemingly easy question. To me compositions, like people, vary in personal impression. Each

155

in its own way may appeal to me strongly. Some arouse within me a feeling of satisfaction and pride for the workmanship as well as the emotional content—something like a fond parent may feel over having a child who proves a real leader in the community." Among other things he said that just as a mother loves her unpopular and unnoticed children, so his neglected, unpublished creations held highest place in his esteem.

Another song writer expressed the same thought in the following lines:

> Oh, my uncared for songs, what are ye worth
> That in my secret book, with so much care
> I write you this one here and this one there,
> Marking the time and order of your birth.

> *Robert Bridges*

Several songbooks were published by Elder Stephens and twenty-six of his compositions appear in *Latter-day Saint Hymns*—more than by any other composer.

Professor Stephens was an ardent lover of nature. Flowers mountain streams, rocky peaks, and pine clad hills allured him. The charm of his early days in Willard was never dispelled and there were few peaks and nooks in those hills that could not show his footprints. His home on State Street was a beauty spot and a rendezvous for lovers. In fact, it is remarkable how this bachelor provided so many romantic nooks for lovers' talks, without himself falling a victim to Cupid's dart.

And this love of Nature was the inspiration that caused him to collaborate with Emmeline B. Wells in bringing forth that beautiful song, "Our Mountain Home, so Dear."

Brother Stephens loved Brighton, in the Cottonwoods, and I have a vivid memory of climbing with him in company of Horace G. Whitney and John D. Spencer to what he called the "Crow's Nest" which we afterwards named "Stephen's Roost." This "nest" was nothing more or less than a native pine tree flattened by the heavy snows which lay on the boughs for eight months in that locality, forming a natural platform on a ledge far up on the side of the Brighton hills. Here, cross-legged, like the Tailor of Tamworth, Professor Stephens would sit and in imagination lead a mammoth choir made up of the forest crowning the basin below. Here on the right, a grove of fresh young pines represented his sopranos. A little below in the colorful rays of the setting sun, were his contraltos. To the north, there on a raised hill, stood his tenors, and to the extreme right, under the full shadow of the hills, waited his fir tree bassos. Interspersed among the pines, the quaking asps sparkled and fluttered and these furnished the brilliant accompaniment for his novel imaginary choir. As the sun slowly sank and the evening breezes played among the soughing pines there seemed almost miraculously to come forth like the legendary "Music of the Spheres," the magnificent harmonies of nature's singers.

Professor Stephens was a powerful personality—self-educated —different from most musicians. He was of the common people and wrote his songs for them. Yet he was in one respect a musical autocrat. He wanted his own way in the conduct of the choir, and when he had it, he succeeded best. He couldn't abide the supervision of committees.

Evan Stephens was a born poet. Had he received a higher education in letters he would no doubt have achieved world renown. As it was, his songs and compositions appealed to the religious emotions of the Latter-day Saints who will forever hold his name in loving remembrance.

The Author

The life story of Emmeline B. Woodward Wells, the author of the exquisite hymn entitled "Our Mountain Home, So Dear" filled as it was with romance, pathos, courage, and devotion, reads like an imagined romance. I am indebted to her daughter, Mrs. Annie Wells Cannon, for the facts here given.

She was born in Petersham, Worcester County, Massachusetts, February 29, 1828. Of Puritan descent and distinguished ancestry, she was proud of the fact that her father, David Woodward, was in the War of 1812, and her grandfather, a soldier of the American Revolution. Having natural talent she was graduated from school at fifteen. She was baptized into the Mormon Church at fourteen and emigrated from New England to Nauvoo with a family named Harris to whose young son she was married in order to leave the state legally. The Harris family apostatized and left Nauvoo, but the young wife refused to leave the people of her chosen faith. She afterwards married Presiding Bishop Newell K. Whitney, and with his family left Nauvoo in the exodus of 1846. Her mother, following in a later company, died of hardships on the journey, and was buried by the wayside in an unmarked grave on the Iowa prairies.

While in Nauvoo Mrs. Wells, under the influence of the Prophet's teaching, obtained a lasting testimony of the divinity of his mission. She was also present at the memorable meeting at the "Grove" when the mantle of the Prophet Joseph fell upon Brigham Young, and so transfigured him that the people marveled.

157

"Aunt Em," as she was known, came to Utah in 1848 and after the birth of two daughters, misfortune again befell her in the sudden death of her husband. After two years of struggle she married General Daniel H. Wells. Three daughters were the fruit of this union. Her home was a gathering place for friends and distinguished guests. Here began her active participation in public affairs. She was a leading figure in the struggle for woman's suffrage. In 1875 she was assistant editor and in 1877 became editor of the *Woman's Exponent*. For thirty-nine years she wrote in behalf of women's progress and in defense of her people. After many years of literary work the Brigham Young University, on February 29, 1912, conferred upon her the honorary degree of Doctor of Literature—this in her eighty-fourth year.

Mrs. Wells was the founder and patron of several literary, patriotic, and study organizations, among them the Utah Women's Press Club, The Reaper's Club, and the Utah Society of the Daughters of the Revolution.

Honors, national and local, came to this remarkable woman. As delegate to American and international councils and conventions her life was flooded. She was chosen to unveil the beautiful Seagull Monument on Temple Square. In October, 1910, she was called to preside over the Relief Society, a position which she held until three weeks before her death, which occurred April 25, 1921. On her one hundredth anniversary a marble bust was presented by the women of the state, which occupies an honored niche in the rotunda of the Utah State Capitol. The inscription reads:

"A Fine Soul Who Served Us."

No. 145

O Ye Mountains High

Words by Charles W. Penrose   **Music Anonymous**

The Hymn

The four-beat measure between the verse and the chorus of "O Ye Mountains High" was changed in the 1950 edition of the Latter-day Saint Hymnal, to a two-beat measure to conform to the common way of singing it.

The Composer

It was in the afternoon of a hot day in July. Salt Lake City "lay sweltering in the summer's sun." But some five thousand feet higher, at the head of Cottonwood Canyon, only a few miles distant, cool breezes were blowing from the snowcapped peaks of the Wasatch, as a genial group, seeking refuge from the heat, gathered before a crackling pine-knot fire in a Brighton cottage. Among the guests were the late Presidents Joseph F. Smith and Charles W. Penrose. The subject of the conversation was the hymns written by Brother Penrose, and he was asked to relate the circumstances under which some of them were written. He gladly responded, and there in the "mountains high, where the clear blue sky arches over the vales of the free," he told the stories of the origin of his hymns.

On another occasion, the sixtieth birthday of President Heber J. Grant, he and his wife were entertaining the General Authorities of the Church. On that day, with one exception, all the hymns rendered were those written by Charles W. Penrose. The one exception, a favorite of John R. Winder, who was present, was "Who Are These Arrayed in White?" sung by President Grant's daughter. Before the singing of Brother Penrose's songs, the interestings stories of their origin were again related. Here is the story of "O Ye Mountains High," in the author's own words. Said President Penrose:

" 'O Ye Mountains High' was written somewhere along about 1854, published in 1856. I was walking on a dusty road in Essex. My toes were blistered and my heels, too. I had been promised that if I would stay in the mission field another year I should be released. That was the cry every year: 'Brother Penrose, if you will stay and labor another year, we will see that you are released to go to Zion.' But it kept up for over ten years. Of course I had read about Zion and heard about the streets of Salt Lake City, with the clear streams of water on each side of th street, with shade trees, and so on. I could see it in my mind's eye and set it to a tune — the Scotch ditty, 'O Minnie, O Minnie, Come o'er the Lea'; those were the opening words. When I got to the place called Mundon, in Essex, we held a cottage meeting, and in that meeting I sang it for the first time it was ever sung. Of course the words were adapted to a person who had never been to Zion then, but it was afterwards changed in a very slight respect or two, to fit people who had gathered with the Saints. It was inspirational and seemed to please President Brigham Young."

With President Penrose's graphic recital in mind, the hymn needs little or no analysis. It tells its own story — the poet's Zion and his intense longing to be there; his love for Zion's "glad tidings" in spite of the ridicule and the revilings of her enemies; his faith in God who would strengthen her feet and cause her to stand without fear or dread of her foes, whose silver and gold should adorn her fair head; his faith in the deliverance of Zion, in the defeat of her oppressors and the ultimate triumph of God's people.

Like all of President Penrose's songs, in common with many

other Mormon hymns, "O Ye Mountains High" was sung to one of the popular tunes of the day. The author names "O Minnie, O Minnie, Come o'er the Lea" as the one to which it was first adapted. But as we now sing it the tune is that of H. S. Thompson's "Lily Dale."

When the song was first published, in 1856, it instantly took its place among the most popular hymns of the Church; and within two years it played a leading part in one of the most thrilling scenes of Church history. When Johnston's Army was in Echo Canyon, on its way to Salt Lake City, a Peace Commission, consisting of Governor L. W. Powell of Kentucky, and Major Ben McCullough of Texas, was sent to Utah, arriving at Salt Lake City in June, 1858. In one of the tense meetings (June 11th) the Commissioners presented their message. Brigham Young responded, and the outlook for peace seemed favorable. Edward W Tullidge, in his *History of Salt Lake City*, tells what followed:

> A well-known character, O. P. Rockwell, was seen to enter, approach the ex-Governor, and whisper to him. He was from the Mormon army. There was at once a sensation, for it was appreciated that he brought some unexpected and important news. Brigham arose, his manner self-possessed but severe:
> "Governor Powell, are you aware, sir, that those troops are on the move toward the City?"
> "It cannot be," exclaimed Powell, surprised, "for we were promised by the General that they should not move till after this meeting."
> "I have received a dispatch that they are on the march for this City. My messenger would not deceive me."
> It was like a thunderclap to the Peace Commissioners: they could offer no explanation.
> "Is Brother Dunbar present?" inquired Brigham.
> "Yes, Sir," responded the one called.
> What was coming now?
> "Brother Dunbar, sing 'Zion.' "
> The Scotch songster came forward and sang—"O Ye Mountains High."

The song deeply impressed the Peace Commissioners, and after several stormy sessions a peaceful solution of the war was agreed upon. The army passed through Salt Lake City, rested temporarily on the west banks of the Jordan River, and then established Camp Floyd on the west side of Utah Lake.

As the clouds of prejudice against the Mormon people disappeared and misunderstandings were cleared up, it occurred to many of our own people that two lines in the third and fourth stanzas should be revised. They were, respectively—"On the necks of thy foes, thou shalt tread," and "The Gentiles shall bow 'neath thy rod."

On one occasion President Heber J. Grant said to Brother Penrose:

"Brother Penrose, when you pass away, with your permission I'd like to change those two lines." He replied, "That will be all right."

Just how fair-minded non-Mormons feel about these lines is indicated in the following circustances gleaned from an interview by the writer with President Heber J. Grant on June 30, 1936.

In 1921 or 1922 Mr. Fred W. Shibley came from New York representing the bankers to whom the Utah-Idaho Sugar Company was indebted $7,000,000. The terrible slump in the price of sugar from $14.00 to $5.00, and the slump in sales, caused the company to lose a vast sum of money. Shibley came out to look the situation over and made a very favorable report on the final triumph of the sugar industry.

President Grant took Mr. Shibley up Emigration Canyon to dinner at Pinecrest Inn. While coming down Emigration Canyon in the automobile the President sang "O Ye Mountains High" and "Come, Come, Ye Saints." Upon the President's finishing "Come, Come, Ye Saints," Mr. Shibley said: "Mr. Grant, give me a copy of that hymn."

The next day the President took him to Brighton, and noticing that Emma Lucy Gates Bowen was visiting with her mother in the cabin next door to the President's, he took Mr. Shibley to their cabin. Brother and Sister John A. Widtsoe were also present. President Grant said: "Emma Lou, please sing for Mr. Shipley 'O Ye Mountains High.' I sang it for him last night, but I would like him to hear it sung by somebody who knows how to sing."

She turned to the President and said, "Of course you want me to sing only two verses."

He replied: "Not on your life, give him all four verses."

When she finished singing, President Grant said: "Mr. Shibley, it must have shocked you for me, the President of the Church of Jesus Christ of Latter-day Saints, to sing that hymn to you, when the Savior's teachings are to turn the other cheek, and love your enemies. I have arranged with the author of the hymn, when he passes away, that we will stop 'treading on the necks of our foes' and making 'the gentiles bow beneath our rod'."

Mr. Shibley said: "Don't you do it. It is only once in a lifetime

161

that a man gets off as inspirational a hymn as that. Leave it just the way he wrote it." He continued: "Mr. Grant, you don't expect actually to tread on the necks of your foes. That is a figurative expression. I am familiar with the Bible, although agnostic. You do expect the neck to bow to the rod of righteousness. Leave it alone. Your people have a greater abiding faith in your final triumph than any other people I have ever met."

Within the next day or two President Grant took him for a ride around Mount Timpanogos, and as they were riding up American Fork Canyon Mr. Shibley repeated the last verse of "Come, Come, Ye Saints"—and remarked: "Mr. Grant, that is the most splendid declaration of a faith in the immortality of the soul I ever read in my life."

"O Ye Mountains High," born of an emotional and yearning heart, has become one of the most beloved of our Mormon hymns.

The Author

On February 4, 1832 in London, England, was born into the world one of the greatest exponents and defenders of Mormonism the Church of Jesus Christ of Latter-day Saints has ever had. Charles W. Penrose joined the Church when he was eighteen years of age— the only member of his family to do so. He was dutifully religious— had a brilliant mind, was devotedly studious, and soon attained a thorough acquaintance with the scriptures. At nineteen, while still in his home town, he was ordained an elder by the Authorities of the Church and sent on a mission to Maldon in Essex, England. He went without "purse or scrip" with poor, inadequate clothing walking all the way to Maldon, sleeping out-of-doors in the chilly nights. In a short time he succeeded in bringing many souls into the Church and established several branches.

He continued his labors in the poor agricultural districts in England for seven years. Such was the character of Charles W. Penrose. He was called from that mission to preside over the London conference. While in this position he began his brilliant career as a writer which was to make his name famous long after his death. Many of his theological articles, his poems, and especially his songs will be preserved always. In 1861 with his wife whom he married in Maldon, and his family, he moved to America—crossed the plains with ox teams and finally settled in Farmington, Utah. He had scarcely become settled when he was called back to England on a second mission. After three years he was released and came home and moved to Logan, Utah. Later he went to Ogden and began his newspaper work which finally projected him to the position of the official paper of the Church, the

Deseret News. Most of his finest literary works came to light during this period in 1880. Charles Penrose held many important Church positions which honors were climaxed by his being chosen a Counselor in the First Presidency in the Latter-day Saint Church. He died in 1925.

Charles W. Penrose

No. 146

How Wondrous and Great

Words by Henry U. Onderdonk   **Music by J. Michael Haydn**

The Hymn

"How Wondrous and Great" was inspired, undoubtedly, by the third and fourth verses of Revelation, chapter fifteen. The most frequently used text for this hymn was written by Sir Robert Grant, a Governor of Bombay, India, entitled "O Worship the King." The choice of Onderdonk's "How Wondrous and Great" was made by the compilers of the 1950 edition of *Latter-day Saint Hymns.*

The Composer

There is some confusion as to which "Haydn" is the composer referred to in the various publications of the tune of "How Wondrous and Great." The Latter-day Saint Hymnal gives J. Michael

Haydn (1737-1806), a younger brother of the great Franz Joseph Haydn, as the composer, while some other hymnals say that the tune is arranged from J. Michael Haydn. Likenesses to the tune are to be found in minuets by Franz Haydn.

The Author

Henry Ustick Onderdonk was born in New York in 1789, and educated at Columbia College where he obtained three degrees, B.A., M.A., and D.D. He then studied in London and Edinburgh where he received an M.D.

On his return to New York, he began the study of theology. In 1815, he was ordained Rector of St. Ann's Church of Brooklyn. He became the co-editor of the *Prayer Book Collection* of hymns, contributing nine of his own. Only one of which survives him—"How Wondrous and Great." In 1844, he was relieved of his church position because of a weakness for alcohol, but two years later, he was reinstated after returning to an exemplary life. He died in 1856.

No. 147

Praise to the Man

Words by William W. Phelps

The Hymn

"Praise to the Man" is one of the few hymns written in praise of a man. Most hymns of praise are to our Father in heaven. This hymn, however, is one of the more popular hymns of the Latter-day Saints.

The Composer

All available information seems to point to the conclusion that the tune for "Praise to the Man" is of Scottish folk song origin. A recent popular song "My Bonnie Lassie" whose melodic line was definitely of Scottish origin, has in it the germ of the tune now used in the Latter-day Saint Hymnal. Another tune, probably the patriotic "Hail to the Chief," was used in the early days for this hymn.

The Author — William Wines Phelps (See No. 213)

No. 148

Jesus, the Very Thought of Thee

Words by Bernard of Clairvaux   **Music by John B. Dykes**

The Hymn

"Jesus, the Very Thought of Thee" was called originally the "Rosy Hymn" and contained one-hundred and ninety-two lines divided into forty-eight verses. It was translated from the Latin by several persons. The one found in the Latter-day Saint hymnal was made by Edward Caswell in 1849.

The Composer

John Dykes was born in Hull, England in 1823, a son of a banker. He studied music with an organist of St. John's Church in Hull. In 1849, he became a full-fledged pastor. He is best known for his hymns, and two are found in the Latter-day Saint Hymnal. Besides "Jesus, the Very Thought of Thee" Dykes wrote "Lead, Kindly Light." Both of these hymns show advanced musical scholarship on the part of the composer. He died in 1876.

The Author

All of the hymn writers of the period in which Bernard of Clairvaux (1090-1153) lived were monks. The religious life of the land came from the monasteries. Bernard, the greatest of the medieval saints, was born in France and came from a noble family. As a youth, he distinguished himself in school and was known for "elegance of speech and gracious manner." Certain mystical events shaped his life, and he dedicated himself to the church. When he was twenty-four years old, he was sent with a party to the valley of Clairvaux, which was nothing more than a wilderness. After much tribulation, the group made the place livable and established a monastery. The story is told of Bernard meeting a condemned robber being led to the gallows. He seized the halter and led the man to the judge where he obtained pardon and the man's custody. Soon he converted the culprit, placed him in the monastery and made a man of him. Bernard was a man of great eloquence and roused all of Europe to the benefits of spiritual life. Crowds came to hear him preach and multitudes of sinners were changed as if by a miracle. His life was spent preaching the principle that that which counts in God's sight is a life of holiness. His writings were numerous "Jesus, the Very Thought of Thee" is one of his best hymns.

No. 149

Praise the Lord with Heart and Voice
Words and Music by Tracy Y. Cannon

The Hymn

Tracy Y. Cannon enlightens with the following comment on the writing and composing of this hymn.

"The music of this hymn came to me before I wrote the words. I was therefore under the necessity of writing words that would fit the music. As I wrote the words, I had a strong desire to make the hymn a song of 'Praise to my Creator.'"

The Composer and Author — Tracy Y. Cannon (See No. 1)

165

Praise to the Lord

Words and Music by Joachim Neander

The Hymn

J. Neander was a poet overflowing with "Praise to God." This theme dominated all of his many hymns. The text used in the Latter-day Saint Hymnal is a translation made in 1863 by Catherine Winkworth. One author characterizes the poem as "A magnificent hymn of praise to God, perhaps the finest production of its author, and of the first rank in its class."

The Composer and Author

Joachim Neander was a genuine musician and capable of writing the music for this famous hymn, but it is fairly well established that he adapted an older tune to his text. Many arrangements and harmonizations are extant today. Mr. Neander was a pastor in St. Martin's Church in his native city of Bremen, Germany where he was born in 1650. When he was a young man he, with a couple of friends, went to hear a famous Pietist preacher "just for the fun of it," but all three fell victims to the well known adage "fools who come to scoff remain to pray." For a short time he served as director of the Latin School at Dusseldorf but was removed by the *reformed* Lutherans who gained control of the institution and who were opposed to his Piestic practices. Death came to him in 1680.

Rejoice, the Lord Is King

Words by Charles Wesley   Music by Horatio Parker

The Hymn

"Rejoice, the Lord Is King" is one of the many hymns of gratitude to our Heavenly Father. It is heroic in character and is sequentially climactic in each of the two-line chorus.

The Composer

Horatio Parker (1863-1919) was one of America's noted composers. His mother was an excellent organist and gave him a thorough musical foundation. He became a church organist at sixteen as well as a composer. His musical education was completed in Europe. On his return, he was given several responsible musical positions, among them being a professorship at Yale University. In 1899 in England Dr. Parker's cantata *Hora Novissima*, was sung at the Worcester Festival, the first American work to be so honored.

Dr. Parker was given an honorary degree at Cambridge University. His most famous works were of large dimension but he has to his credit, some outstanding smaller numbers such as anthems, organ numbers, secular songs, etc.

The Author — Charles Wesley (See No. 10)

No. 152

O Sons of Zion

Words by Ed M. Rowe   **Music by Robert P. Manookin**

The Hymn

Robert Manookin says of his hymn:

> The hymn was one of ten submitted by myself. I received a list of selected sacred poems from Tracy Y. Cannon. I chose ten and wrote hymn tunes to them. Because I had not heard of the hymn contest sponsored by the Church until a late date, these hymns were composed rapidly to permit their being submitted before the closing date of the contest. I remember no special "feeling" associated with the composition of this hymn. I do remember, however, my total surprise when I learned that one of my hymns had been chosen for the new hymnbook. Since its publication, I have experienced a curious feeling of detachment from it, as if it were not mine at all, so rapid and fleeting was my handling of it. Perhaps worthy of note is that I have never really liked the hymn, I submitted it with the others so that I could send in an even ten. The melody I feel seems lacking in imagination and the harmony poor. My interest and lifelong concern over the status and quality of church music seems to be contradicted by my own pen. The words of this hymn are words of glory, praise, joy, and majesty. The attempt was made to provide a musical setting which would best clothe these inspiring thoughts and express their message. It is almost a "march" of the Sons of Zion, glorious and triumphant, and consequently should, under no circumstance, be rushed. Observation of the indicated metronome speed will best express this. The music is an endeavor to provide a musical note of praise so well expressed in the text, to furnish a harmonious medium by which to give voice to this message of gladness and inspire those who sing it to "Lift up your hearts in gratitude and serve the Living God."

The Composer

Robert Manookin was born in Salt Lake City, in April 1918, the son of Kerrigan Mark and Agnes Park Midgley Manookin. He began to study piano with Lulabelle Elldredge at the age of eight. Then he studied piano and organ with Frank Asper and Alexander Schreiner, composition under B. Cecil Gates, choral conducting with J. Spencer

Cornwall. He attended East High School, Brigham Young University where he worked for a B.A. degree in Music Theory. Also studied with Dr. Leon Dallin, Carl Fuerstner, and Newell Weight, and J. J. Keeler. In 1955-1956 did graduate study at the B.Y.U. and took counterpoint under Crawford Gates. He is now doing graduate work at the University of Illinois.

The Author

Ed M. Rowe was born Dec. 9, 1878 in Spanish Fork, a son of Owen J. and Anna Creer Rowe.

He received his early education in Spanish Fork schools and at Brigham Young Academy, where he was editor of the Blue and White newspaper 1898-1899. He was graduated from Brigham Young University in 1923 and became instructor in English the next year. He also did graduate work at Brigham Young University, University of Utah, Utah State Agricultural College, University of Chicago, University of Wales and Cornell University.

He married Minnie Barry, June 3, 1908, in the Salt Lake Temple, and they moved to Spanish Fork where he was principal of Spanish Fork High School and a member of the city council. They had four sons and two daughters.

Ed M. Rowe

Robert Manookin

Ed M. Rowe was superintendent of Utah State Industrial School at Ogden, 1912-1915, and later served as state parole agent for that institution.

He was active in the Church and filled a mission to Ireland. Also he was an active worker in the Republican party and backed sports in Provo.

He joined the BYU faculty as an instructor in Englsh in 1924 and became a full professor in 1935. He retired in 1949 with the rank of Professor Emeritus in English.

He was chief organizer in getting the Welsh National Library placed at BYU. The BYU library also received many books from his personal collection, and he was an authority on Wordsworth. Also he authored several collections of poetry.

He died in November 1951 in Salt Lake City while returning from a Republican convention.

No. 153

Poor Wayfaring Man Of Grief

Words by James Montgomery   Music Anonymous

The Hymn

"A poor Wayfaring Man of Grief" was not an own song-child of the Latter-day Saints, but a dearly beloved adopted one.* It might never have gained the prominence given it among our hymns had it not been so closely associated with the most tragic scene in Mormon history—the assassination of the Prophet Joseph Smith and his brother, Hyrum in Carthage Jail, June 27, 1844.

The long story of the exciting days in Nauvoo is well-known to every Latter-day Saint. However, a brief sketch of events immediately leading up to the martyrdom may be enlightening to those who are not acquainted with Mormon history.

The enemies of the Prophet were wrought up to such a pitch of hate that Joseph's life was not safe in Nauvoo. After consultation with some of his friends, he decided to escape from the dangers of the city he had founded and seek refuge in the West. In fact, Hyrum recorded that the Lord had warned Joseph to flee to the Rocky Mountains. So, on June 22nd at midnight, the Prophet, with a number of his friends, rowed across the Mississippi, arriving on the Iowa side Sunday morning, the 23rd.

O. P. Rockwell, one of the party, was sent back to Nauvoo for horses to carry them farther West, but he returned at the request of

---

*From George D. Pyper's *Stories of Latter-day Saint Hymns*.

Emma Smith, the Prophet's wife, with an appeal for Joseph to return to Nauvoo. A letter from Emma also entreated him to give himself up, and carried the further message that the governor had pledged his faith and the faith of the state to protect him. Some even accused the Prophet of cowardice for leaving the Saints. That was the deciding factor. Joseph said: "If my life is of no value to my friends, it is of no value to myself." And so, through the importunities of his wife and some friends, Joseph went back to Nauvoo and the warning of the Lord went unheeded.

From then until the fatal hour of the martyrdom, every minute of the time was fraught with history-making episodes. Gathering clouds pointed inevitably to a tragic ending. Joseph sensed this and urged his brother and his friends to leave him to his fate. He said, "Could my brother Hyrum be released it would not matter so much about me."

His remarks at various times along the way to Carthage indicate his frame of mind: "I go like a lamb to the slaughter." To Squire (Daniel H.) Wells he said: "I wish you would cherish my memory."

On June 27th the friends of the Prophet and Patriarch, except John Taylor and Willard Richards, were hustled from Carthage, and these four went into the cell at Carthage Jail. The Prophet was depressed. Seeing this, John Taylor, to cheer him up, sang "A Poor Wayfaring Man of Grief," a favorite song of the Prophet, and popular in Nauvoo previous to the martyrdom. Soon after, Hyrum Smith asked Elder Taylor to sing the song again. Elder Taylor said: "Brother Hyrum, I do not feel like singing." And Hyrum said: "Oh, never mind, commence singing, and you will get the spirit of it."

It was not long after the song was sung the second time that the mob attacked the jail. Brigham H. Roberts, in his book says:

> How quickly disastrous things happen! Three minutes after the attack was commenced upon the jail, Hyrum Smith lay stretched upon the floor of the prison—dead. John Taylor lay not far from him savagely wounded. The Prophet was lying outside the jail by the old well curb—dead: The mob in consternation and disorder had fled in the direction of Warsaw; the plighted faith of a state was broken, its honor trailed in the dust and the stain of innocent blood affixed to its escutcheon that will remain a blot which time cannot efface.

The Composer

It had been thought by our song compilers that the composer of the music was unknown, but since looking up references in this series, it is recorded that the words were put to George Coles' tune "Duane Street." Up-to-date we have been unable to find that tune and cannot say whether or not it is the same as that used by John Taylor and reprinted since that time in our songbooks.

The Author

James Montgomery was born at Irvine, Ayrshire, Scotland, November 4, 1771. His father was the Rev. John Montgomery, a Moravian minister, who, with his wife, went to the West Indies as a missionary and died there. James was apprenticed at the age of sixteen to a grocer but ran away two years later. He was writing poetry at the age of nineteen and went to London to arrange for publication of his efforts, but Mr. Harrison, the publisher to whom he applied, did not warm up to the poetry, although he engaged him as a shop man. Here began his newspaper work. In 1792 he engaged to work in the *Sheffield Register, a* revolutionary paper, the owner of which fled to America to avoid imprisonment. Montgomery took over the paper in 1795, renaming it the *Sheffield Iris,* and continued its publication until July, 1825. His reform principles met with the antagonism of the government, and he was fined twenty pounds and imprisoned for three months. Later, he was convicted of sedition, fined thirty pounds, and imprisoned for six months.

In spite of the government's hostility to him, his power and popularity grew. His Christian virtues finally won the favor of the government, and he was given an annual pension of two hundred pounds. His closing years were serene and lovely. He died April 30, 1854.

Montgomery wrote four hundred hymns and poems, all published in his lifetime.

"A Poor Wayfaring Man of Grief," originally written in four eight line stanzas, is a great sermon, based on Matthew 25:35. It is said that when the hymn was first published "it made every heart beat time," and "that the coldest heart kindled with the gospel warmth as the story swept on."

No. 154

Raise Your Voices to the Lord

Words and Music by Evan Stephens

The Hymn

"Raise Your Voices to the Lord" is a closing hymn of prayer. It is written in chorale style.

The Composer and Author — Evan Stephens (See No. 144)

171

Savior, Redeemer of My Soul

Words by Orson F. Whitney   **Music by Harry A. Dean**

The Hymn

The hymn "Savior, Redeemer of My Soul" is a hymn of gratitude for life and being.

The Composer — Harry Dean (See No. 142)

The Author — Orson F. Whitney (See No. 292)

No. 156

Shall We Meet beyond the River

Words by Horace L. Hastings   **Music by Elihu S. Rice**

The Hymn

"Shall We Meet" is a favorite funeral hymn with many people. It is a sentimental gospel song—a product of revivalism.

The Composer

Elihu S. Rice was a clerk in a hardware store. Later he became a preacher. Further information in unavailable.

The Author

Horace Lorenzo Hastings was born in Blandford, Mass. in 1831. He began preaching and writing hymns at the age of seventeen. In 1856 he established a monthly paper *The Christian* in which many of his hymns were published. In his three collections of hymns which he published and which totaled one thousand five hundred and thirty three, four hundred and fifty were of his own writing. His best known hymn is "Shall We Meet beyond the River." He died in 1886.

No. 157

Shall the Youth Of Zion Falter

Words and Music by Evan Stephens

The Hymn

"Shall the Youth of Zion Falter?" is not a hymn in the strict sense but rather an exuberant song whose sub-title could well be "Faith in the Youth of Zion."

Composer and Author — Evan Stephens, See No. 144.

The late Evan Stephens, the most prolific composer of Latter-day Saint hymns, who wrote "True to the Faith"* had a clear con-

---

*From George D. Pyper's *Stories of Latter-day Saint Hymns.*

ception of the requisite fundamentals of Latter-day Saint hymnody. On the subject he wrote:

> The songs and music of the Latter-day Saints are in perfect accord with the spirit of the newly revealed gospel of Jesus Christ, as restored in modern times through the medium of the Prophet Joseph Smith.
>
> In contrast to that generally used by the churches of the day in which this Church was set up anew upon the earth, they are as light to darkness, or brightness to gloom. Expressions of fear and sorrow, the terrible confessions of and lamentations over sin, the constant dwelling upon the sufferings of our crucified Savior, and the eternal tortures in store for sinners, give place in the songs of the Latter-day Saints to expressions of hope, joy, and the sense of sins forgiven. More emphasis is placed upon the love and the glorious conquest of our Redeemer than upon his earthly sufferings; more on the final redemption of all erring humanity than upon a never-ending suffering of souls. When the heartstrings and the fount of tears are to be touched at all, it is with tenderness, sympathy, and joy, rather than with terror and sorrow. This is equally true of the keynote of text and music. when the songs are really characteristic of the prevailing spirit of Mormonism.
>
> A young professor of music recently put to me the question, "What would you term the 'Mormonistic' in music?" I replied, "That which breathes optimism and not pessimism, music in which the sombre must not predominate, but be used only as a means of contrast to heighten the effect of the bright."

When Evan Stephens was conductor of the Tabernacle Choir he was thrilled on one occasion by a sermon delivered by the late President Joseph F. Smith on the subject of "The Third and Fourth Generations."

At the close of the service Professor Stephens strolled alone up City Creek Canyon pondering the inspired words of the President. Suddenly the muse came upon him and seated upon a rock which was standing firm under the pressure of the rushing water and happily symbolic of his theme, he wrote with a pencil the words of "True to the Faith" and with roughly drawn staves composed the music.

> It isn't words or music to dream over; it is that pulsating with the life and action of today. Yesterday was the dreamer's day. Today belongs to the active wideawake worker, and our religion is pre-eminently in harmony with today and its unparalleled activity. Our songs and music, to a degree, at least, are here again in harmony with our religion, as they should be; and, true to its active, optimistic character, our young people sing:

173

We will work out our salvation,
    We will cleave unto the truth,
We will watch and pray and labor
    With the fervent zeal of youth, Yes!

True to the faith that our parents have cherished,
    True to the truth for which martyrs have perished,
To God's command, soul, heart, and hand,
    Faithful and true we will ever stand.

"True to the Faith" was first published in *The Juvenile Instructor*, Volume 40, page 95, and was proposed by the Sunday School General Board to be sung at their conferences in 1905. On the copy was written: "Lovingly dedicated to my 20,000 pupils of Zion."

This song, more than any other, in the opinion of the writer of this sketch, contains more of the composer's emotional enthusiasm than any other of his writings. Professor Stephens loved the youth of Zion. He was companionable with them and did much for those who came within his charmed circle. The song was his spiritual advice to them.

No. 158

Sing Praise to Him

Words by Johann J. Schultz Music from the Bohemian Brethren's Songbook

The Hymn

"Sing Praise to Him" is a joyous hymn of praise to the Lord. Its Bohemian tune has a musically savory flavor.

One outstanding characteristic of Bohemian music is the simple beauty of its melodic lines. "Sing Praise to Him" is no exception.

The Composer

It is not absolutely established that Schultz (1640-1690) is the composer of "Sing Praise to Him," but it is established that it came from the publications of Bohemian Brethren. The Bohemian Brethren was a sect which broke away from the Catholic Church. Three men whose names were Peter, Gregory, and Lucas, effected the organization about the year 1467. In 1546, a man by the name of John Augusta succeeded in uniting many factions who had left the central group, but this unity only lasted until 1621 when disastrous wars finally destroyed the entire cult. With all of their tribulations, they gave to the world several fine hymns among which is the tune to "Sing

Praise to Him." Just when this tune became associated with the Cox translations of Schutz' hymn is not known.

The Author

Johann Jacob **Schultz**(Shuitz, Shuetz) was born at Frankfurt-am-Main, Germany. He studied and practiced law. His religion was that of the Separatists. In 1683 he had some land dealings with William Penn in Pennsylvania. He died in his home town of Frankfurt.

The Translator

John Wesley discovered the great wealth of Christian hymns written by German authors. He translated many of them, but after he died, a century passed before any further translations were made. Then Francis Elizabeth Cox, (1812-1897) an Anglican and a native of Oxford, England, rediscovered the fineness of the German hymns and set herself to the task of translating more of them. Miss Cox, by her translations, placed renewed emphasis on the ecumenical character of Christianity. "Sing Praise to Him" was one of her translations, the German author being Johann Jacob Schutz.

No. 159
Should You Feel Inclined to Censure
Music by Philip Paul Bliss

The Hymn

Probably the most prevalent and insidious failing of human beings is that of indulging in censure or as it is commonly called "faultfinding." Fixing the blame or noting by word of mouth the infirmities of a fellow being seems to be basic to man's uninhibited make-up. In a world of "live and let live" or "peacable co-existence," unmitigated and oft-times unwarranted censure is the greatest obstacle to "goodwill toward men" and its resultant "Peace on earth."

The Composer — Paul Bliss (See No. 301)

The two songs credited to Paul Bliss, found in the Latter-day Saint Hymnal indicate that he was a successful writer of gospel songs.

The Author

The anonymous author of the simple but potent lines of this hymn, has brought home without any uncertainty, a great principle of human relationship.

Silent Night

Words by Joseph Mohr   **Music by Franz Gruber**

The Hymn

Inspiration to pen the words of this soulful carol came to Joseph Mohr, an assistant pastor at Oberdorf, near Ansdorf, Germany, on Christmas eve, 1818.* The young priest was attending a celebration in the schoolhouse at Arnsdorf with his dear friend Franz Gruber, a village schoolmaster, song writer, and church organist. These two friends talked earnestly and regretfully over the fact that there was no really great Christmas song. Pondering the thought, young Mohr that same evening in his church study saw the picture—*"and there were shepherds in the same country, abiding in the fields, and keeping watch over their flocks by night."* (Luke 2:8)—a flash and the inspiration came, and so on the peaks of the Tyrolian Alps were framed the words of the carol that was to be heard around the world.

Next morning, Christmas, (some writers say it was the same night), Mohr went to the home of Franz Gruber and presented him with a folded copy of his carol. Franz opened it, read it and exultingly exclaimed, "You have found it!—the right song!— God be praised!" He then repaired to his own room and, inspired by the words, composed the tune as we now have it. Franz hurried back to his friend saying: "Your song—it sings itself: the tune came to me at once, and while you were gone I played to the Strasser sisters, and we have together composed it."

Mohr and Gruber then sang it as a duet, the author singing the melody, the composer the bass. The Strasser sisters, under the name of the "Strasser Quartette" learned it, and later it was sung at the great cathedral of Leipzig. The song was first called "The Tyrolian Song" because of its place of birth. It was not printed, however, until 1840. In 1854, thirty-six years after it was written, the Berlin Church Choir sang it before Emperor Frederick Wilhelm IV. The emperor was so delighted with the beautiful song that he ordered it given first place in all Christmas programs.

Music histories contain very little, if anything, concerning the lives of Joseph Mohr and Franz Gruber. Only the years of birth and death are recorded. Mohr, 1792-1848; Gruber, 1787-1863.

Speaking of "Silent Night," Mme. Schumann-Heink paid this tribute:

---

*From George D. Pyper's *Stories of Latter-day Saint Hymns.*

Oh, that is such a lovely song! It was composed by this man Gruber in a tiny village near Salzburg, where he lived. The author didn't think much of it at the time, but it got so popular that now on Christmas Eve, everywhere in the world they sing "Stille Nacht." I sang this song, and my records went even to South America. I got letters once from the nurses in a hospital there, and they told me how they put on that record on Christmas Eve, and that they all cried, nurses and doctors as well as the sick ones; and they all thanked me for it. That touched me very much. Yes—these simple songs have reached the hearts of and given pleasure to thousands and thousands of people all over the country.

The Composer — Franz Gruber

The Author — Joseph Mohr

Franz Gruber

No. 161

Sing We Now at Parting

Words by George Manwaring   **Music by Ebenezer Beesley**

The Hymn

"Sing We Now at Parting" is the best closing song in the Latter-day Saint Hymnal. Because of the line "Rend this Sabbath Air" it can only be sung with propriety on Sundays. This hymn will never

177

become trite or worn out. It has a genteel loveliness about it which makes it beloved. It is beautifully written in both text and music.

The Composer — Ebenezer Beesley (See No. 94)

The Author — George Manwaring (See No. 136)

(See No. 94)
(See No. 136)

No. 162

Softly Now the Light of Day

Words by George W. Doane   **Music by C. M. von Weber**

The Hymn

Evening, twilight, sunset, the fading day, have all kindled many a poet's mind to introspective quiet contemplation.

The solemnity of the day's ending presages, in a way, the end of life. Tennyson's "Sunset and Evening Star" and "Softly Now the Light of Day," the hymn under discussion, and many others bring to us the beauty and peace of the day's passing.

The Hymn

Carl Weber with his three great operas, *Der Freischutz, Euryanthe,* and *Oberon,* disposed of Italian opera in Germany. At the same time he set the stage for Richard Wagner's transcendent operas, which were to surpass all previous efforts everywhere in the world in the writing of opera. Von Weber's life was filled with vicissitudes but he managed to obtain some very fine musical training from Wallishauser in Munich, Vogler the teacher of Meyerbeer, in Vienna, and finally Michael Haydn in Salzburg. He died suddenly, while supervising a production of *Oberon* in Covent Gardens, London.

The tune of "Softly Now the Light of Day" came from the theme of the opening chorus in the opera *Oberon.* The adaptation was made by Henry Wellington Greatorex in 1851. Carl Von Weber was born in 1786 and died in 1826.

The Author

George W. Doane, born in 1799, was one of the most prominent churchmen of his time. He was thoroughly trained for the ministry in New York City. His son, also a Bishop, gave tribute to his father by saying that "His heart is full of song." He wrote poems and sermons constantly whether traveling or at home. Four volumes of his works were published after his death in 1859. "Softly Now the Light of Day" was written by Bishop Doane for St. Mary's Hall, a girls' seminary in New Jersey which he founded. It is sung traditionally at every weekly assembly of the school.

Sons of Michael, He Approaches

Words by Edward L. T. Harrison   **Music by Charles J. Thomas**

The Hymn

The contents of the hymn "Sons of Michael" are based on the following passages from the Doctrine and Covenants; section 27:11, section 76:16, section 88:112-113, section 107:54,55,56.

The Composer

Charles John Thomas was born November 20, 1832 in Burnley, Lancashire, England, the son of Joseph K. Thomas, and Margaret Spotswood. When only seven years of age, he exhibited natural ability for music and at the age of nine he played with his father in an orchestra at the Theatre Royal New-Castle-on-Tyne. While still a lad he went to London and studied harmony under the tutorship of Professor Thirwall of the Theatre Royal Covent Garden where he graduated with honors. Soon after becoming a convert to Mormonism in 1851, Charles took sick and continued to grow worse until his life was despaired of, and the doctor said he would die. His father's heart was touched, and he exclaimed: "My son, if there is anything on earth that you wish, and I can get for you, you shall have it." Charles asked that the Latter-day Saint elders be sent for, to pray for him. The elders came, and after they had administered to him, he was instantly healed. Soon after this the whole family joined the Church. In 1853 Charles traveled with an Italian opera company. In 1854 he published some of his compositions which were played at several London theaters. In 1856 he was offered the position of band master on board *H.M.S. Great Marlborough* but had to decline because of ill health. After being a member of the Church for ten years, he set sail for America with a large company of emigrating Saints who crossed the Atlantic in the ship *William Tapscott*. To Professor Thomas belongs the distinction and honor of being the first orchestral leader for the Salt Lake Theatre and for the first to receive a testimonial benefit in that historic house. He was also musical director of the first male glee club in Salt Lake City, which was organized under the name of the "Union Glee Club" in March 1876 with a membership of sixteen. The object of the organization was mutual improvement in the "Divine art of vocal music and to assist in charitable purposes." From 1875 to 1885 Elder Thomas had charge of the temple block by special appointment from the Presidency of the Church. In 1887 he filled a mission to Great Britain. Among his church assignments were the following: leader of the temple choir, composer of many church anthems, vocal and instrumental teacher, and a band director. He married Charlotte Gibbs and was the father of one son. One of his colleagues in the music world, speaking of Professor Thomas says: "In summing up this noble, earnest teacher's work, it may be said that his advent into these valleys marked an epoch in early musical history of Utah."

The Author

In about the year 1868 a merchant of Salt Lake City by the name of W. S. Godbe started a literary publication called *The Utah Magazine*. He selected for its editor Edward L. T. Harrison, a gifted writer who was the author of the hymn "Sons of Michael."

The magazine soon became financially impoverished, and Mr. Godbe lacked goods for his store. Godbe and Harrison took a coach trip to New York City to seek merchandise and also aid for the periodical. It is reported that they took with them a copy of the Book of Mormon to read in their leisure time of which they had "a plenty." Their reading led them to questioning and to skepticism of the Book of Mormon writings because they did not follow the admonition of Moroni in the final chapter, verses four and five of the book which gives the key to the knowing of its truthfulness. These verses are as follows:

> And when ye shall receive these things, I would exhort you that ye would ask God, the Eternal Father, in the name of Christ, if these things are not true; and if ye shall ask with a sincere heart, with real intent, having faith in Christ, he will manifest the truth of it unto you, by the power of the Holy Ghost.
> And by the power of the Holy Ghost ye may know the truth of all things.

These two men read with a spirit of faultfinding.

When they returned, they voiced their differences and disbeliefs in a newspaper which they established. This gained for them a following of other disgruntled Latter-day Saints. Mr. Godbe organized these people into a sect which assumed the name of *Godbeites*. All were subsequently excommunicated from the Church. Soon after, the organization disintegrated and the "Church of Zion," (its official name) was abandoned.

Although Edward L. T. Harrison lost his standing in the Church he left to his credit a worthy hymn.

180

Stars of Morning, Shout for Joy

Words, Anonymous   Music by Thomas Durham

The Hymn

"Stars of Morning, Shout for Joy" was composed in 1860. It has been in all of the Latter-day Saint Church Hymnals since it was written by Thomas Durham. The text was undoubtedly written by a Latter-day Saint author unknown to us. It was evidently inspired by verses four to seven of the thirty-eighth chapter of Job which declare the pre-existence of man.

The Composer

Parowan, Utah was settled January 13, 1851 by a group of settlers headed by Apostle George A. Smith, a cousin of the Prophet. Brigham Young made it a policy to send to each community some sort of musician to direct and develop the activities of that art. Thomas Durham was the man in the case of Parowan.

Born in Oldham, Lancashire, England on May 2, 1828, he crossed the Atlantic in a sailing vessel at the age of twenty-eight. After landing in Boston, he journeyed by rail as far west as the road then went.

Continuing westward he crossed the plains with the ill-fated Martin Handcart Company in the fall of 1856. A large percentage of the group perished in the cold as, barefoot, they pushed their handcarts through the snow. The company, or what was left of it, arrived in Salt Lake in the dead of winter.

Brigham Young personally called Brother Durham to proceed immediately to Parowan to direct the musical activities there. He arrived at his destination December 12, 1856. Two days later, on a Sunday, he took charge of the Parowan choir and directed it until his death fifty three years later in 1909.

Thomas Durham was a joiner by trade, an expert craftsman trained in the old country. But his first love was always music. Much of the music for his group he copied by hand where only one copy was available. He also composed many hymns for predecessors of the present LDS hymnbook.

He had a fine background of musical training in England. He was a student of the reed organ, composition, harmony, and sight reading at Stalybridge, and during the ten years prior to his departure for America he directed the church choir in his home town.

As early as 1864 we discover in our perusal of the records the first tangible results of his work in Parowan, when, in November of that year, he was instrumental in organizing "The Parowan Harmonic Society, for the cultivation of sacred and secular music." (*Deseret News*, November 21, 1864.)

A memorable high light of the Harmonic Society was reached five years later — a thrilling event never to be forgotten by any member of that group of music-lovers.

It was at "October Conference" time in 1870. At this particular conference, the merits of the Parowan Harmonic Society had been recognized, and they had been invited by Brigham Young to journey to Salt Lake to furnish the musical selections for the meetings — an honor for which the various ward choirs vied constantly.

It so happened that when they arrived in Salt Lake that the Chief Commander of the United States Army was spending a few days in that city. This official was none other than the famous General Sherman, hero of the Union army forces in the Civil War. At this time, he was en route to his home in the east after an extended trip of inspection in the Pacific Coast area.

Sherman's famous march to the Sea had made him the day's national hero and his attentions were solicited on all sides wherever he made his way.

Whitney, in his *History of Utah*, tells how the eminent soldier, accompanied by his daughter, General Schofield, and other military officers, registered at the Townsend House, present site of the Hotel Utah, and during their stay had a very sociable interview with President Young and other church leaders, at the President's office.

> One evening, while Sherman was still in Salt Lake City, the townspeople gathered outside his hotel, clamoring for a view of their idol. The war-worn veteran had been serenaded the same evening by the Camp Douglas Band, but in spite of all this he had declined to put in an appearance and address the throng.
>
> An hour later, after the throng had dispersed to a small degree, the members of the Parowan choir, who were in Salt Lake to attend the Conference, made their appearance and sang two or three pieces, which were followed by cries of "Sherman," "speech." This was followed by a call for "Hard Times, come again no more," which was very effectively rendered by the choir.
>
> General Sherman then made his appearance, and in a few well-chosen words acknowledged the compliment paid him by the singers.

The clamorings and pleadings of a throng, plus the serenading of one of Uncle Sam's military bands had failed to impress the general. What they had failed to do, the Parowan Mormon choir had been able to accomplish with their sweet, sincere singing.

182

That the hero of the March to the Sea was deeply touched is evident by his words to the choir:

> I address myself not to the crowd, but to this little band of singers who, I understand, have travelled by team and wagon two hundred and fifty miles to sing at their church conference.
>
> So far as it is in my power, I promise them that "hard times shall come again no more" to this people.

These words were especially significant to these Mormon pioneers, for surely they, above all others, had experienced more than their share of "hard times" as they were persecuted and driven from state to state.

He stated further that he did not intend to make a speech. He had heard the singers were from Parowan; he did not know Parowan, only by having seen it on a map. He was gratified to behold the beautiful homes which the people, while facing difficulties and trials of the severest kind, had built up in the desert, and "his sincere wish was that they might live to enjoy them." *Journal History*, October 4, 1870.)

The Author — Anonymous

No. 165

O Little Town of Bethlehem

Words by Phillips Brooks   **Music by Lewis H. Redner**

The Hymn

"Thank God, Christmas comes every year, for we need to be reminded," so says the sage. In December 1865, Phillips Brooks went to Palestine. To relive the ancient journey, he rode on horseback from Jerusalem to Bethlehem. His own words describe the journey.

> Before dark we rode out of town to the field where they say the shepherds saw the star. It is a fenced piece of ground with a cave in it in which, strangely enough, they put the shepherds. . . . Somewhere in those fields we rode through, the shepherds must have been. As we passed, shepherds were still "keeping watch over their flocks," or leading them home to fold.

He also states that he attended the service on the site thought to be the place of the nativity. The service lasted from ten p.m. to three a.m. After returning to Philadelphia with the memories of his pilgrimage to the Holy Land, he wrote for a Sunday School Christmas celebration, the immortal carol "O Little Town of Bethlehem."

The Composer

Lewis H. Redner (1831-1908) was the organist in the Holy Trinity Church in Philadelphia where Phillips Brooks was pastor. Brooks came to Redner on Saturday night before Christmas in 1868 with what he called "a simple carol." Redner retired with the words of the carol in his mind. He relates that just after midnight he awoke, hearing in his mind strains of music. These strains were to carry the carol to the ends of the earth. He wrote the melody down in a great hurry, filling in the harmony a few hours later. It was sung the next day in the Sunday Christmas service.

The Author

Phillips Brooks was born in Boston in 1835, educated at Harvard University, and trained for the ministry in the Episcopal Theological Seminary in Alexandria, Va.

When he became Pastor of Trinity Church, he drew such large crowds by his preaching that the people of the parish had to build a larger church. When he preached, the words flowed forth at the rate of two hundred and fifty a minute. He was loved by all of his compatriots. He never married. As long as the world sings "O Little Town of Bethlehem" Phillips Brooks will be remembered. He died in 1893.

No. 166

Sweet Hour of Prayer

Words by W. W. Walford   Music by William B. Bradbury

The Hymn

This hymn is appealing to large numbers of people, due to its solemnity and its contemplative character.

The Composer

The hymn tune, "Sweet Hour of Prayer," is really a precursor to the gospel song. The composer, William Bradbury (1816-1868), was a rather well-trained musician, having studied in Boston, New York and two years in Leipzig, Germany.

He was a popular conductor of musical festivals. In 1854, he went into the business of manufacturing pianos, and together with Lowell Mason and George F. Root did much for earlier American church music. He was editor of the New York *Musical Review*.

The Author

Reverend William W. Walford was a blind English minister. He recited the poem to a fellow pastor who took it down and brought it to New York where it was published in the New York *"Observer."* In addition to his preaching, Walford, though blind, used his mechanical skill in making useful articles out of bone and ivory.

No. 167

Take Courage, Saints

Words by James Crystal   Music by Frank W. Asper

The Hymn

"Take Courage, Saints" is a hymn of exhortation and encouragement to "faint not by the way."

The Composer — Frank W. Asper (See No. 96)

The Author

James Crystal was born in Scotland in 1839. He joined the Latter-day Saint Church in 1848. He cared for seven brothers and sisters and his mother after his father was killed in a mine accident.

He came to America with his eldest sister in 1866 settling in American Fork, Utah.

James Crystal was a writer and contributed articles to several magazines. He also held many prominent positions in the Church. Death came to him in 1924.

No. 168

Sweet Is the Work

Words by Isaac Watts   Music by John J. McClellan

The Hymn

In the first collection of hymns by Emma Smith "Sweet Is the Work, My God, My King" was included, and has never been omitted from our compilations.* The beautiful song of praise appealed to Emma Smith as it has to the compilers since her time. However, it is not classed by critics among Watts' best hymns. Most hymnologists place "When I Survey the Wondrous Cross" among the finest of Christian hymns. Of the thousand written by this author more are of a high standard of excellence and suitable for congregational use than those of any other English writer.

The hymn that is the subject of this sketch is beloved by everyone who experiences happiness and joy in praising God and giving thanks to him from early dawn, through the day and into the night; who finds peace and rest in every hour and puts his heart in tune with the infinite; who triumphs in the work of God, and, when in realms of joy can meet his Lord face to face, when sin shall vex the eyes and ears no more and inward foes be slain; when knowledge and intelligence — the glory of God — and every power "find sweet employ in that eternal world of joy." The tune of the first phrase is the diatonic scale.

---

*From George D. Pyper's *Stories of Latter-day Saint Hymns.*

This hymn has been used since the initiation of the Latter-day Saint Church of the Air broadcasts as the signature music.

The Composer

In every walk of life there occasionally appear on the horizon, men and women who tower above their fellows. In science, literature, art, industry, these giants, by the sheer force of their talents, come into prominence. One of these excelling spirits was John J. McClellan, who rose to unusual prominence as an organist and who more than any other man made the pipe organ loved by the American people.

John J. McClellan, the son of John Jasper and Elizabeth B. McClellan, was born in Payson, Utah, April 20, 1874. His musical precocity was manifest at a very early age. He began the study of music at ten years of age and was a Church organist at eleven; studied under local teachers until July, 1891, when he left Utah for Saginaw, Michigan. There he worked hard, and later, at Ann Arbor, studied under competant internationally known teachers. He engaged in many public musical functions, taught classes, and founded a symphony orchestra. His student life in America and Europe was filled with unusual activity, and included courses with Xaver Scharwenka, the noted Hungarian pianist.

Upon taking up his residence in Salt Lake City, he became Tabernacle organist and director of the Salt Lake Opera Company. He married Mary Douglass, and was the father of five children. He died August 2, 1925.

At the time of Professor McClellan's death, the writer of these song stories published "An Appreciation" in the *Juvenile Instructor*, part of which is as follows:

> Professor John J. McClellan was a child of art. The very lineaments of his face were classical, and his performances truly indicated the refinement of his nature. He did more than any other man to make the people love the organ, and he knew well how to make it reach their hearts. How often, during his playing have we experienced the thrill of spiritual exaltation which the organ alone could produce. It was the soul of John J. McClellan. He was highly temperamental. His artistic bow seemed to be always bent to the limit. It was seldom unstrung.
>
> How grateful I am that the spirit of John J. McClellan was reserved through the ages to be clothed with mortality in this generation; that he came here in our time and that we have had the privilege of knowing him and sharing the blessings resulting from his supreme art; that he used his great gift in God's service; that he was able to put such soul into the grand old Tabernacle organ of ours and through its instrumentality preach the gospel to the world. Millions

have heard him perform upon the great organ, and many of these who came here with hatred toward us have been uplifted and have gone away with their hearts softened and their impressions changed through his soulful playing.

Professor McClellan, above most musicians that could be named, possessed the instinct to read the hearts of his audience and to tell what they wanted from his instrument. No matter whether that audience consisted of the cultured or the untutored, he could satisfy their desires. This was one of the secrets of his popularity.

Such was the man who wrote the music to Isaac Watts' soulful hymn. No romantic or dramatic occurrence inspired the tune used by the Latter-day Saints, but it is said to have been written when Brother McClellan was only eleven years old. His artistic soul budded early in life.

Prof. Tracy Y. Cannon, now the Chairman of the Church Music Committee, in appraising this composition says:

> Several musical factors contribute to the beauty and effectiveness of this hymn: It is natural and singable; it is easy to remember as it is built on simple scale passages; its harmonies are natural and interesting; it is expressive as its phrase rise and fall in natural sequence, thus preserving its musical unity, and giving it pleasing variety.

The compiler of this book is grateful for the musical instruction he received from John J. McClellan.

The Author

Southampton, England, was the city where the stork left Isaac Watts, July 17, 1674, the first of eight like visits which followed. His father was the keeper of a boarding house.

Isaac Watts was a precocious child. He was poring over the classics in his fifth year and is said to have written religious verses, to please his mother, at seven or eight. In religious conviction he was a non-conformist and for that reason was not permitted to attend the universities but studied at Haberdasher's Hall, a London academy. Here overwork brought on a physical weakness from which he never completely recovered. He was engaged as tutor in the family of Sir John Hartopp at Stoke Newington and wrote two book, viz; *Logick, or the Right use of Reason in the Inquiry after Truth*, and *The Knowledge of the Earth and the Heavens made Easy*. At twenty-seven he became assistant to Dr. Chauncey an independent pastor, and two years later succeeded him at Mark Lane, London. In 1712 he became ill and went to stay with his friend Sir Thomas Abney for a weekend, but he remained there 36 years until he died in 1748.

His time was spent in the writing of hymns and in the publication of sermons. His *Psalm of David* is said to be the foundation of English Hymnody, and *Divine and Moral Songs for Children* (1720), the first of its kind ever published. This contains the poem, popular with our forefathers—"How Does the Little Busy Bee." .

Isaac Watts died November 25, 1748, and was buried at Bunhill Fields. There is a memorial tablet in Westminster Abbey and a Memorial Hall at Southampton, erected in his honor.

Isaac Watts   John J. McClellan

No. 169   **There Is Beauty All Around**
Words and Music by John Hugh McNaughton

The Hymn

This song is "a tender lyric in praise of the home where love dwells." Especially true are the lines, "All the earth is filled with love, When there's love at home."

The author here recognizes the wide influence of the home, the primary social institution, where individuals learn the first lessons of Christian life. A nation's peace and prosperity stems from the quality of life found in its homes.

The deep-seated moral and the ever-important lesson of this hymn text, together with the singability of its musical setting, make it a great favorite among Latter-day Saints where the sanctity of the home is so sacred to every faithful member of the Church.

Composer and Author

John Hugh McNaughton, author of both words and music, was born in 1829, in Caledonia, New York, of Scottish parentage. He is the composer of many popular songs of the past, including "The Blue and The Gray," and "Faded Coat of Blue."

Dearest Children, God Is Near You

Words by C. L. Walker   Music by J. M. Macfarlane

The Hymn

The hymn "Dearest Children, God Is Near You" contains a loving message to God's children of his tender care and watchfulness over them.

The Composer — J. M. Macfarlane (See No. 33)

The Author

Charles Lowell Walker was born at Leek, Staffordshire, England, November 17, 1832, a son of William Gibson Walker—ribbonmaker, scholar, teacher — and Mary Godwin Walker — milliner — philosopher. One of her choice precepts was, "Let thy neighbor live quietly by thee." When Charles was seven years old, his parents moved to Manchester where they heard and accepted the restored gospel. He was baptized by his father April 22, 1845.

At seventeen the young man found himself unemployed. The invention of machines to make tassels and braid, at which he worked for several years, clinched his desire to go to Zion. Charles left England in February 1849 aboard the ship *Henry* and with 209 Saints landed at New Orleans in April. Continuing his journey, he worked his passage to St. Louis on the *Grand York*. During the summer cholera broke out, and many of his companions died, so he moved into Kentucky where he found work and began saving his earnings to help his parents emigrate. Later he returned to St. Louis, stayed there four years and was made second counselor to a Bishop Seal. In the meantime his father, mother, and little sister, Mary Lois, came from England. Preparations to go to Utah were underway when his mother died, so Charles went on alone. He was hired as teamster to transport a threshing machine and other merchandise to Salt Lake City, where he arrived in September 1855.

He went to work for his brother-in-law, Parley P. Pratt, and lived with his sister Ann Agatha (wife to Elder Pratt). When famine came upon the people that winter, the Pratts were no longer able to provide food for him. Charles recorded in his journal "From then on until 1857, I will not attempt to describe what I passed through—hardships, hunger, starvation. Digging roots to subsist upon—living on greens, cornmeal, siftings—and not enough of that."

Charles took up the trade of blacksmithing, secured a small home, and with ecclesiastical duties was fully occupied. He was married September 28, 1861, in the Endowment House to Abigail Middlemass, convert from Pope's Harbor, Nova Scotia. Together they shipped up their home and were getting comfortably situated when in October a year later, Charles was called to Dixie—a sentence hard to endure. In his journal he wrote,

> Well, here I have worked for the last 7 years through heat and cold, hunger and adverse circumstances, and at last have got me a home, a lot with fruit trees just beginning to bear and look pretty. Well, I must leave it and go do the will of my Father . . . I pray God to give me strength . . . obedience is a great principle in Heaven and on earth.

Life in the Dixie Cotton Mission was hard—often grim. Even so, Charles had a God-given talent—mirth. He learned to laugh in spite of poverty, heat drouth, and heartbreak, and helped others to join him. People often said that their desert homeland was conquered with faith, toil, and Charley's songs. When hunger and death stalked the colony, Apostle Erastus Snow would turn to this devoted Saint and say, "Charley, write a song to lift our sadness." Thus such lines as these were composed and sung at a concert in honor of Brigham Young and George A. Smith at one of their visits in the latter 1860's. Humorously Charles call it

ST. GEORGE AND THE DRAG-ON
Oh, what a desert place was this
When first the Mormons found it;
They said no white man here could live
And Indians prowled around it.
They said the land it was no good,
And the water was no gooder,
And the bare idea of living here
Was enough to make one shudder.
The wind like fury here does blow,
That when we plant or sow, Sir,
We place one foot upon the seed,
And hold it till it grows, Sir.

During the forty years that Charles Walker lived at St. George, he composed scores of poems and songs which were used at celebrations, concerts, weddings, and funerals. He wrote daily in his journals which today are considered priceless by historians and students of early Mormon Americans. Copies of the journals are found at the University of Utah, Brigham Young University, Utah State Historical Society Library, Dixie College at St. George, and the Henry Huntington Library at San Marino, California.

The first manuscript newspaper produced in Utah came from the Dixie Cotton Mission at St. George. Charles L. Walker was one of the first four editors; his associates in this unique venture were Orson Pratt, Jr., Joseph Orton, and George A. Burgon. They kept this handwritten, three-columned four page newspaper coming out regularly bi-weekly for well over a year in 1864-1865. He accepted the principle of plurality of wives, and was married to Sarah Smith in 1877. Each wife bore him eight children.

The Washington County News said this of him at the time of his death on January 11, 1904.

> He was a faithful member of his Church and was endowed with more than ordinary intelligence. His poetical productions have a fame extending beyond the range of his acquaintances. He was ever willing to respond with suitable lines to commemorate any important occasion. He was a good citizen and will be greatly missed.

His hymn, "Dearest Children, God Is Near You," was selected by the Primary general board as its theme song for the year and was sung the world over.

> It is fitting that this history be concluded by quoting a verse written for public rendition by the pioneer whose writings so faithfully reflect the aspirations, hopes, and dreams of the Cotton Mission . . . . It was the last gracious act of a life dedicated to public service.

DIXIE PIONEERS

> Forty years have we spent in this country so dreary,
> Subduing the mineral, thorns, cactus and sands;
> Our spirits are bright, though our bodies are weary,
> In filling the mission required at our hands.

Written by Katherine Miles Larson, a granddaughter.

No. 171

God Speed the Right

Words by W. G. Hickson   Music Anonymous

The Hymn

One of the most forceful devices for emphasis is that of reiteration. The repetitive line "God Speed the Right" gives to this hymn a challenging importance which arrests attention and interest.

The Composer

The tune for "God Speed the Right" is of German origin ascribed to Ernst Moritz Arndt (1796-1860). This hymn tune has a revered place in your compiler's memory since it was the first piece in the hymnbook that he learned to play on the parlor organ when only a small boy of five years.

The Author

William Edward Hickson (1803-1870) was an English boot manufacturer. In 1835 he felt the need of a new English National Anthem. The line "God Save Our Gracious King" according to Mr.

191

Hickson, did not apply to the hated King William the IV. Consequently, he wrote a fourth stanza to an already existent translated German hymn "God Bless Our Native Land" in which he couched his opposition to existing political conditions.

"God Speed the Right" was also a hymn from his pen praying for more righteousness.

No. 172

There Is an Hour of Peace and Rest

Words by Hans Henry Peterson   **Music by Hans Henry Peterson**

The Hymn

"There Is an Hour of Peace and Rest" is written in the form of a gospel song with a verse and chorus. The particular emphasis given to the value of secret prayer is of ever present importance. The author is unknown.

The Composer — H. H. Peterson (See No. 127)

The Author — See No. 127

No. 173

They the Builders of the Nation

Words by Ida R. Alldredge   **Music by Alfred M. Durham**

The Hymn

"They the Builders of the Nation" is a splendid, poetic tribute to the Pioneers.

The Composer — Alfred M. Durham (See No. 42)

The Author

Ida Romney Alldredge was born January 7, 1892 at Colonia Juarez, Mexico. She was a daughter of Miles and Catherine Cottam Romney. She lived in Mexico until 1912 when she went to Douglas, Arizona.

Her husband, Lew Alldredge, engaged in the mercantile business. Later they moved to Mesa, Arizona, where they were residing at the time of her death. She died in Pheonix, Arizona June 14, 1943.

No. 174

There Is Sunshine in the Soul

Words by E. E. Hewitt   **Music by John R. Sweeney**

The Hymn

This number is a gospel song with its characteristic verse and chorus. It is popular because of its "catchy" melody and joyful text.

192

The Composer — John R. Sweeney (See No. 103)

The Author

Mrs. Hewitt was born in Philadelphia, Pennsylvania in 1851. She was an ardent Sunday School worker in the Calvin Presbyterian Church.

Her career as a teacher, however, was cut short by a spinal malady which made her a "shut-in" for a long time. It was during this period that she wrote many hymns. The following ones have persisted:

"There Is Sunshine in My Soul today"
"Will there be any Stars in My Crown?"
"Stepping in the Light"
"More about Jesus Would I Know"

No. 175

Who's on the Lord's Side, Who?

Words by Hannah Last Cornaby   Music by Henry H. Russel
                                         Arr. by George Careless

The Hymn

The hymn "Who's on the Lord's Side, Who?" was a great rally hymn in the early days of the Latter-day Saint Church. When Elder George Goddard sang it he would call for all those who were "on the Lord's side" to rise and sing the refrain. Brother Goddard, who possessed a fine baritone voice, was a popular hymn singer in the Church during his lifetime. He traveled extensively singing the songs of Zion, but he is particularly remembered for his singing of "Who's on the Lord's side, Who?"

The Composer

The tune of "Who's on the Lord's Side" was taken from a popular song entitled "A Life on the Ocean Wave" composed by Henry H. Russel. George Careless (1839-1932) made the arrangement found in the Latter-day Saint Hymnal 1908 edition. In the 1950 edition the song was made into a four-voice form by the editors. During the Civil War, parodies were written on the original words such as "A Life in the Soldier's Camp" and "A Life on the Vicksburg Bluff." Henry Russel was born in 1812 and died in 1900.

The Author

Hannah Last Cornaby, although not a noted author, was a sweet humble person who appreciated beauty of every kind, found the good in everything about her and bore a sincere and beautiful testimony to the truthfulness of the gospel of Jesus Christ.

Although her life was full of reverses, she always praised God and was never bitter in any way because of any hardship she was

193

called upon to bear. She was an invalid for ten years during which time she was administered to many times through her extended illness. One day Bishop Thurber of Spanish Fork, Utah came accompanied by Apostle Orson Pratt. The doctors had told her she would never walk again, but Orson Pratt administered to her and promised her she should yet arise from her bed and stand on her feet and be able to go to church again. He also confirmed upon her the gift to write—with many other gifts and blessings. On this occasion, Bishop Thurber remarked that it seemed worth being sick as long as she had been to be the recipient of such blessings. Although her recovery did not come until fifteen months later, it came suddenly and in a miraculous manner in which she gave all thanks and recognition to God. Following her recovery she spent the remainder of her life in faithful service and the development and use of her talent to write in which she wrote her own autobiography and poems and had them published; any quotes hence forth will have been taken from her own book.·

> Surely goodness and mercy have followed me all the days of my life—I realize that if I have received but one talent, I am accountable to the Giver for the proper use of the same; which consideration has induced me to write a short history of my life in order that my verses may be better understood.

She was born on 17 March 1822, the eldest child of William Last and Hannah Hollingsworth of the Parish of Hoten, near the town of Halesworth, County of Suffolk, England. Her parents were devout members of the Episcopal Church, and the Bible was her mother's constant companion. Hannah committed to memory much of the New Testament and the Psalms before she was old enough to read. Good books played an important part in her entire life.

Hannah Last was married to Samuel Cornaby 30 January 1851 in St. Georges Church, a venerable structure celebrated for it's antiquity and architectural beauty.

This couple were very dissatisfied with their religion and prayed for guidance in finding a true religion. They owned a bookstore in England. One night during a storm, they saw a man sheltered under the awning of their store. They invited him in and it so happened he was a Mormon missionary. They were converted to the Church, and Samuel Cornaby was soon baptized. Shortly after the birth of their first child, Hannah requested baptism; and although she received baptism amid a mob of angry people trying to prevent her baptism she says, "We then made our way back, as best we could, followed by the mob; and though the stones whizzed around us thick as hail not one touched us and we reached home safely, thanking God for our miraculous deliverance; determined, more than ever, with the assistance of the holy spirit, to adhere—through evil, as well as good report to the principles we had embraced. At the next meeting of the saints I was confirmed, and knew for myself that the work was of God."

They were so persecuted by their friends that they decided to come to America. They left Norwich on the 9th of Jan. 1853 on the *Ellen Maria.* Hannah wrote a very lengthy poem called "Crossing the Atlantic" that very beautifully portrayed the entire journey.

She and her husband walked the entire journey across the plains, and she did not complain as was told in her book. "I often think that the weeks spent crossing the plains were as full of instruction and interest as any part of our lives. Admiring nature, we had abundant opportunities of beholding its varied beauties. Especially did we admire the flowers—growing in some places in great profusion, handfuls of which daily adorned the wagon and delighted our child, who was in the care of a sister, who was too feeble to walk. Delicious wild fruits met with at different stages of the journey were much relished, and afforded wholesome variety to our diet."

They arrived in Emigration Canyon 12 Oct. 1853.

They were endowed 21 Mar. 1856, and moved to Spanish Fork, Utah, 27 July 1856, where they resided the balance of their lives.

Hannah L. Cornaby

Hannah Cornaby gave birth to 7 children, only 2 lived to maturity, Edith and Samuel Last Cornaby.

Hannah Cornaby died 1 Sept. 1905 at the age of 83. She was on the Lord's side from the time she embraced the gospel, and I feel that because of her firm convictions she was inspired to write the words to the song, "Who's on the Lord's Side, Who?"

No. 176
This House We Dedicate to Thee

Words by Henry W. Naisbett   Music by Frank W. Asper

The Hymn

"This House We Dedicate to Thee" is one of the very few hymns of dedication in the Latter-day Saint Hymnal.

With the rapid growth of the Church and the consequent expanding building program, more hymns on this subject would be a welcome addition to the music literature of the Church.

The Composer — Frank W. Asper (See No. 95)

The Author — Henry W. Naisbett (See No. 278)

No. 177
Thanks for the Sabbath School

Words by William Willes   Music by James R. Murray

The Hymn

"Thanks for the Sabbath School" is a youth hymn of thanks and admonition to youth to cherish virtue and "decry vice." The musical movement in this song gives it a likable character. It is sung often in the Sunday Schools of the Church.

The Composer — James R. Murray (no information)

The Author — William Willes (See No. 19)

No. 178
God Loved Us, So He Sent His Son

Words by Edward P. Kimball   Music by Alexander Schreiner

The Hymn

This music was written in response to assignment. It is a sacramental hymn, quiet, devotional, thought-provoking in quality both as to text and accompanying melody. There is a fervent emotion expressed in the text, in addition to the doctrinal statements, or rather the doctrinal statements are couched in fervent, emotional expression. This quality is paralleled in the hymn melody and its poignant harmonies.

The Composer — Alexander Schreiner (See No. 24)

The Author

Edward P. Kimball was educated in the Salt Lake City Schools, the Latter-day Saints College, and Brigham Young University. He went on a mission for his Church to Germany in 1906. In 1914 he went back to Germany to study. He served on the Deseret Sunday School Union Board and was a member of the General Church Music Committee.

Elder Kimball composed several hymns, most beloved of which is "Wintry Day." He was appointed Tabernacle organist October 5, 1905, and served in that capacity for twenty-five years. In 1929 he was sent to Europe to preside over the German-Austrian Mission. In 1933 he was appointed director of the Bureau of Information in Washington, D.C., which post he held until his death on March 15, 1937. Edward P. Kimball with his versatile, active personality was an effective speaker and always a faithful, vigorous church worker. He was one of the few musicians to hold civic positions, being made at one time president of the Salt Lake City Rotary Club, and later District Governor of the organization. He was born in 1882 and died in 1937.

No. 179
The Day Dawn Is Breaking

Words by Joseph L. Townsend   **Music by William Clayson**

The Hymn

The song "The Day Dawn Is Breaking" is distinct and interesting due to its chorus which is rhythmically different from the verse part, but beautifully co-ordinated with the tune and form of the verse. The symbolism of the first stanza taken from nature, together with the atmosphere of joyousness, created by the line "Beautiful Day of Peace and Rest" makes it a delight to sing.

The Composer — William Clayson (See No. 64)

The Author — Joseph L. Townsend (See No. 64)

We Give Thee but Thine Own

Words by W. Walsham How   **From Cantica Laudis**

The Hymn

"We Give Thee but Thine Own" was written for the Offertory in the church. It goes beyond our duty just to give as the third stanza indicates. We give "to comfort and to bless, to find balm for woe." In the Latter-day Saint Church, it has an application to the law of tithing.

The Composer

The Latter-day Saint Hymnal credits this hymn as being from a collection known as "Cantica Laudis" compiled by George James Webb and Lowell Mason. Dr. William Leroy Wilkes, Jr., in his comprehensive dissertation on *Borrowed Music in Mormon Hymnals*, is of the opinion that compilers Webb and Mason, may have had much to do with the composition of this hymn, at least the arrangement of it. One well-known Hymnal attributes this tune to Robert Schumann (1810-1856).

The Author

William Walsham How was a friend of the poor. The fact that he was the Bishop of the slum district of London, with a small salary and no social prestige, gave him no worry whatever. He was a benefactor to all people especially those who were unfortunate. How wrote sixty hymns, twenty-five of which became popular. "A good hymn," said he, "should be like a good prayer—simple, real, earnest, and reverent." He was born in 1823 and died in 1897.

Thou Dost Not Weep Alone

Words by Eliza R. Snow   **Music by George Careless**

The Hymn

"Thou Dost Not Weep Alone" is a lovely funeral hymn that was probably written for a particular person whose identity cannot be established by this writer.

The Composer — George Careless (See 269)
The Author — Eliza R. Snow (See No. 139)

No. 182
Hail to the Brightness of Zion's Glad Morning
Words by Thomas Hastings   **Music by Edwin F. Parry**

The Hymn

Usually the most telling line in a successful hymn text is the first one. "Hail to the Brightness of Zion's Glad Morning" is a splendid example of this characteristic. After this exultant outburst, the entire hymn continues with exclamatory gladness for the restored gospel.

The Composer — Edwin F. Parry (See No. 135)

The Author — Thomas Hastings (See No. 82)

No. 183
Awake! O Ye People, the Savior Is Coming
Words by W. W. Phelps   **Music by Samuel B. Mitton**

The Hymn

Preparation for the second coming of the Savior is the theme of the hymn, "Awake! Ye People."

The Composer

Samuel B. Mitton was born in Wellsville, Utah, in March 1863. He was the son of Samuel C. and Mary Bailey Mitton. His training was deeply religious, and he early exhibited a great interest in music—an interest which became one of the chief joys of his life.

As a boy he urged his father to get him a musical instrument. At great sacrifice for pioneer days, he bought him a cabinet organ which, for want of a teacher, he diligently taught himself to play. At the age of fourteen years he became the organist of Wellsville Ward. He was active in promoting music and organized and directed choirs, choruses, and operettas, also a band in Wellsville which won the state-wide contest in 1897. When living in Ogden, Utah, he served as the Ogden Tabernacle organist.

Returning to Cache Valley he directed the musical activities at the State Agricultural College. Then he served for one year as director of music in the Logan City Schools. For five years beginning in 1915 he directed the Logan Tabernacle Choir.

Before retiring from the leadership of the choir he rendered, with his choir of 160 voices, *The Vision* composed by Evan Stephens.

Stephens was always a source of encouragement and inspiration to him and until Stephens' death they conducted a frequent correspondence.

When he no longer had the choir responsibilities, he took a keen interest in composition, writing well over one hundred hymns and anthems and numerous songs—in all over five hundred compositions. Many of his hymns have been published in church hymnals and periodicals. Among the best known are a setting for "Sweet Is the Work," "Why Should I Falter," "Awake! O Ye People," "Dark the Battle Clouds Are Closing," and "With One Accord We'll Sing Thy Praise." Aside from his musical activities, he served as a home missionary, as a member of the Cache Stake high council, and for many years was a Patriarch of the Logan Stake. With his brother-in-law Lorenzo Hansen he helped to organize and develop the condensed milk industry in Cache Valley and was active in that business until the time of his retirement. He passed away in Logan, February 25, 1954 at the age of ninety one.

The Author — William Phelps (See No. 213)

No. 184
The Time Is Far Spent

Words by Eliza R. Snow   **Music Anonymous**

The Hymn

"The Time Is Far Spent" is a missionary hymn of exhortation. Frequently it is mistaken to be a closing hymn. This is due to the fact that the first line is often read out of its context. Such is far from its real import—that of "publishing glad tidings by sea and by land."

The Composer

The tune which in some way became associated with "The Time Is Far Spent" is a German drinking song called "Krambambule" Probably the choice of this tune was for the reason that it had been used previously in at least two other hymn collections with religious texts. These collections were evidently known to the early Mormon hymn-writers.

The Author — Eliza R. Snow (See No. 139)

Mid Pleasures and Palaces

Words by John Howard Payne   Music by Sir Henry Bishop

The Hymn

"Home, Sweet Home" is the most popular of all the home songs. The one famous line "Be it ever so humble, there's no place like home" has made it immortal. It is not a hymn, but, its particular content, that of love of home, justifies its inclusion in a hymn collection.

The Composer

Sir Henry Bishop (1786-1855) was an English dramatic composer-conductor, he produced more than one-hundred and twenty-five operas, two-thirds of which were his own. In 1822, in one opera *Clair-The Maid of Milan* he incorporated "Home, Sweet Home" a song which he had composed earlier. This song has outlived most of his other creations. As a conductor in major theaters of London, he was highly esteemed.

The Author

John Howard Payne was born in New York City in 1791. When only a boy of fourteen he established and edited a paper. Soon after, he published his first play *Julia*. Three years later, he assayed the role of actor and became well-known in both America and England. While in England, he adapted more than sixty novels for the stage. Two of his plays, *Brutus* and *Charles the Second* became very popular, but it was not until he wrote, in 1823, *Clair, The Maid of Milan* in collaboration with Sir Henry Bishop, that he made himself immortal. It was in this opera that "Home, Sweet Home" came to light. The opera was first performed in Covent Garden, London, and Ann Maria Tree sang the famous song for the first time. In 1832 Payne ·returned· to America and espoused the cause of the Cherokee Indians who were having trouble with the Government. In 1832, Payne was appointed American consul to Tunis where he died ten years later in 1842.

To Nephi, Seer of Olden Time

Words by Joseph L. Townsend   Music by William Clayson

The Hymn — (See No. 64)

The Composer — William Clayson (See No. 64)

The Author — Joseph L. Townsend (See No. 64)

'Tis Sweet to Sing the Matchless Love

Words by George Manwaring   Music by Ebenezer Beesley

The Hymn

" 'Tis Sweet to Sing the Matchless Love" is a reverent sacra-mental hymn written in the gospel song style of a verse and chorus.

The Composer — Ebenezer Beesley (See No. 94)

The Author — George Manwaring (See No. 136)

No. 188

Truth Reflects upon Our Senses

Words by Eliza R. Snow   Music by C. D. Tillman

The Hymn

"Truth Reflects upon Our Senses" is a versification of the first part of the 7th chapter of the Gospel of St. Matthew. "Judge not that ye be not judged. For with what judgment ye judge, ye shall be judged: and with what measure ye mete, it shall be measured to you again."

The Composer

The tune of "Truth Reflects upon Our Senses" is accredited to a gospel song writer, Charles D. Tillman. Its first publication in Jackson's *Another Sheaf of White Spirituals* was titled "Life's Rail-way to Heaven," and may have been written by someone other than Tillman. The chorus of this song seems to have been added by some unknown person.

The Author — Eliza R. Snow (See No. 139)

No. 189

Truth Eternal, Truth Divine

Words by Parley P. Pratt   Music by Alexander Schreiner

The Hymn

"Parley P. Pratt, apostle of the latter-days, martyr to the faith, missionary, prince of latter-day poets, here again expresses doctrines of the newly restored gospel. The truth of the eternal gospel frees people from the fetters of superstition and falsehoods and fears and darkness of fallen creeds. The hymn melody forms one long arch with the high points in the middle, and so is eminently suited in its frank, straightforward style to congregational singing. It is devoid of such ornaments as would distract from the thoughts expressed by the hymn text. The hymn-melody is accompanimental to the hymn itself, the text by Alexander Schreiner."

The Composer — Alexander Schreiner (See No. 24)

The Author — Parley P. Pratt (See No. 20)

No. 190

Welcome, Welcome, Sabbath Morning

Words by R. B. Baird   **Music by Ebenezer Beesley**

The Hymn

"Welcome, Welcome, Sabbath Morning" is undoubtedly the most popular Sunday School song in the Latter-day Saint Hymnal.

In the early printings of this song it began on the "down beat." Undoubtedly it was written that way, but in the 1950 edition of the Latter-day Saint Hymnal, it was changed to a more logical form—that of an "up-beat" beginning, with each succeeding phrase following the same pattern.

The Composer — Ebenezer Beesley (See No. 94)

The Author — R. B. Baird (See No. 73)

No. 191

Sweet Is the Peace the Gospel Brings

Words by Mary Ann Morton   **Music by Alfred M. Durham**

The Hymn

"Sweet Is the Peace the Gospel Brings" is a beautiful delineation of one of the greatest blessings of the gospel—that of peace.

The Composer — Alfred M. Durham (See No. 42)

The Author — Mary Ann Morton (See No. 133)

No. 192

We Are Sowing

Words Anonymous   **Music by H. A. Tuckett**

The Hymn

The words of "We Are Sowing" are a paraphrase and development from the Parable of the Sower found in Matthew 13th chapter verses 3-9. To sound as the composer intended, the third line of this hymn should be sung in four parts because composer Tuckett saw fit to make the bass the most melodic part with the other three voices acting as accompaniment. This section of the hymn is unconventional as hymn tunes go traditionally, for the reason that the standard form always keeps the melodic line in the soprano part.

The Composer — Henry A. Tuckett (See No. 110)

The Author — Anonymous

No. 193

We Meet Again in Sunday School

Words by George Manwaring   Music by Ebenezer Beesley

The Hymn

Gladness for the Sabbath School and its teachings is the theme of this Sunday School hymn.

The Composer — Ebenezer Beesley (See No. 94)

The Author — George Manwaring (See No. 136)

No. 194

We're Marching on to Glory

Words and Music by J. M. Chamberlain

The Hymn

The marching trend of "We're Marching on to Glory" has endeared it to the youth of the Church. Older folk also enjoy singing it.

The Composer

Your compiler well remembers John M. Chamberlain. As a small boy, I went into his music store in Salt Lake City, with my father. As soon as Brother Chamberlain found out that I was interested in music and attempting to learn to play, he sat down at the piano and played some of his piano compositions for me. They were filled with elaborate arpeggios and other flourishes. As a youngster I was intrigued. His tall stature and grey hair were very becoming to his gentle words. As we left he gave me a printed copy of one of his compositions and told me to take it home and learn to play it.

The Author

John Marvin Chamberlain was born in Leicester, Leicestershire, England, May 27, 1844. He emigrated with his parents to Zion when a small boy of eight years, traveling by sailboat to New Orleans, thence journeying across the plains to Utah by ox-team. He stated that most of the way he walked along with the oxen over the new and dusty trail.

Arriving in Salt Lake City the family occupied a quarter block just south of the present City and County Building, and he followed the career of a carpenter during his early years. But he was always musically inclined, and was credited with having received the first organ to arrive in the valley.

Besides teaching the piano and organ he was partner with the musical firms of Taggart & Chamberlain, and then San Sant & Chamberlain, and finally his own Chamberlain Music Company, in which several of his seven sons were interested.

He married Louise M. E. Rawlings in the Manti Temple. Both he and his wife were members of the Tabernacle Choir and were choir director and organist of the Eighth Ward choir for many years.

Besides "Marching Homeward," he was the composer of numerous other hymns and piano and organ selections, some of which are: "When Jesus Shall Come in His Glory" (1874), "A Sunday School Call" (both in the earlier Sunday School songbook), and the ever popular "Heart Tones" (piano solo), the piano transcription "Oh, My Father," and the vocal duet "Music of the Pines." "Marching Homeward" was composed in 1879 when he was in the superintendency of the ward Sunday School.

He retired when about seventy-two years of age and became interested in organizing youth choruses and taking them to the local

John M. Chamberlain

205

hospitals to serenade the patients. Elder Chamberlain passed away in 1928 at the age of eighty-four and during his funeral services, Alvin A. Beesley played "Marching Homeward" as a fitting last tribute.

No. 195

Redeemer of Israel

Words adapted by W. W. Phelps   **Music by Freeman Lewis**

The Hymn

"Redeemer of Israel" was based on a song credited to Joseph Swain, an engraver, who was born in Birmingham, England, in 1761.* Swain was fond of writing verses and loved poetry passionately. A spiritual awakening changed his life, and he was baptized by Dr. John Rippon, and studied for the ministry. At twenty-five years of age he took charge of a Baptist church at Walworth where he remained until his death in 1796. There was produced the *Walworth Hymns* which contained one loved and sung for more than a century, entitled "O Thou in Whose Presense My Soul Takes Delight."

William W. Phelps (See No. 213) no doubt came across this song and following its trend and meter composed "Redeemer of Israel," breathing into it the breath of life. It first appeared in *Evening and Morning Star,* June 1832. Brother Phelps retained a few words and lines of Swain's hymn as the reader will notice by the italicized type in the following stanzas:

O Thou in whose presence my soul takes *delight*
    On whom in affliction *I call;*
My comfort *by day and my song* in the *night,*
    My hope, my salvation, my *all.*
Where dost thou, dear shepherd, resort with thy *sheep*
    To feed *them* in pastures of *love?*
Say *why in the valley of death should I weep,*
    Or alone in the wilderness rove.
O why should I *wander an* alien from Thee,
    Or *cry in the desert* for bread?
Thy foes *will rejoice when* my *sorrows* they'll see
    And smile at the tears I have shed.

"Redeemer of Israel" was also included in Emma Smith's collection and is still one of the most popular of Mormon hymns—a Restoration song. It is truly poetical and embodies all the requisites of technical hymnody. It is scriptural in sentiment and expression; it is devotional, lyrical, and surely fills the more modern definition

---

*From George D. Pyper's *Stories of Latter-day Saint Hymns.*

206

as heretofore expressed—"a sacred poem, expressive of devotion, spiritual experience. . . fitted to be sung by an assembly of people in a public service."

Its four stanzas center in the idea of group redemption. The first is in praise of the Redeemer, "our King, our Deliverer, our all." The second expresses the feeling that Jesus the Christ is to come to redeem his people. In the third are suggested the sufferings of the Saints in the desert, amid enemy rejoicings. It closes with expressions of joy at the "good tidings" of deliverance.

The Composer

This hymn has been printed in many of our songbooks without giving credit to the composer of the music. After considerable research we are now able to name the composer—he was Freeman Lewis, a surveyor, of Uniontown, Pennsylvania, who lived between 1780 and 1859. This is the only tune credited to him. It is associated with Joseph Swain's "Oh, Thou, in Whose Presence My Soul Takes Delight," under the titles of "Beloved" and "Meditation."

No. 196
We Thank Thee, O God, for a Prophet

Words by William Fowler   **Music by Mrs. C. E. S. Norton**

The Hymn

"We thank Thee, O God, for a Prophet to guide us in these latter days"—have sung the Saints at every general conference of the Church of Jesus Christ of Latter-day Saints since the song, penned by William Fowler, was published in 1863.* In every stake, in every ward, it is rendered by the congregations next if not equal in frequency to "The Spirit of God like a Fire is Burning."

What is the secret of the popularity of this song?

It cannot be called the greatest hymn ever written by any of our authors. In fact, it does not compare in literary merit or poetic beauty with many of the other gems contained in our hymnbooks; but it has something different from our other hymns. In simple language it expresses deep gratitude to our Father in heaven for revealing anew the everlasting gospel, and setting up prophets to guide us in these latter days.

The first stanza, especially, is full of praise; a song-prayer of much emotional value, expressing the joy of service and the satisfactions of obedience.

---

*From George D. Pyper's *Stories of Latter-day Saint Hymns.*

207

The second stanza sings of the smiling star of hope and the absolute faith of the Saints in the power of God to deliver them from "the clouds of trouble" whenever these threaten to destroy their peace and happiness; a fearless reliance upon him who had already been their friend and protector in days past.

The last stanza is first of all a paeon of praise for the goodness and mercy of God and the life-giving light of his glorious gospel. The last half shows that the author, though far from the fountainhead of the Church, fully understood one of the greatest principles of the restored gospel—the doctrine of eternal progression; that "when we have lived according to the full value of the life we possess, we are prepared for eternal advancement in the scale of eternal progression . . . ; that there is no period, in all the eternities, wherein organized existence will become stationary, when it cannot advance in knowledge, wisdom, power and glory. . . ."

The hymn closes with a warning that while the honest and faithful shall reach the promised goal, they who reject the message will fall short of such happiness.

The Composer

The story of the origin of the tune to "We Thank Thee, O God, for a Prophet" is most interesting and not generally known. The composition is credited in our songbooks to "Mrs. Norton;" and questions are often asked us as to who she was, when and where she lived, and whether or not she was a Latter-day Saint.

Mrs. Norton's full maiden name was Caroline Elizabeth Sarah Sheridan. She was an English author born in 1808, the granddaughter of the amazingly brilliant Richard Brinsley Sheridan, actor, playwright, Member of Parliament, and owner and manager of the historic Drury Lane Theatre, London. He was the author of *The Rivals*, *School for Scandal*, and other well-known plays.

Mrs. Norton gained for herself a prominent place among the women writers of England. A greater part of her career, however, was shadowed by an unfortunate marriage with George Chappel Norton. On Norton's death she married Sir William Sterling-Maxwell, but her happiness was short-lived, as she died the following year. Through her own suffering she became a forerunner of the movement which by gradual steps had finally resulted in the full enfranchisement of women.

During the Crimean War (1854-56) between the English and French on one side and the Russians on the other, the battle of Balaklava was fought. This was in 1854. In that historic struggle an English officer of high rank, whose wife was no doubt a friend of Mrs. Norton, was killed. Mrs. Norton wrote the words and music of a song called "The Officer's Funeral March." This was sung at the officer's funeral service and the music was played by the band over the grave of the British hero. Here are the words of that song:

THE OFFICER'S FUNERAL MARCH

Hark to the shrill trumpet calling!
　　It pierces the soft summer air;
Tears from each comrade are falling,
　　The widow and orphan are there.
The bayonets earthward are turning,
　　And the drum's muffled breath rolls around;
Yet he heeds not the voice of their mourning,
Nor wakes to the bugle sound.

Sleep, soldier, though many regret thee,
　　Who stand by thy cold bier today;
Soon, soon shall the kindest forget thee,
　　And thy name from the earth pass away.
The man thou didst love as a brother,
　　A friend in thy place will have gained;
Thy dog shall keep watch for another,
　　And thy steed by a stranger be reined.

Though friends that now mourn for thee sadly,
　　Soon joyous as ever shall be;
Though thy bright orphan boy may laugh gladly
　　As he sits on some comrade's kind knee;
Yet there's one who will still pay thee duty,
　　In tears for the true and the brave,
As when first in the bloom of her beauty
　　She wept o'er her soldier's grave.

Lord Byron wrote:

" 'Tis strange—but true; for truth is strange,—stranger than fiction"—

And surely the old adage has been exemplified in this case for William Fowler, a humble English elder searching for a tune to put to his hymn, found and adapted Mrs. Norton's composition to the present setting of "We Thank Thee, O God, for a Prophet."

Could Mrs. Norton enter a Latter-day Saint chapel today she would be astonished to learn that the music which she dedicated to a fallen soldier of war is now frequently sung to a new song of praise in honor of a modern prophet of peace.

The Author

William Fowler, who wrote the words of "We Thank Thee, O God, for a Prophet," was born May 9, 1830, thirty-three days after the Church of Jesus Christ of Latter-day Saints was organized. His father, John Fowler, a native of Sheffield, Yorkshire, England, enlisted in the British Army at the age of 21, and went to Ireland, where he married Bridget Niel. From Ireland he was sent with his regiment to Australia, in which country, William, the subject of this sketch, was born. When William was about three and a half years old the family made another move to the East Indies where, after five years of service, the father was honorably discharged and returned with his family to Sheffield, England. William was then nine years old. Two years later his father died and in three and a half more the mother followed, leaving him an orphan before he was fifteen years of age. Originally his mother was a Roman Catholic, his father a Protestant, but previous to their demise both had joined the Wesleyan Methodists.

At eighteen William began to think seriously of religion and attended Methodist services, but was not satisfied. It seemed to him Methodism was all hope and trust—no reality. It was then that he first heard the sound of the gospel through a young friend whose father, Peter Poulucci, was a priest in the Church of Jesus Christ of Latter-day Saints. This friend took William to hear the Mormons at the Hall of Science, Rockingham Street, in the winter of 1848. His search for the truth was ended, and on July 29, 1849, he was baptized by Elder J. V. Long. He was ordained a priest, March 3, 1851, and labored in the Deepcar branch under Elder William Memmott. He worked as a cutler in a factory at Sheffield, but was discharged on

William Fowler

account of having joined the Latter-day Saints. He married Ellen Bradshaw, by whom he had three children.

The daily diary of William Fowler, containing the record of four years of missionary service up to 1854, has been perused by the writer and is of intense interest. It shows the deep and abiding faith of the man in the restored gospel; how he traveled on foot and endured revilings and all sorts of persecutions for the gospel's sake. It is full of such entries as "walked 21 miles, rode 7 today." One of March 27, 1853, reads: "Mob assembled and broke up the afternoon meeting. In the evening we met at Brother Craig's house and had a good meeting. The mob assembled outside expecting to pelt us with goose eggs, but as we did not open the door they did not know where to look for us, so they pelted each other."

William Fowler was a self-educated man. He understood the gospel and believed implicitly in the doctrine of "eternal progression," as the last stanza of his hymn will show, and trained himself accordingly. He studied and gave instruction in music, and learned the Pitman system of shorthand. His diary, under date of September 9, 1853, records in shorthand that he received the book of instruction from the founder, Sir Isaac Pitman, himself.

There is no evidence to show the exact date on which "We Thank Thee, O God, for a Prophet," was written. President Joseph F. Smith in his lifetime related that when he was in England Brother Fowler brought his new song to meeting where it was sung for the first time. As President Smith's mission was from 1860 to 1863, it was probably written somewhere between those dates. It was published in the 12th edition (1863) of the Latter-day Saint Hymnbook.

Brother Fowler wrote other songs and hymns which were printed in the *Millennial Star*. He sailed for America June 3, 1863, on the ship *Amazon*, arriving in New York July 25, 1863, finally settling with his family in Manti, where he taught school. He died August 27, 1865, and the Church erected a monument in the Manti Cemetery in his honor.

Brother Fowler's three children survived.

No. 197
What Glorious Scenes Mine Eyes Behold
Words Anonymous   Music by Ebenezer Beesley
The Hymn

The anonymous writer of "What Glorious Scenes Mine Eyes Behold" was undoubtedly a Latter-day Saint else he could not have

211

written with such knowing and understanding of the contents of "Ephraim's records." Also the gathering of Israel from every clime, another Latter-day Saint belief, is prophetically declared in the fourth stanza.

The Composer — Ebenezer Beesley (See No. 94)

The Author — Anonymous

No. 198
When First the Glorious Light of Truth
Words by William Clayton   **Music Anonymous**

The Hymn

The hymn "When First the Glorious Light of Truth" is a touching tribute to the early pioneers who lost their lives in a valiant battle to establish the Church in the latter days. A line in the first stanza of the hymn reveals that William Clayton used an old war song as an impetus to write the hymn. In the song "The Field of Monterey" appears this line "Who Now in Death Are Sleeping." Clayton's line reads "And in their graves are sleeping."

The Composer

William Clayton adapted the tune for "When First the Glorious Light of Truth" from M. Dix Sullivan's soldier's song "The Field of Monterey."

The Author — William Clayton (See No. 13)

No. 199
When in the Wondrous Realm
Words by Frank I. Kooyman   **Music by Alexander Schreiner**

The Hymn

This hymn is definitely a sacramental hymn.* "We take the bread and cup this day." Excellent poetry, and feelingful presentation of the story of the universal sacrifice offered by our Savior, Jesus the Christ.

Like the three other contributions by this song-writer, found in *Hymns*, this song was written in response to a call from the Church Music Committee for additional sacred songs to be included in a contemplated new hymnbook.

This being another sacrament song, what has been stated in this volume about "In Memory of the Crucified" is also applicable here. "Thy will be done" is here the leading idea, the motif. The premortal selection of our Savior in "the wondrous realms above," and his departure from "worlds of light," only to find on the earth he came

---

*The comments on this hymn were written by A. Schreiner and F. I. Kooyman.

to save, a "crown of thorns" and a "cruel cross," are stated in four brief stanzas.

What a field for contemplation is opened here for heart and mind to enter while the sacred emblems of the body and blood of the Sinless One are being passed!

The Composer — Alexander Schreiner (See No. 24)

The Author — Frank I. Kooyman (See No. 99)

Frank Kooyman

No. 200

When the Rosy Light of Morning

Words and Music by R. B. Baird

The Hymn

"When the Rosy Light of Morning" is a song filled with joyous exhortation and gratefulness for the Sabbath School. The writer of this fine Sunday School song, Robert B. Baird, was both poet and musician. He composed the song in the form of the gospel song with verse and chorus. It is a favorite number with Sunday School groups.

The Composer and Author — R. B. Baird (See No. 73)

There Is a Green Hill Far Away

Words by Cecil Frances Alexander   **Music by John H. Gower**

The Hymn

Certain lines of this hymn have been controverted by some hymnologists (1) on the grounds of being topographically inaccurate and (2) theologically unsound. Albert Edward Baily in *The Gospel in Hymns* contends that the descriptive bits "green hill" and "without a city wall" cannot be substantiated. "The hills of Judea" says he, "are rocky and barren and the exact place of the crucifixion has never been accurately determined." One story concerning the "green hill" relates that Mrs. Alexander often had to drive by a grassy hill in County Derr, Ireland, and she tells how in her fancy she imagined it to be like Calvary, which she had never seen. Mr. Baily, continuing, says of the theological controversy, "One can only regret that this hymn perpetuates an outworn theology." Such controversy, we know, can only be cleared up by modern revelation and may we hasten to say that true theology can never be "outworn." It is either right or wrong in the first place.

Mrs. Alexander wrote a number of hymns, of which "There Is a Green Hill" is one to teach children the meaning of the Abstractions found in the Apostle's Creed. This hymn attempted to make understandable, the phrase in the Creed "Suffered under Pontius Pilate." She published this series in 1848 under the title of *Hymns for Little Children*.

The Composer

Many tunes are extant for "There Is a Green Hill." In a previous volume of Latter-day Saint Hymns, this hymn was given the old ballad tune of "Drink to Me Only with Thine Eyes." This kind of combination of music and words can hardly be condoned. The setting in the 1950 edition of the *Latter-day Saint Hymns,* by John H. Gower is very appropriate and lovely—especially so in the third phrase. Gower was an English organist who, in his later life, came to America to engage in mining. John H. Gower was born in 1855 and died in 1922.

The Author

Mrs. Alexander was born in Dublin, Ireland in 1818. As a young girl, she was a great religious teacher of children. When she became the wife of Reverend Wm. Alexander, she became more zealous than ever in the education of children. Her errands of charity and helpfulness among the poor of the parish, were numerous. As the wife of the Bishop, she entertained many distinguished men and women in her home. At her death in 1895, people gathered from all England to pay homage to her.

No. 202
When upon Life's Billows

J. Oatman, Jr.   **Music by Edwin Othello Excell**

The Hymn

"When upon Life's Billows" is a hymn for the moralist. Its value cannot be gainsaid, because many a worshipper on hearing or singing it is induced to contemplation on the blessings with which he is surrounded.

The Composer — E. O. Excell (See No. 74)

The tune of "When upon Life's Billows" is of the rhythmic variety of the gospel hymn. Its message is accentuated by some con-gregational conductors in the *ninth measure of the chorus,* by slowing the tempo and counting it out much as one would do in making a numerical calculation. It was composed by Othello Excell and first published in his gospel hymnal in 1899.

The Author

The only information available concerning the Reverend Oatman is that he was born in 1856 and died in 1926.

No. 203
We Love Thy House, O God

Words by William Bullock   **Music by Leroy J. Robertson**

The Hymn

This hymn, as the title indicates, might be used at dedicational services, but it could also be sung in most any part of the regular church service except sacramental service. It is especially suited for congregational singing.

As a young naval officer, William Bullock was greatly distressed with the moral conditions along the coast of Newfoundland. After resigning from the English Navy, he returned to Trinity Bay in Nova Scotia and erected a small chapel. He wrote the hymn "We Love Thy House, O God," for the dedication service of the new chapel.

The Composer — Leroy J. Robertson (See No. 45)

The Author

William Bullock (1797-1874) was a man of many accomplish-ments. He spent several years in the English Navy as a lieutenant.

215

Then he became a Bishop in the Church, a medical doctor, the Coroner, a Magistrate, and finally the Dean of the Cathedral of Nova Scotia. He was awarded a Doctorate by Kings College.

No. 204

Thy Spirit, Lord, Has Stirred Our Souls

Words by Frank I. Kooyman   **Music by Alexander Schreiner**

The Hymn

A spiritual experience such as this song mentions is a private possession, and when put into the words of a hymn, it becomes a personal testimony as "I know that my Redeemer lives." It may or may not strike a responsive chord in the hearts of others, but usually does.

"Thy Spirit, Lord, Has Stirred Our Souls" was "born" in a very spiritual meeting. We all, no doubt, have partaken in such gatherings when during a spirit-prompted address a profound silence falls upon the congregation, a hushing spell that is felt by all present. This song is intended to be a grateful closing hymn after a rich outpouring of the "glowing power" of the Lord has moved the souls of the listeners and filled them with new determination to carry on, or newborn resolutions to do better.

"Did not our heart within us burn?" is, of course, a quotation from Luke 24:32. These words were used by the two disciples who were on their way to Emmaus when "Jesus himself drew near, and went with them." They did not recognize him at the time, but later "their eyes were opened, and they knew him." Then, when he had vanished out of their sight, "they said one to another, Did not our heart burn within us while he talked with us by the way, and while he opened to us the scriptures?"

The "burning bush near Sinai" in the first stanza is in reference to Exodus 3:2. The angel of the Lord appeared unto Moses in a flame of fire out of the midst of a bush. "And, behold, the bush burned with fire, and the bush was not consumed." The preceding Bible verse mentions "the mountain of God, even Horeb." Horeb is also called Sinai.

The Composer — Alexander Schreiner (See No. 24)

The Author — Frank I. Kooyman (See No. 99)

216

We'll Sing the Songs of Zion

Words .by William G. Mills   Music by Felix Mendelssohn

The Hymn

"We'll Sing the Songs of Zion" is truly a song of Zion, the gathering place from which "shines the gospel of light."

The Composer — Felix Mendelssohn (See No. 370)

The tune for this hymn is the same one used for "O God the Eternal Father." (No. 125)

The Author — William G. Mills (See No. 225)

No. 206

Put Your Shoulder to the Wheel

Words and Music by Will L. Thompson

The Hymn

"Put Your Shoulder to the Wheel" is a thorough going gospel song. Due to its exuberance of exhortation it has been unofficially adopted as the theme song of the Latter-day Saint's welfare workers.

The Composer and Author

Will L. Thompson was born in Beaver County, Pennsylvania in 1847. He received his musical education in Boston and Leipzig. He organized a publishing house in Ohio, from which place many American song collections mostly sacred, have come. He is well-known as a writer of gospel songs and glees including "Softly and Tenderly," "Come Where the Lilies Bloom," and many others. Mr. Thompson wrote both the words and the music for "Put Your Shoulder to the Wheel." He died in 1909.

No. 207

Rejoice, Ye Saints of Latter-days

Words by Mabel Jones Gabbott   Music by Frank W. Asper

The Hymn

"Rejoice, Ye Saints of Latter-days" is a hymn of thanksgiving for a new temple wherein the work for the dead can be performed.

The Composer — Frank W. Asper (See No. 96)

The Author — Mabel Jones Gabbott (See No. 49)

You Can Make the Pathway Bright

Words Helen Dungan   **Music by J. M. Dungan**

The Hymn

"You Can Make the Pathway Bright" is another of the several gospel songs found in the Latter-day Saint Hymnal. It has the usual verse and chorus, and conjecture would prompt that is was written and composed by near relatives, J. M. Dungan and Helen Dungan. E. O. Excell, a gospel song writer and publisher, incorporated it in his Gospel Hymnal of 1898.

The Composer — J. M. Dungan (No information)

The Author — Helen Dungan (No information)

No. 209

With Wondering Awe

The Hymn

This Christmas carol is completely anonymous. Its text, however, raises the age-old question as to whether the "wise men" and the "shepherds" were or were not the same people. Matthew, in the second chapter, records that the "wise men" saw the star and that they followed it at the bidding of King Herod, to the place "where the young child was," while in the second chapter of Luke verses 8-20, Luke says that an angel appeared to the shepherds in the field and told them of the Savior's birth in Bethlehem and "suddenly there was with the angel a multitude of the heavenly host praising God, and saying, 'Glory to God in the Highest, and on earth peace, good will to Men.' " Then the shepherds journeyed to Bethlehem "and found Mary and Joseph, and the babe lying in a manger." In Matthew's account there is no mention of a heavenly choir and in Luke's account there is no mention of a star.

Often the great event is represented pictorially by showing the shepherds following the "star" and the wise men hearing the "angel's choir." Other Christmas carols present the same confusion as "The First Noel," verse two, for example. (No. 39)

No. 210
We Are All Enlisted till the Conflict is O'er

Words Anonymous   Music by W. B. Bradbury

The Hymn

There are two kinds of gospel songs—the sentimental ones and the dominantly rhythmical ones. "We Are all Enlisted" is of the latter category.

The Composer — William B. Bradbury (See No. 166)

No. 211
Ye Chosen Twelve, to You are Given

Words by Parley P. Pratt   Music by A. M. Fox

The Hymn

The hymn "Ye Chosen Twelve" is unique in that its subject matter has to do with the calling and commission of the twelve apostles. No other hymn in the Latter-day Saint Hymnal has a like content.

The Author — Parley P. Pratt (See No. 20)

The Composer — A. M. Fox (See Appendix, page 295).

No. 212
Zion Stands with Hills Surrounded

Words by John Kelly   Music by A. C. Smyth

The Hymn

What the author had in mind when he wrote his impressive lines is said to have been "the safety of the Church," but he must have foreseen a condition that did not exist until seventy-seven years after he penned the lines, when the Saints established Zion, "with hills surrounded."* He might have had in mind the City of David (2 Kings, 8:11), Jerusalem (Psalm 125), The Tribe of Judah (Psalms 58, 68), or he might have envisioned the latter-day "Zion, the Pure in Heart," spoken of in modern revelation (D & C 97:19-21). In any case it was an inspired prophecy; for no Latter-day Saint could have more perfectly described the belief of the Mormon people than did John Kelly back in the eighteenth century.

ZION
And the nations of the earth shall honor her, and shall say:
Surely Zion is the city of our God, and surely Zion cannot fall,

---

*From George D. Pyper's *Stories of Latter-day Saint Hymns.*

neither be moved out of her place, for God is there, and the hand of the Lord is there;

And he hath sworn by the power of his might to be her salvation and her high tower.

Therefore, verily, thus saith the Lord: Let Zion rejoice, for this is Zion—the pure in heart, therefore, let Zion rejoice, while all the wicked shall mourn. (Doctrine and Covenants 97:19-21.)

ZION IS A PLACE

We believe in the literal gathering of Israel and in the restoration of the Ten Tribes; that Zion will be built upon this (the American) continent; that Christ will reign personally upon the earth; and, that the earth will be renewed and receive is paradisiacal glory.

—Tenth LDS Article of Faith

The Composer — A. C. Smyth (See No. 136)

The Author

John Kelly, the author of this song, was an Irish judge, born in Dublin, July 13, 1769, sixty-one years before the Church of Jesus Christ of Latter-day Saints was organized. He was educated for the bar at Trinity College, Dublin, and became a London judge of the Court of Common Pleas. Experiencing a spiritual awakening the judge left the Bench and took Holy orders but later seceded from the established Anglican Church and became an independent non-conformist preacher, building churches for his own use. He is said to have been a man of great learning, a noted Bible critic, skilled in Oriental languages, having great wealth which he distributed liberally. He died May 14, 1854.

John Kelly wrote 765 sacred songs and published a number of hymnbooks during a period of fifty-one years.

No. 213

The Spirit of God like a Fire

Words by William W. Phelps   **Music Anonymous**

The Hymn

> The Spirit of God like a fire is burning!
> The latter-day glory begins to come forth.

This inspiring hymn was composed by William Wines Phelps, one of the most gifted and prolific hymn writers of the early days of the Church of Jesus Christ of Latter-day Saints.* Neither the date

---

*From George D. Pyper's *Stories of Latter-day Saint Hymns.*

on which it was written, nor the particular circumstances under which it was penned is known. It was a Restoration product, included in Emma Smith's collection which was first published in 1835. Is was sung by the Saints in their meetings before the completion of the Kirtland Temple; but the full measure of its emotional and spiritual power was not reached until it climaxed the dedicatory services of that temple, which occurred March 27, 1836. The Kirtland Temple was erected by the command of the Lord, at a cost of seventy-five thousand dollars, which was a very large sum for that day, especially considering the small membership of the Church and the poor condition of its members financially. Too, it was built in spite of the jeers, ridicule, and dire prophecies of the enemies of the Saints. It is said that the sparklers seen in the finished walls of the temple were caused by glass jewels contributed by the Latter-day Saint women, which were ground into the mortar and plastered on the outer walls of the edifice.

During the dedicatory service, Sidney Rigdon, of the First Presidency, referred to the sacrifices made by those who had labored on the building and had wet the walls with their tears while praying to God to stay the hands of the ruthless spoilers who vowed that the walls would never be reared.

A vote sustaining the Authorities of the Church was taken; then an unusual dedicatory prayer was offered by the Prophet Joseph Smith. This prayer constitutes section 109 of the Doctrine and Covenants from which the following paragraphs are taken:

> Thanks be to thy name, O Lord God of Israel, who keepest covenant and showest mercy unto thy servants who walk uprightly before thee, with all their hearts—
>
> Thou who hast commanded thy servants to build a house to thy name in this place.
>
> And now thou beholdest, O Lord, that thy servants have done according to thy commandment.
>
> And now we ask thee, Holy Father, in the name of Jesus Christ, the Son of thy bosom, in whose name alone salvation can be administered to the children of men, we ask thee, O Lord, to accept of this house, the workmanship of the hands of us, thy servants, which thou didst command us to build.
>
> For thou knowest that we have done this work through great tribulation; and out of our poverty we have given of our substance to build a house to thy name, that the Son of Man might have a place to manifest himself to his people.

221

By way of admonition and plea for mercy, the prayer continued:

... Seek ye diligently and teach one another words of wisdom; ... seek learning even by study and also by faith;

Organize yourselves; prepare every needful thing, and establish a house, even a house of prayer, a house of fasting, a house of faith, a house of learning, a house of glory, a house of order, a house of God...

Have mercy, O Lord, upon all the nations of the earth; have mercy upon the rulers of our land; may those principles, which were so honorably and nobly defended, namely, the Constitution of our land, by our fathers, be established forever.

Remember the kings, the princes, the nobles, and the great ones of the earth, and all people and the churches, all the poor, the needy, and afflicted ones of the earth; ...

O Lord God Almighty, hear us in these our petitions, ...

... And accept the dedication of this house unto thee, the work of our hands, which we have built unto thy name. (Doctrine and Covenants 109:1-5, 7-8, 54-55, 77-78.)

At this point the singers, stationed in the four corners of the temple, together with the assembly sang, "The Spirit of God Like a Fire Is Burning" with such emotional fervor as to bring to mind the record of the dedication of the temple of Solomon:

"And it came to pass, as the trumpeters and singers were as one,—and when they lifted up their voice . . . and praised the Lord saying, For He is God; for His mercy endureth forever; that then . . . the glory of the Lord had filled the House of God."

Originally the hymn contained six stanzas with chorus. Our present hymnbook contains four stanzas—the *Deseret Sunday School Songbook* has only three. The fourth and fifth omitted stanzas are as follows: and the wisdom of omitting them in our new hymnbook is apparent:

> We'll wash and be washed and with oil be anointed
> Withal not omitting the washing of feet,
> For he that receiveth his penny appointed
> Must surely be clean at the harvest of wheat,
>
> Old Israel, that fled from the world for his freedom,
> Must come with the cloud and the pillar amain,
> A Moses and Aaron and Joshua lead him
> And feed him on manna from heaven again.

The hymn is a herald of the restoration. It tells of a return to the earth of visions and blessings; of the visitation of angels; of the advancement of the Saints in understanding, in the knowledge of God and the expansion of his power; of the bursting of the veil of ignorance and the spread of the gospel to the nations of the earth, culminating in an era of peace and the coming of Christ to the earth.

The chorus is a stanza of exultation in which the Saints join with the "angels of heaven" in the cry which embodies the most sacred shout of the Latter-day Saints, viz: "Hosanna, Hosanna, Hosanna, to God and the Lamb!"

This song has been featured in the dedicatory services of each of the temples built by the Latter-day Saints and of many ward chapels.

Up to this writing I have not been able to discover who wrote the tune to this hymn. It probably was among the old Southern folk-songs originating in England and adopted by the early Latter-day Saints, among whom there were no composers.

The Author

William Wines Phelps was born February 17, 1792, at Hanover, Morris County, New Jersey. He received what in that day was considered a good education; married Sally Waterman by whom he had several children. In his early life he became interested in politics and was one of the aspirants for nomination to the office of Lieutenant Governor of New York. He became interested in Mormonism through reading the Book of Mormon and after a ten hours' talk with Sidney Rigdon, who declared he knew through the power of the Holy Ghost that the book was true.

William W. Phelps visited Kirtland in June, 1831, and placed himself at the disposal of the Prophet. He is the subject of a revelation contained in section 55 of the Doctrine and Covenants. In it he was instructed to be baptized and to be ordained an assistant to Oliver Cowdery to do the work of printing and selecting and writing books for the schools of the Church. Brother Phelps was baptized soon after this revelation was given and thereafter became an active spirit in preaching the gospel and assisting the Prophet in the great work of establishing the Church in Jackson County, Missouri. Under the Prophet he established the *Evening and Morning Star*, and was one of the stewards over the revelations given to the Prophet, prior to their publication.

It would take more space than is allowed in this book to relate the activities of Wm. W. Phelps in those days. The whole story is published in the third volume of Jenson's *Biographical Encyclopedia*. It would be well, however, to name a few of the high points in the life of this wonderful man. He was one of the presidency of the stake organized in Missouri. He lived with the Prophet Joseph in Kirtland and subscribed personally five hundred dollars toward the building of the temple erected there. He was one of the Prophet's scribes in translating the Book of Abraham from the papyrus found with the Egyptian mummies and when the vote on the Doctrine and Covenants was taken, he bore record that the book was true. He was appointed to revise the hymns selected by Emma Smith under revelation, and to prepare them for publication. He himself contributed a large number which were included in that volume, among which was the song treated in this article. Returning to Missouri he was appointed postmaster of Far West and in expectation of a temple being built in that locality he subscribed one thousand dollars to it. On Febrary 6, 1838, William W. Phelps, together with his co-laborers in the presidency, was rejected by the Saints.

He became disaffected and was finally excommunicated at a conference held at Quincy, Illinois, March 17, 1839. Repenting, he was restored to fellowship in 1841 and filled a mission to the Eastern States. Returning to Nauvoo he became a special messenger of the Prophet in his communications to the governor of the state.

W. W. Phelps

In Nauvoo he labored diligently in the interest of the Church but received little compensation for the labors he performed. He was a member of the city council and became involved in the difficulty surrounding the destruction of the *Expositer*. He was arrested in connection with that incident but acquitted. Upon the assassination of the Prophet Joseph Smith, William W. Phelps espoused the cause of the twelve and acknowledged Brigham Young as the head of the Church. It was upon his motion at the meeting held October 5, 1844, that Sidney Rigdon was excommunicated. In 1844, he assisted Willard Richards in getting material for a history of the Church. He was also one of those summoned to Carthage to be tried on the charge of treason, but was promptly discharged.

William W. Phelps and his wife were among the first to receive their endowments in the Nauvoo Temple. They crossed the plains in 1848 and were active in the early history of the Territory. He was one of the first regents of the University of Deseret, and in 1851 was elected a representative in the Utah legislature and reelected in 1853-4-5-6-7; was also an ordinance worker in giving the first endowments in the valley. He died March 7, 1872.

No. 214
Praise God from Whom All Blessings Flow

Words by Thomas Ken

The Hymn

The term doxology is applied to any praise of the Trinity, usually given at the end of a religious service.* Many doxologies have been written, but "Praise God from Whom All Blessings Flow" — by Bishop Thomas Ken—more than two centuries ago, is the popular one sung around the world by Christian denominations. It was not included in the first Latter-day Saint hymnbook, although two other hymns by Bishop Ken were selected by Emma Smith for that collection, viz: "Awake, My Soul and with the Sun," and "Glory to Thee, My God, This Night." Neither of these beautiful poems is found in the latest edition of *Latter-day Saint Hymns*.

H. Augustus Smith in his book, *Lyric Religion*, has this to say of Bishop Ken's "Doxology" which has been a rich contribution to Christian hymnody:

"Ken's 'Doxology' is a masterpiece of amplification and compression; of amplification on the thought 'Praise God,' repeated in every line; of compression, by including in the short space of four

---

*From George D. Pyper's *Stories of Latter-day Saint Hymns*.

225

lines God as the object of praise for all His blessings, by every creature, above, below, and in each of His manifestations as Father, Son and Holy Ghost."

The Composer

The tune to Bishop Ken's "Doxology," called "Old Hundred," is of the old Gregorian type. Some have claimed Martin Luther as the composer. Others have attributed it to Louis Bourgois, editor of the French *Genevan Psalter*. Now the hymnologists place the authorship on Guillaume le Franc (William Franc) of Rouen, France, who established a music school in Geneva, in 1541. He died at Lausanne in 1570.

The Author

Bishop Thomas Ken was born in Birkhampstead, Hertfordshire, England, in 1637. He was a prominent prelate and hymn-writer.

Seventeen years after he took holy orders, Bishop Ken became Chaplain to Mary, Princess of Orange, by appointment of her brother, King Charles II. In 1665 he was made Bishop of Bath and Wells. Under James II in 1688, he refused to publish the "Declaration of Indulgences" and with eight other bishops was imprisoned in the Tower of London. Having given his allegiance to the Stuarts, he refused it to William of Orange, and in 1691 was deprived of his see. He spent the remainder of his life in poverty in a home gratuitously offered him by Lord Viscount Weymouth. He died March 17, 1711. In fulfillment of his wish, six of the poorest men in the parish bore him to his final resting place.

No. 215

Today While the Sun Shines

Words and Music by Evan Stephens

The Hymn

The text of the hymn "Today While the Sun Shines" amplifies in a most forceful manner, the old saying "yesterday is gone, tomorrow may never come, but today is here."

The Composer and Author — Evan Stephens (See No. 144)

No. 216

With All the Power of Heart and Tongue

Words by Isaac Watts   **Music by Lowell Durham**

The Hymn

Lowell Durham gives the following account of the writing of the hymn "With All the Power of Heart and Tongue."

Of the list of hymn-texts submitted to me in 1944 by the General Church Music Committee, this particular one was the most appealing. I composed the music very quickly the morning following receipt of the text. It seemed to lend itself to a rather straightforward chorale treatment. Although I did not include written fermatas at the end of each phrase, I rather assumed that the spirit of the music would dictate such pauses.

The Composer

Lowell Durham was born in Boston, Mass., on March 4, 1917. His life to the present writing has been most eventful. He seems to be gifted with outstanding qualities of leadership. During his school he was elected or appointed to offices of trust from the elementary grades to college. In his scholastic studies he was always in the first ranks. At the present time he is Dean of the College of Fine Arts at the University of Utah. He holds three degrees—B. A., M.A., and a Doctorate. Dr. Durham is a thoroughly trained musician and has to his credit several fine compositions both vocal and instrumental. Some of his instrumental works have been played by the local symphony orchestra. Lowell's church activities have been quite complete in the various organizations up to the filling of a mission for the Latter-day Saint Church in the British Isles. He has always been a faithful church member and has held many important offices in the Church.

The Author — Isaac Watts See No. 168)

Lowell Durham

While of These Emblems We Partake

Words by John Nicholson   **Music by Alexander Schreiner**

The Hymn

Mr. Schreiner advises that the hymn, "While of These Emblems" should begin quietly and devotionally, gradually rising in melody to the high point "let us remember" and subsiding into devotional calm. The words are outstanding in poetic beauty. The contemplation of such thoughts is a religious duty asked of Latter-day Saints at the time of partaking of the emblems of the Lord's supper.

It is the opinion of this compiler that the musical setting given this hymn by Alexander Schreiner bids fare to become one of the most cherished sacramental hymns in the Church.

The Composer — Alexander Schreiner (See No. 24)

The Author

John Nicholson was born in Boswells, Roxburghshire, Scotland, in 1839. When he was ten-years-old the family moved to Edinburgh. He had to help support the family as a boy and couldn't go to school. He worked in a tobacco factory for 36 cents a week. Later he became an apprentice painter and paperhanger. In 1861 he joined the Latter-day Saint Church after becoming interested through reading a tract given him by Orson Pratt. He became a local missionary and spent his entire time in the work. In 1866 he came to Utah where he continued his work as painter and wall-paper hanger. In 1878 he went on a mission to England where he became the editor of the *Millennial Star*. When he returned home, he worked at the *Deseret News* and later was the chief recorder at the Salt Lake Temple.

John Nicholson's chief trait of character was integrity coupled with inherent goodness. He wrote many articles and was a fine speaker. He was a fearless man as exemplified by his dispelling a mob in England who threatened harm to him, with a lecture on "cowardice and brutality." He had a rich, expressive vocabulary. This accounts for the fineness of the phraseology in his two hymns; "Come Follow Me" and "While of These Emblems We Partake." He died in 1909.

We'll Sing all Hail to Jesus' Name

Words by R. Alldridge   **Music by Joseph Coslett**

The Hymn

"We'll Sing all Hail to Jesus' Name" is a Latter-day Saint sacramental hymn. All of the stanzas should be sung when it is used, to make the meaning complete. It is an excellent hymn. The best principles of hymn composition such as interesting melodic line, integration of the various phrases, proper balance and emphasis, and simple but good harmonization, are in evidence throughout.

The Composer
No information is available concerning Joseph Coslett.

The Author
Richard Alldridge was born May 3, 1815 in Birmingham, England. He was married to Ann Blunt of Northampton, England, and came to America for the Latter-day Saint Church.

The following hymns were composed by Richard Alldridge, and along with the other hymns comprised the first English edition of *Latter-day Saint Hymns*. These were published under the direction of Brigham Young, John Taylor, and Parley P. Pratt, Manchester, England in 1840.

> Lord Accept Our True Devotion
> We'll Sing All Hail to Jesus' Name
> O Lord Accept Our Songs of Praise
> How Dark and Gloomy Was the Night
> O Lord Preserve Thy Chosen Seed

Richard Alldridge died in Cedar City, Utah Feb. 14, 1896.

No. 219

I Heard the Bells on Christmas Day

Words by Henry W. Longfellow   **Music by J. Baptiste Calkin**

The Hymn
"I Heard the Bells on Christmas Day" by Henry W. Longfellow shows the touch of a master hand. It is blessed with all of the elements of longevity.

The Composer
John B. Calkin was an English composer and organist having been taught by his father. He held many important positions; organist and choir master at St. Columbia's College in Ireland and professor at the Guildhall School of Music were two of them. His compositions consist of sacred music, songs, glees, and numbers for strings, organ, and piano. He was born in 1827 and died in 1905.

The Author
Longfellow was born in Portland, Maine in 1807. Early in life he showed interest in letters. He went to Europe in 1826, perfecting his knowledge of French, Italian, and Spanish. In 1834, he studied

in England, Sweden, and Denmark. After his wife died, he went to Germany and Switzerland. After his return he spent his time teaching and lecturing in principal colleges and universities of America, later turning to writing verse as a profession. His success with "The Spanish Student," "Evangeline" and other shorter poems led him to this decision. Soon, "Tales of Wayside Inn," "Hiawatha," and "The Courtship of Miles Standish" came to light. His translations of Dante's *Divine Commedia* and *Christus* were the greatest works of his later years. He was honored with degrees from Cambridge and Oxford Universities and elected to membership in the Royal Spanish Academy. At the present time, his works are read as much as those of any other American poet. After Longfellow died in 1882, a monument was erected to him in Westminster Abbey. He was the first American to receive such an honor.

No. 220

Prayer Is the Soul's Sincere Desire

Words by James Montgomery   **Music by George Careless**

The Hymn

In a lecture delivered in New York, by J. Arthur Thomas, Professor of Natural History at Aberdeen, Scotland, on the subject of prayer, he expressed himself as follows:*

> A well-educated modern man has a conception of the Order of Nature which forbids him expecting or wishing any providential intervention for his own sake. We may pray for peace, if only since part of the answer comes in the asking; but we do not any longer pray for rain.

From another learned writer, a minister, we get the following:

> Prayer is an art, a science, and it must be learned by studying its laws and submitting to them in our experiments in praying. All the great geniuses in the realm of prayer have understood the necessity of studying carefully all the laws of prayer.

To a Latter-day Saint these ideas concerning prayer have not the right ring. To be tied down to principles of art and science in prayer would take the heart out of it. Looking for a better definition we turn to the inspired teachings of our late President Joseph F. Smith, who says:

---

*From George D. Pyper's *Stories of Latter-day Saint Hymns*.

True, faithful, earnest prayer consists more in a feeling that rises from the heart and from the inward desire of our spirits to supplicate the Lord in humility and in faith, that we may receive His blessings. It matters not how simple the words may be if our desires are genuine and we come before the Lord with a broken heart and contrite spirit, to ask Him for that which we need. Where is there a soul upon the earth that does not need something that the Almighty can give? . . . . We do not have to cry unto Him with many words. What we should do as Latter-day Saints, for our own good, is to go before Him often to witness unto Him that we remember Him and that we are willing to take upon us His name, and keep His commandments with righteousness; and that we desire His Spirit to help us. Then if we are in trouble let us go to the Lord and ask Him directly and specifically to help us out of the trouble we are in; and let the prayer come from the heart. . . . Let us speak the simple words expressing our need that will appeal most directly to the Giver of every good and perfect gift. He can hear in secret; and he knows the desires of our hearts before we ask; but He has made it obligatory and a duty that we shall call upon His name; that we shall seek that we may find.

How like an inspired Prophet are these simple words as compared with those first quoted! How like the teachings of the Master who gave us the Lord's Prayer as an example!

Our Father which art in heaven,
Hallowed be thy name.
Thy kingdom come. Thy will be done in earth, as it is in heaven.
Give us this day our daily bread,
And forgive us our debts, as we forgive our debtors.
And lead us not into temptation, but deliver us from evil:
For thine is the kingdom, and the power, and the glory, forever.
Amen.

There is no art in it, no science; just a simple exposition of how to pray. So, when we lack rain, let's pray for it; and likewise for our every righteous, unselfish need.

It was through prayer that the heavens were opened, that the gospel was restored in these last days. The youth Joseph Smith, confused at the cries of "lo here" and "lo there!" among the religious leaders of his day, while searching the scriptures found this promise, contained in the first chapter of James, which reads:

If any of you lack wisdom let him ask of God that giveth to all men liberally and upbraideth not and it shall be given him. But let him ask in faith, nothing wavering. For he that wavereth is like a wave of the sea, driven with the wind and tossed.

Joseph Smith obeyed, went to the woods to pray, and then came the great vision,—the Latter-day Saint Theophany.

231

Almost every revelation contained in the book of Doctrine and Covenants came in answer to a prayer uttered by the Prophet. Even so in some form or another, come blessings to us all, in answer to prayer—the comfort and solace of every human heart.

The Composer — George Careless (See No. 269)

The Author — James Montgomery (See No. 153)

No. 221

Upon the Cross of Calvary

Words by Vilate Raile   **Music by Leroy J. Robertson**

The Hymn

The hymn "Upon the Cross of Calvary" is an Easter hymn. It might also be used for the sacramental service.

The Composer — Leroy J. Robertson (See No. 45)

The Author

Vilate Schofield Raile was born in Salt Lake City in 1890.

She received her early education in the schools of Salt Lake and her college training at Brigham Young University, the University of Utah, the Utah State University at Logan, Utah, and at Mills College Oakland, California.

Leroy J. Robertson

232

As a member of the general board of the Primary Association, Church of Jesus Christ of Latter-day Saints, she was instrumental in the founding of the Primary Children's Hospital.

Mrs. Raile was a writer of note having several of her poems published in national magazines. She published a book of poems for children.

Her poem "Pioneers" was placed on the "This Is the Place Monument" at the mouth of Emigration Canyon.

She was the author of two hymns—one "Upon the Cross of Calvary" is published in the 1950 edition of the Latter-day Saint Hymnal.

She wrote the popular "Trail Builder's" song for the Primary Association.

All the words for the choral part of the dedication ceremony of the Brigham Young Monument in Washington D.C. were written by Mrs. Raile.

She was active in the public relations department of the Utah Medical Association.

A malignancy took her life in 1954 after a long illness.

No. 222

While Shepherds Watched Their Flocks by Night

Words by Nahum Tate   **Yorkshire Melody**

The Hymn

This carol is a paraphrase of verses 8-15 of Luke the second chapter.

The Composer

Song and dance were joined in many religious rituals of the earliest ages of mankind. Especially was this true of the carols. This Yorkshire carol has the dance element strongly emphasized in its make-up. In 1822 a Davis Gilbert edited a group of eight ancient Christmas carols with traditional tunes which he remembered singing when a boy. "While Shepherds Watched Their Flocks by Night" was included in this volume. No composer of this hymn is given.

The Author

Nahum Tate, Esquire (1625-1715) was the Poet-Laureate to his Majesty King William of England. He published, in collaboration with N. Brady, *The Psalms of David* in 1696.

All Hail the Glorious Day

Words by Joel H. Johnson   Music by Evan Stephens

The Hymn

"All Hail the Glorious Day" is a typical Latter-day Saint hymn. It embodies Mormon doctrine and is written and composed by two prominent Latter-day Saints.

The Composer — Evan Stephens (See No. 144)

The Author — Joel Hills Johnson (See No. 62)

No. 224

An Angel from on High

Words by Parley P. Pratt   Music by John Tullidge

The Hymn

As "An Angel from on High"* was neither included in Emma Smith's collection nor Parley P. Pratt's book of poems copyright in 1839, but was included in the first edition of the Latter-day Saint hymns published in 1840, it must have been written in that year. So alleges Samuel Russell in a collection of Pratt's hymns called *Millennial Hymns* published in 1913. In the new *Latter-day Saint Hymns* this prolific song writer has thirty-eight numbers to his credit, eight more than Wm. W. Phelps, his nearest competitor.

The hymn tells in five graphic, effective stanzas the story of the coming forth of the Book of Mormon; that the long silence has been broken by the announcement from an angel to the boy Prophet that the sacred record, for ages concealed in the Hill Cumorah, is at last to speak out of the dust, to usher in Christ's reign on earth; that the bursting of the seals would send light and glory into the world and reveal the fulness of the gospel. The last stanza is a mighty prophecy now being literally fulfilled—that Israel "shall now be gathered home" and build Jerusalem with their wealth and means† "while Zion shall arise and shine and fill the earth with truth divine."

"An Angel from on High" belongs distinctly to Mormon hymnology. It is a song of the restoration—a revelation of a divine truth of which Parley P. Pratt was an inspired torchbearer.

---

*From George D. Pyper's *Stories of Latter-day Saint Hymns*.

†Within a year from the time this song was written Orson Hyde, on the Mount of Olives, dedicated and consecrated the land of Palestine for the return of Judah's scattered people.

This truly remarkable hymn has been sung to many tunes, but the one composed by John Tullidge, published in *Latter-day Saint Hymns*, is the setting now generally accepted.

The Composer

Weymouth, a noted seaport on the south coast of England, is said to be second in the world for beauty—that of Naples being scarcely its superior. Beautiful indeed is Weymouth Bay when its waters are stirred by the approaching storms of the rough coast or lie sleeping in placid beauty under the misty light of the summer moon. It was here in this town of ever-changing beauty that John Elliot Tullidge, the composer of the tune "An Angel from on High" was born, in the year 1806, the son of Edward and Mary Elliot Tullidge. His father, being a wealthy man, gave his son every advantage. At the age of three years, showing signs of a very remarkable voice and a love for music, he was placed under the care of a tutor. At the age of ten years he led the choir at a concert in London. He received his education at Eton and at the same time studied voice culture. Later, he studied composition and technique under the celebrated musician and composer Hamilton.

At the age of twenty he married Elizabeth Daw, granddaughter of Squire Horsey, a wealthy land owner of Brighton. Five children were born to them, three sons and two daughters, the youngest son died when a child.

In his youth Professor Tullidge won the position of principal tenor of the Philharmonic concerts and became one of the four conductors of the York Harmonic Society. Mrs. Sunderland, known as the "Yorkshire Queen of Song" and later as the greatest oratorio singer in England, was at that time the leading soprano of the society. With her Mr. Tullidge was frequently sent out by the society to fill engagements as the principal singers at the oratorio concerts in the northern parts of England. It was one of these professional tours that led him into Wales, where he became the conductor of St Mary's Cathedral choir of Newport, South Wales. He was founder of the Newport Harmonic Society in 1843. This same organization, years later, took the laurels form the choral societies of all England, and to this day this choral society is known by the same name, and has never ceased to be active.

During the years he lived in Wales he gave concerts, taught voice culture and composition. Professor Evan Stephens' musical teacher was a student of Professor Tullidge.

In 1836 he was invited to spend the Christmas holidays at Lord

Reynolds' castle. It was there he sang for Princess Victoria, who became Queen of England the following year.

In 1850 he returned to Weymouth. About one year later his son Edward (the Utah historian) was converted to the Mormon Church by William Bowring, a distant relative of Sir Henry Bowring, his mother's cousin. Edward was a traveling elder for seven years, only coming home long enough to get clothes and some much-needed food. During these brief visits he converted his sisters and brother.

In 1855 Professor Tullidge and his family moved to Liverpool where Edward became editor of the *Millennial Star*. In 1860 his daughters, Elizabeth and Jane, sailed for America, and in 1861 Edward followed them.

It was the spring of 1863 that Professor Tullidge and his wife decided to make the long trek to Utah. His son John and his wife and baby emigrated with them. The child died and was buried on the plains. They arrived in the valley in September 1863. Professor Tullidge did not join the Church until almost a year after his arrival in the city. His wife never did join the Church. She and her family had always been Episcopalians, and the gospel coming to her later in her life, as it did, she was unable to make the change. However, she came to Utah, braving all the hardships of the plains and pioneer life to be with her children.

Professor Tullidge gave his first concert in Salt Lake City in September, 1864. There was little in Salt Lake for a man of his ability, but he accomplished as much as possible, giving concerts, teaching and composing. He was the first musical critic in Utah. Recently published in one of the local newspapers, this article appeared:

> The earliest evidence of music criticism in Utah is very probably Professor John Tullidge's reaction to a concert witnessed upon his arrival in Salt Lake Valley, Saturday, October 31, 1863. This criticism expressed is the oldest of evidence used by Basal Hansen, N. A., of the Brigham Young University in a thesis dealing with the history of music in Utah.

Professor Tullidge arranged the musical scores for the Salt Lake Theatre orchestra and was composing music for the orchestra at the time of his death which occurred in January, 1874, resulting from a fall which killed him instantly.

Professor Tullidge's daughter Jane became the wife of Bishop Alexander C. Pyper, and their children and children's children, faithful Church members, have reflected the musical genius of their talented ancestor.

The Author — Parley P. Pratt (See No. 20)

Arise, O Glorious Zion

Words by William G. Mills   Music by George Careless

The Hymn

If there are distinctive characteristics in Latter-day Saint hymns, "Arise, O Glorious Zion" has all of them. It reflects the principles and teachings of the restored gospel. Also it has in it the hope and joy of latter-day truth. Choir hymns as found in the Latter-day Saint Hymnal are distinctly different from the general character of congregational hymns. (See preface)

The Composer — George Careless (See No. 269)

The Author

There is no information available concerning the life of author William G. Mills.

No. 226

While of These Emblems We Partake

Words by John Nicholson   Music by S. McBurney

The Hymn — (See No. 217)

The Composer — S. McBurney (See No. 14)

The Author — John Nicholson (See No. 217)

No. 227

Arise, My Soul, Arise

Words by Charles Wesley   Music by George Careless

The Hymn

"Arise, My Soul, Arise" is a sacramental hymn from the pen of the great hymn writer Charles Wesley. It is obviously a choir hymn and should not be used with the congregation.

The Composer — George Careless (See No. 269.)

The Author — Charles Wesley (See No. 10)

Author of Faith, Eternal Word

Words by Charles Wesley   Music by George Careless

The Hymn

"Author of Faith" is another of the many hymns of Charles Wesley. The phraseology in the various lines bespeak an experienced hymnist. To sing this hymn most effectively, a good four-voiced choir is required as the part writing in it is musically impressive.

The Composer — George Careless (See No. 269)

The Author — Charles Wesley (See No. 10)

No. 229

Awake, Ye Saints of God, Awake!

Words by Eliza R. Snow   Music by Evan Stephens

The Hymn

The hymn "Awake, Ye Saints of God, Awake!" is in its spirit, a reflection of·the trials, tribulations, and persecutions of the Latter-day Saints in the early days of the Church. It is a typical Latter-day Saint hymn. The music of the hymn is dynamically accentuated.

The Composer — Evan Stephens (See No. 144)

The Author — Eliza R. Snow (See No 139)

No. 230

Behold the Great Redeemer Die

Words by Eliza R. Snow   Music by George Careless

The Hymn

"Behold the Great Redeemer Die" is an exalted poem of the great atoning sacrifice of Jesus Christ. Its arched tone-line phrases make it musically expressive.

The Composer — George Careless (See No. 269)

"Behold the Great Redeemer Die" is a perfectly written choir hymn. Choir hymns are peculiar only to the *Latter-day Saint Hymnal*.

The Author — Eliza R. Snow (See No. 139)

Before Thee, Lord, I Bow My Head

Words and Music by Joseph H. Dean

The Hymn

Both words and music of this hymn were written in the year of 1921 by Joseph H. Dean. It is a great favorite with Latter-day Saint choirs. The style of the first and last parts of this hymn, with the tenor and bass reiterations, harks back to a simple anthem form used in Protestant church music. It is a kind of variation from pure hymn style wherein all voices when singing harmonically, sing simultaneously.

The Composer

Joseph H. Dean was born in 1855. He left England with his parents in 1859, came to Utah and settled in Morgan. He moved to Salt Lake City in 1870. He was a stone cutter for seven years for the Salt Lake Temple At the dedication of the temple in 1893, he was appointed chief caretaker of the temple. He established a mercantile business in Mencos, Colorado, and in Fruitland, New Mexico. He filed on 240 acres of land in what is now Redmesa, Colorado. He moved to Shelley, Idaho, in 1913 and was employed there by Utah-Idaho Sugar Company for eight years.

Joseph Dean filled three missions for the Church—to the Hawaiian Islands, and the Samoan Islands, where he opened the Samoan Mission in 1888. He assisted in translation of songs of Zion into the Samoan language and did similar work for the Hawaiian Mission in 1918.

Elder Dean held numerous positions in the wards and stakes of the Church and in 1940 was ordained a patriarch in the Shelley Stake, Idaho.

He kept a daily journal from seventeen years of age to the end of his life, and it is on file in the Church Historian's Office, valued highly for the amount of historical details pertaining to missionary work in Hawaii and Samoa. He died in 1947.

No. 232

As the Dew from Heaven Distilling

Words by Parley P. Pratt   **Music by Joseph J. Daynes**

The Hymn

Your compiler, after hearing "As the Dew from Heaven Distilling" played on the organ every Sunday morning on the broadcast of the Tabernacle Choir for twenty-two years while he was its conductor, is of the opinion that the tune is a better instrumental selection than a vocal one. The flowing lyric character of its melodic line gives it an appealing quality which is long lasting. When it is sung, a smooth legato style must be used to make it thoroughly satisfying.

The Composer

Joseph J. Daynes, who wrote the tune to "As the Dew from Heaven Distilling,"* was a man of unusual musical ability—not only as an organist but also as a composer. He wrote many anthems, and twenty-seven of his compositions are included in the recently compiled *Latter-day Saint Hymns*—giving him third place in the number of tunes contributed. He wrote no words but was an adept in fitting his tunes to the hymns of Latter-day Saint poets.

Joseph J. Daynes was born April 2, 1851, in Norwich, England, the son of John and Eliza Miller Daynes. Early in life he displayed rare musical talent. At four years of age he could play "The Rat-catcher's Daughter," and at six was in demand for concerts and special entertainments. The father and mother were converted to the doctrines of the Church of Jesus Christ of Latter-day Saints, and in 1862, with two children, immigrated to Utah. Joseph, the subject of this sketch, was then eleven years old. Up to this time a strange affliction had come to this young man. Every fall he went blind, and each following spring he recovered his sight. This occurred annually until he arrived in Utah, when the blindness ceased.

A few years later a pipe organ, constructed by Joseph H. Ridges at Sidney, Australia, where he resided, was donated by the Saints in that mission and after much tribulation was brought to Salt Lake City and in March, 1867, installed in the old Tabernacle by its builder, who came all the way from Australia for the purpose. Joseph J. Daynes, then a youth of sixteen, was appointed organist and played there until the new Tabernacle was completed. He was small of stature and was obliged to put cork extensions on his shoes in order to reach the organ pedals.

The old Tabernacle organ was blown by hand power, and an eccentric brother named Charley Moore worked the bellows. One day a newspaper article appeared in which Professor Daynes, in describing the details of playing the organ used the personal pronoun "I" quite frequently. Brother Moore took exception to the "I," believing, as did Charles A. Lindbergh, later, when he named his book "We" that the performance on the organ was a joint affair. So, when the next

---

*From George D. Pyper's *Stories of Latter-day Saint Hymns*.

rehearsal occurred, there was no power in the organ. Professor Daynes asked what was the matter, and Brother Moore said there would be no more organ until the organist acknowledged that "We did it." Some talk and laughter ensued. Professor Daynes said, "All right, Brother Moore. We did it," and after that all went "merry as a marriage bell."

Professor Daynes continued as organist of the new Tabernacle under Professor Charles J. Thomas, George Careless, Ebenezer Beesley, and Evan Stephens. Pressed by personal business, he was honorably released in 1900, and was succeeded by John J. McClellan. He did not cease his active work in the Church, however, for as conductor of the Twentieth Ward Choir, Salt Lake City, he brought that organization up to be an outstanding one. In 1884 he wrote, "The Nations Bow to Satan's Thrall" for the dedicatory services of the Salt Lake Temple, and later a book of his anthems was published. He wrote marches for the funerals of Brigham Young and Wilford Woodruff. To him, also, is due the honor of instituting the first recitals in the Tabernacle on the Great Organ.

In 1872 Brother Daynes married Miss Mary Jane Sharp, daughter of Joseph and Ellen Condie Sharp, by whom he had seven children.

He died January 15, 1920.

Joseph J. Daynes, Sr.

In Parley P. Pratt's hymn, "As the Dew from Heaven Distilling," Professor Daynes caught the gentle spirit of the author, and has given us a beautiful song prayer. And when it is sung with the proper, emotional feeling, a reverential seal is put upon the spoken word, through the power of music; and the congregation is guided into a spirit of adoration and confession and drawn one step nearer to the Infinite.

The Author — Parley P. Pratt (See No. 20)

No. 233

Blessed Are They that Have the Faith

Words by Herbert S. Auerbach   **Music by Anthony C. Lund**

The Hymn

Herbert Auerbach, the writer of the poem "Blessed Are They that Have the Faith" was of Hebrew descent. His intimate association with Anthony C. Lund, Tabernacle Choir Director and other Latter-day Saint people, evidently convinced him of the rightness of their faith. The lines of this hymn seem to bear out this conclusion.

The Composer

Anthony C. Lund, the ninth conductor of the Tabernacle Choir, was born on February 25, 1871 in Ephraim, Utah. Hilda Peterson, his aunt, gave him lessons on the organ at eight years of age. At the age of eighteen he was appointed choir leader in Ephraim. He graduated from Brigham Young University in 1891. In 1892 he enrolled in the Royal Conservatory in Leipzig, Germany, graduating in 1899. He studied in Paris in 1902 and in London in 1909. In 1897 Professor Lund became the head of the music department at Brigham Youn University. While in this position he directed one hundred operas. In 1915 he became a member of the Utah Conservatory faculty and later joined the faculty of the McCune School of Music. In these capacities he became the outstanding vocal teacher in the state of Utah. On July 28, 1916, he was appointed conductor of the Tabernacle Choir. On July 15, 1929, he directed the choir in their first national broadcast. He directed the music for the *Message of the Ages* pageant in 1930 which was presented for one month. Professor Lund received many favorable comments for the standard of music which he introduced to the choir. He culminated his career as the director of the Tabernacle Choir when it sang at the Century of Progress Exposition in Chicago during September 1934. He died June 11, 1935.

242

Herbert Auerbach

Anthony C. Lund

The Author

Herbert S. Auerbach was born in Salt Lake City in 1882. He received his higher education in Fresenius, Weisbaden, Germany and in Lausanne, Switzerland. Later he was graduated from the School of Mines, Columbia University with an MA degree. Mr. Auerbach engaged in the real-estate business, building, and merchandising in Salt Lake City, Utah, and was manager of the Auerbach Company of Salt Lake City. He was also a director of the Federal Reserve Bank in Salt Lake, a Major in the Army, president of the Utah State Historical Society and a member of the American Society of Authors and Composers. His club activities included the Rotary Club, the Sons of Pioneers, and the Timpanogos Club. Mr. Auerbach was a lifelong friend of Anthony Lund, Tabernacle Choir Director. This sketch is from *Who's Who in America*. Herbert Auerbach died in 1945.

No. 234

Great Is the Lord; 'Tis Good to Praise

Words by Eliza R. Snow   **Music by Ebenezer Beesley**

The Hymn

Eliza R. Snow was in every way a latter-day hymn writer. The restored gospel message permeated all of her writings. The universality

243

found in the hymns of so many of the great hymnists is not a characteristic of the many hymns of Eliza R. Snow. Hers are largely of the restored gospel. "Great Is the Lord" is a fine exemple of Latter-day Saint gospel teachings, couched in poetic lines.

The Composer — Ebenezer Beesley (See No. 94)

The Author — Eliza R. Snow (See No. 139)

No. 235

Cast Thy Burden upon the Lord

Psalms   Music by Felix Mendelssohn

The Hymn

The text of "Cast Thy Burden upon the Lord" is an amplified version of Psalm 55; verse 22.

The Composer — Felix Mendelssohn (See No. 370)

This hymn is a chorale and was used by Mendelssohn in his oratorio *The Elijah*.

The Author — Psalm 55:22.

No. 236

Captain of Israel's Host and Guide

Words by Charles Wesley   Music by Gioacchino Rossinni

The Hymn

The text of "Captain of Israel's Host" was written by the great hymn writer Charles Wesley. When this text and Rossinni's music became wedded is not known.

The Composer

Rossinni was one of the most noted musical luminaries of the nineteenth century. He was born in 1792 and as a boy, received a musical education from his father and mother together with several of the best musicians in the country. A short time after he began the study of harmony, his teacher, Mattei, told him that he was ready to write operas. His first opera *The Matrimonial Market* was a huge success. After this beginning, one opera after another followed. In 1816, he composed the ever popular *Barber of Seville* and in 1829 his masterpiece *William Tell* was written. Only one more composition of note was written after *William Tell*, and that was *The Stabat Mater*, a religious work. The intrinsic worth of Rossinni's music is a controversial subject among critics, but some of the music has per-

244

sisted, nevertheless, and is enjoyed today as formerly. "Captain of Israel's Host" is from one of his shorter works and has been made into a four part choir number in the *Latter-day Saint Hymnal*. He died in 1868.

The Author — Charles Wesley (See No. 10)

(See No. 10)

No. 237
Come, Dearest Lord

Words by Isaac Watts   **Music by Evan Stephens**

The Hymn

"Come, Dearest Lord" is an eloquent prayer from the pen of Isaac Watts. The hymn is a great favorite with Latter-day Saint choirs.

The Composer — Evan Stephens (See No. 144)

The Author — Isaac Watts (See No. 168)

No. 238
Come, Let Us Sing an Evening Hymn

Words by William W. Phelps   **Music by Tracy Y. Cannon**

The Hymn

"Come, Let Us Sing an Evening hymn" suggests a very beautiful group or family custom. To sing a hymn is an appropriate closing of the day as line two of the first stanza avers, "To calm our minds for rest."

The Composer — Tracy Y. Cannon (See No. 1)

Tracy Cannon gives the following account of writing this hymn:

"The words, written by W. W. Phelps, were assigned to me by Elder Melvin J. Ballard when the 1927 edition of the Latter-day Saint Hymnbook was being prepared. I immediately composed the music for these words and the hymn was first printed in the 1927 edition of the hymnbook."

The Author — William W. Phelps (See No. 213)

No. 239
Break Forth, O Beauteous Heavenly Light

Words and Music by Johann Schop

The Hymn

"Break Forth, O Beauteous Heavenly Light" is a Christmas chorale, translated from the German. It was first published in Rist's

Himmlische Lieder in 1641 and included in Cruger's *Praxis Pietatis Melica*, 1648. The text is based on Isaiah 9:2-7.

The Composer

This dignified chorale was composed by Johann Schop in 1641. He was a prominent German musician of that period. Schop is credited with being the auothor of the words as well as of the music.

The present form of the tune and its harmonization is that used by J. S. Bach in Part 2 of his Christmas Oratorio, 1734.

No. 240

Come, Thou Glorious Day of Promise

Words by Alex Neibaur   Music by A. C. Smyth

The Hymn

There is no need of any analysis of this hymn. The three concise stanzas, written over a hundred years ago call upon the Lord to redeem his ancient people, to end their unbelief and misery, and set them free. If Alexander Neibaur were living today he could not write a hymn more applicable to the present sad condition of his race than the one presented here.

The Composer — A. C. Smyth (See No. 37)

The music of "Come, Thou Glorious Day of Promise" is written in chorale style. It is a dignified piece of writing. The duet in it places it in the realm of choir hymns.

The Author

Alexander Neibaur, who wrote this hymn was a Jew, the first of his race to join The Church of Jesus Christ of Latter-day Saints.* An unpublished sketch of his life, in the files of the Church Historian's Office, is one of the most interesting sagas of pioneer life. He was born January 8, 1808, in Ehrenbriestein, Alsace-Lorraine, then French but afterwards German territory. His parents were Nathan and Rebecca Peretz Neibaur, the father a well-to-do physician and surgeon in the French army under Napoleon Bonaparte. It is said that upon Nathan's retirement from the army the great Napoleon personally visited him urging him to re-enter the army as a spy, but, though offered great inducements, Nathan declined, and in this bloodless battle Napoleon was defeated.

Alexander Neibaur was educated for a Rabbi, but at seventeen decided against the ministry and chose the profession of surgeon and dentistry. He was graduated from the University of Berlin before he

*From George D. Pyper's *Stories of Latter-day Saint Hymns*.

was twenty. Becoming converted to the Christian faith, he left his home and after much travel, located in Preston, England. Here he met and on July 30, 1837, married Ellen Breakel. And here he met the first Mormon elders, who were preaching in the "cock pit."

Brother Neibaur was first attracted to Mormonism through a dream in which he was shown a new book, and when he saw and read the Book of Mormon he was converted to the religion of the Latter-day Saints, baptized April 9, 1838, by Elder Isaac Russell, and sailed from Liverpool, February 7, 1844, on the *Sheffield*. At Nauvoo he worked on the Nauvoo House and Temple and taught the Prophet Greek and Hebrew. He, himself, spoke seven languages. After the martyrdom he suffered many persecutions. At the battle of Nauvoo his wife had just been confined and could not be moved. His journal contains the following items:

"1846—Sept. 1—Mob advanced toward Joseph's farm—fired three cannon shots at night. Quartered at Squire Wells'—mob moved North toward William Law's field, firing 35 cannon balls—myself being placed in a corn field opposite Hyrum's farm to spring a mine. —Two forts erected at night—On 12th mob made an attack to get into Nauvoo.— Brother William Anderson and his son, belonging to the 5th Quorum of Seventies, being shot—Mob repelled with a number wounded."

The Neibaur family moved to Winter Quarters in 1847 and with borrowed wagon and oxen entered Salt Lake Valley in 1848. There Brother Neibaur became the pioneer dentist and also the pioneer matchmaker. His daughter Rebecca married Charles W. Nibley who became one of the First Presidency of the Church. On December 15th, 1883, this fine and valiant Hebrew Saint passed away, the father of 14 children, 83 grandchildren, 13 great-grandchildren, and at the time the sketch of his life was written his flock numbered 427.

No. 241   For the Strength of the Hills

Words by Felicia D. H. Brown   Music by Evan Stephens
Altered by Edward L. Sloan

The Hymn

"The hymn of the Vaudois Mountaineers in Times of Persecution," from which "For the Strength of the Hills" was adapted by Edward L. Sloan, is as follows: (The Vaudois Mountains are in Switzerland in the Lausanne area, north of Geneva).

Hymn of the Vadois Mountaineers in Times of Persecution

"Thanks be to God for the Mountains!"
Howitt's *Book of the Seasons*

For the strength of the hills we bless thee,
　　Our God, our father's God!
Thou hast made thy children mighty
　　By the touch of the mountain sod.
Thou hast fixed our ark of refuge
　　Where the spoilers ne'er trod;
For the strength of the hills we bless thee,
　　Our God, our fathers' God!

We are watchers of a beacon
　　Whose light must never die;
We are guardians of an altar
　　'Midst the silence of the sky:
The rocks yield founts of courage,
　　Struck forth as by thy rod;
For the strength of the hills we bless thee,
　　Our God, our fathers' God!

For the dark, resounding caverns,
　　Where thy still, small voice is heard;
For the strong pines of the forests,
　　That by thy breath are stirred;
For the storms, on whose free pinions
　　Thy spirit walks abroad;
For the strength of the hills, we bless thee,
　　Our God, our fathers' God!

The royal eagle darteth
　　On his quarry from the heights,
And the stag that knows no master
　　Seeks there his wild delights;
But we, for thy communion,
　　Have sought the mountain sod!
For the strength of the hills we bless thee,
　　Our God, our fathers' God!

The Composer — Evan Stephens (See No. 144)

　　C. Sylvester Horne made an altered adaptation of the "Hymn of the Vaudois Mountaineers" and published it in an American Hymnal. Evan Stephens either knowingly or by coincidence, patterned his setting of "For the Strength of the Hills" after the Horne setting. The rhythm and many of the melodic phrases are similar.

The Author

　　(Altered by Edward L. Sloan)

　　Felicia Dorothea Browne was born in Liverpool, England in 1795 and died in Redesdale (near Dublin), Ireland in 1835. She was a poet of marked distinction. The last London edition of her poems was published in 1856 by Phillips, Samson, and Company, Boston, Massachusetts.

Again We Meet around the Board

Words by Eliza R. Snow   Music by George Careless

The Hymn

"Again We Meet around the Board" is a sacramental hymn especially written for choirs. It is thoroughly Latter-day Saint in character and stands as a representative Mormon hymn. This hymn is individualized by the three sequential phrases of the soprano and alto duet. When sung well by a choir of good voices, it has a lovely reverent appeal.

The Composer — George Careless (See No. 269)

The Author — Eliza R. Snow (See No. 139)

No. 243

Glorious Things Are Sung of Zion

Words by William W. Phelps   Music by Joseph J. Daynes

The Hymn

"Glorious Things Are Sung of Zion" is a typical Mormon hymn. The text proclaims the Latter-day Saint version of the city of Enoch, and the music is by the first Tabernacle organist, Joseph J. Daynes. This hymn has a happy, exuberant mein which is characteristic of many of the Latter-day Saint hymns, but it in no way leans toward the frivolous as do the lighter gospel song tunes. It is musically substantial.

The Composer — Joseph J. Daynes (See No. 232)

The Author — William W. Phelps (See No. 213)

No. 244

Glorious Things of Thee Are Spoken

Words by John Newton   Music by J. S. Hanecy

The Hymn

The hymn "Zion," as it was originally called, is based on chapter 33:20-21 of Isaiah. It was first published in 1779 in a collection known as John Newton's *Olney Hymns*. Two hundred and seventy-nine additional hymns of Newton, together with sixty-eight by William Cowper, writer of "God Moves in a Mysterious Way" also appear in this collection.

The Composer

"Glorious Things of Thee Are Spoken" was first sung to a

"Croatian" folk song which Franz Joseph Haydn had arranged as the national hymn of Austria.

Subsequently, Hanecy composed the setting found in the *Latter-day Saint Hymnal*.

The Author

John Newton in his early life was a slave trader. Fate brought him in contact with the Wesleys, John and Charles, who converted him to Christianity. He determined to join the ministry and after diligent study, he was ordained by the Bishop of Lincoln. He wrote his own Epitaph which reads; "John Newton, clerk, once an infidel and Libertine, a servant of slaves in Africa, was by the rich mercy our Lord and Savior, Jesus Christ, preserved, restored, pardoned, and appointed to preach the faith he had long labored to destroy." John Newton was born in 1725 and died in 1807.

No. 245

Does the Journey Seem Long?

Words by Joseph Fielding Smith **Music by George D. Pyper**

The Hymn

"Does the Journey Seem Long" is a hymn of exhortation and encouragement to "Look Upward in Gladness, Where all Trouble Doth End."

According to Elder Joseph Fielding Smith the words of this hymn were written while he was riding on a train to Arizona. When George D. Pyper saw the hymn, he asked for the privilege of writing the music for it.

The Composer

George D. Pyper was born November 21, 1860, in Salt Lake City, Utah, a son of Alexander C. Pyper and Christiana Dollinger. He was baptized when eight years old, officiated in the offices of the Aaronic Priesthood and was ordained an elder in 1883, and later ordained a high priest.

He was manager of the Salt Lake Theatre from 1904 until 1929 when the edifice was torn down. For a period of over thirty years he had brought to the people the finest attractions the stage afforded and during that period also brought to the Tabernacle, Salt Lake City, many world-famed artists and musical organizations. In 1928 he published the story of the Salt Lake Theatre and early drama in Salt Lake, under the title of *The Romance of an Old Playhouse*. Among the side activities he was a member of the first Salt Lake Board of

Education, and of the first Library Board; also president of the Oratorio Society and Musical Arts and Civic Music Association. He was first assistant to Elder Melvin J. Ballard in the Church music committee. Elder Pyper was chairman of the Century of Progress Church Committee and in connection with the Fairbanks family (J. B., J. Leo, and Avard) supervised the preparation of that wonderful exhibit. In November 1911, he managed the Tabernacle Choir in a 6000 mile tour to the National Irrigation Congress held in Madison Square Garden, New York City, and extended the tour to Washington and other cities of the United States. In 1934 he conducted the tour of the choir to the Century of Progress Fair in Chicago where it sang for a week in the Ford Auditorium. In 1929 he was named as chairman of the Latter-day Saint Pageant Committee which produced the great spectacle *Message of the Ages*, in the Tabernacle in Salt Lake City, April 6, 1930 as part of the exercises celebrating the one hundredth anniversary of the organization of the Church. He visited the Hawaiian Islands and was among the first fliers from Hilo to Honolulu. For twenty-seven years he was associate editor of the *Juvenile Instructor*, now *The Instructor*.

He also wrote a book entitled *Stories of Latter-day Saint Hymns*. Fifty-four hymns were included in the volume. It has been said of Elder Pyper that he knew more about Latter-day Saint hymns than anyone else in the Church.

In 1918 he was chosen as second assistant to David O. McKay in the general superintendency of the Deseret Sunday School Union. This position he held until he was chosen the general superintendent in 1934.

Elder Pyper was a symbol of the faith of the Latter-day Saints. Three interesting activities marked his earlier life. The first was when he planted two hundred mulberry trees near the mouth of Emigration Canyon and raised silkworms for a silk factory which had been established in Salt Lake City. Then because of his beautiful singing, he was sent on a short-term mission to the Eastern and Southern states with Brigham H. Roberts—he to sing and the eloquent Roberts to preach.

The third experience was when he returned from this mission he became secretary to Heber J. Grant of the Heber J. Grant Insurance Company.

At the time of Elder Pyper's death on January 16, 1943 the buildings were closed on Temple Square as a precautionary war measure, but by a special concession the Assembly Hall was opened for his funeral.

Joseph Fielding Smith

George D. Pyper

The Author

Joseph Fielding Smith was born July 19, 1876, the son of Joseph F. Smith the sixth President of The Church of Jesus Christ of Latter-day Saints, and Mary Fielding Smith. Elder Smith is known for his unbending devotion throughout his life to the revealed word of God. As Church Historian he has edited and written a complete history of the Church and seven doctrinal books as well as a score of illuminating pamphlets. He served as a missionary to Great Britain 1899-1901. Many ward, stake, and general church responsibilities have been entrusted to him. He is at present the President of The Church of Jesus Christ of Latter-day Saints. Hymn No. 245, "Does the Journey Seem Long?" written in collaboration with George D. Pyper, gives him a lasting place in the *Latter-day Saint Hymnal*. As a scriptorian, President Smith hasn't a peer in the Church.

No. 246

God Is in His Holy Temple

Words Anonymous   Music by Frank W. Asper

The Hymn

The symbolism used in the two last lines of "God Is in His Holy Temple," wherein the body is termed the temple of the soul, is a beautiful figure of speech. Our bodies are God given, and they should be kept in purity so that the Spirit of the Lord may ever abound therein.

The Composer — Frank W. Asper (See No. 96)

The Author — Anonymous

No. 247
Go, Ye Messengers of Glory

Words by John Taylor   **Music by Ebenezer Beesley**

The Hymn

According to Leroy J. Robertson the hymn "Go, Ye Messengers of Glory" is written on the missionary movement. It is best suited to the choir but could be effective when sung in unison by the congregation with organ accompaniment.

The Composer — Leroy J. Robertson (See No. 45)

The Author — John Taylor (See No. 296)

No. 248
Great God, Attend while Zion Sings

Words by Isaac Watts   **Music by Joseph J. Daynes**

The Hymn

"Great God, Attend" is one of the six hundred hymns from the gifted pen of the creator of the modern English hymn, Issac Watts. Most of his best hymns were written between the age of twenty and twenty-two. The effect produced in this hymn by this type of composition is very pleasing.

The Composer — Joseph J. Daynes (See No. 232)

The main charm of the music of this choir hymn is in its unorthodox hymn form—a sustained melody in the soprano part with a chordal chant accompaniment in the alto, tenor, and bass parts.

The Author — Isaac Watts (See No. 168)

No. 249
Hark, Ten Thousand, Thousand Voices

Words by Thomas Raffles   **Music by Joseph J. Daynes**

The Hymn

"Hark, Ten Thousand, Thousand Voices" is a jubilant hymn

of praise and triumph. The doctrine that "he that is warned, let him warn his neighbor" is found with slight variation in the lines of the first stanza: "Speed the gospel! Let its tidings gladden every human mind."

The Composer — Joseph J. Daynes (See No. 232)

The Author

Thomas Raffles was born in London, the son of a solicitor. He studied for the ministry at the suggestion of the pastor of his church—the English Congregational—and was ordained in 1808. Dr. Raffles became pastor of the great George Street Congregational church in Liverpool where he served for forty-nine years. He is credited in Julian's *Encyclopedia* with being the author of sixteen hymns.

No. 250

The Happy Day Has Rolled On

Words by Philo Dibble   **Music by Ebenezer Beesley**

The Hymn

"The Happy Day Has Rolled On" is a Latter-day Saint hymn in praise of the restoration of the gospel.

The Composer — Ebenezer Beesley (See No. 94)

The Author

Philo Dibble (1805-1895) was a staunch friend of the Prophet Joseph Smith. He was with the Prophet in 1833 during the troublesome times in Jackson County, Missouri. He was wounded by a shot from a mob and carried the bullet in his body for the remainder of his life. His testimony at the time of his death was that he knew that the Latter-day Saint Church was established by divine revelation through Joseph Smith. He often told of seeing the Prophet's body after he had been martyred. Elder Dibble died in Springville June 7, 1895. Philo Dibble had and was witness to some of the most astounding miracles, healings and manifestations ever recorded in the history of the Church.

No. 251

Again, Our Dear Redeeming Lord

Words by Theodore E. Curtis   **Music by Alfred M. Durham**

The Hymn

"Again, Our Dear Redeeming Lord" is a choir sacramental hymn, reiterating in reverential verse, the purpose for which we partake of the Sacrament.

Theodore E. Curtis

The Composer — Alfred M. Durham (See No. 251)

The Author — Theodore E. Curtis (See No. 294)

No. 252

Hushed Was the Evening Hymn

Words by James D. Burns   **Music by Arthur Sullivan**

The Hymn

"Hushed Was the Evening Hymn" is a versification of the second and third chapters of 1st Samuel. With its narrative type of subject matter, it can hardly be classified in the category of hymn literature.

The Composer — Sir Arthur Sullivan (See No. 128)

The real charm of this choir hymn is found in the smooth flowing style of Arthur Sullivan's music.

The Author

James D. Burns was born in Scotland in 1823. He was educated for the ministry, but ill health constantly interrupted his work as a preacher. It is said that he broke down completely in delivering his first sermon but in doing so, he won the hearts of the worshipers. His spirit rose continually above his vitality in his effort to carry on.

While on an assignment in Edinburgh, he contracted a severe cold which caused his death in 1864.

No. 253

Hark, Listen to the Trumpeters

Words Anonymous   Music by George Careless

The Hymn

"Hark, Listen to the Trumpeters" is a hymn of jubilation, using figuration from the military to enlist sinners to the cause of Christ. This hymn should be sung with a firm, martial, rhythmical tread.

The Composer — George Careless (See No. 269)

The Author — Anonymous

No. 254

I'll Praise My Maker while I've Breath

Words by Isaac Watts   Music by J. G. Fones

The Hymn

The way in which Isaac Watts preserved individuality in his thousand hymns is one of the great literary feats of hymn writing, but the hymns speak for themselves on this question.

Every successive line of this hymn is logical, and the rhyming is natural—never forced. The content of each stanza is impressive and gives lasting qualities to the hymn.

The Composer — Joseph G. Fones (See No. 78)

The Author — Isaac Watts (See No 168)

No. 255

I Saw a Mighty Angel Fly

Words Anonymous   Music by George Careless

The Hymn

The theme of "I Saw a Mighty Angel Fly" is that of the gospel restoration as predicted by John the Revelator. (Revelation 14:6-7.) "And I saw another angel fly in the midst of heaven, having the everlasting gospel to preach unto them that dwell on the earth, and to every nation, and kindred, and tongue, and people, saying with a loud voice, Fear God, and give glory to him; for the hour of his judgment has come."

The Composer — George Careless (See No. 269)

256

No. 256

Give Us Room that We May Dwell

Words Anonymous   Music by Wm. N. B. Shepherd

The Hymn

This anonymous hymn "Give Us Room that We May Dwell," is a Latter-day Saint song of Zion.

> Zion is like one who dreams
> Filled with wonder and delight.

The Composer

William Nathaniel Budge Shepherd was born at Southampton, England, September 18, 1854, third of a family of ten children. His parents, William Shepherd and Mary Ann Tracy, were already members of the LDS Church. They and their family eventually emigrated to America in 1877, settling in Paris, Idaho.

Mr. Shepherd and his wife, Emily Mary Phipp, resided in Paris until 1897, raising a family of ten children, three of whom became distinguished in the musical world: Arthur, composer, pianist, and teacher; Charles Lorenzo, pianist; and Albert Thoroughgood, violinist.

At the end of twenty years, the family moved to Salt Lake City, but wherever their residence, Mr. Shepherd always participated actively in church and civic affairs. In Paris he taught school, served in the Idaho legislature, and was chorister of the Bear Lake choir from the time is was organized until his departure. His first position in Salt Lake was that of bookkeeper for H. Dinwoodey Furniture Company, his experience in the same post on a large estate in England standing him in good stead. In 1911 he entered the employ of the ZCMI, working in the general offices until the end of his life. He was Ensign Stake Sunday School chorister for thirty-seven years.

Aside from his musical accomplishments, Mr. Shepherd was a penman of no little talent, and his beautiful handwriting (script) was famous. As a child at school he always carried off first prize in penmanship. But his great love was music. As he said in his own words: "My chief church activities have been connected principally with the musical service in the Church, in which service I have taken great delight."

William Shepherd's love of music probably began in his father's home, where the family took great interest in musical matters and enjoyed themselves in part-singing. At the early age of six he enjoyed standing up in Church with his mother as the hymns were sung. One hymn which particularly appealed to him was "Come, Come, Ye

Saints." Later on he and his brother Tracy sang in the choir of the Fawley village church at the invitation of the rector. On the arduous sea voyage to the United States, the family spent many pleasant hours singing part songs, and anthems, which they were invited to sing the last day on board by one of the officers.

Two days after the family's arrival in Paris, they were asked to sing at the Sunday evening service. This was the beginning of long years of active contribution to the musical activities of both church and community on the part of Mr. Shepherd.

Soon after moving to Salt Lake City, he joined the Tabernacle Choir and was a member up until just before his death, on September 24, 1945, at the age of 91.

His religion and music were the two great motivating forces of William Shepherd's life. He served both with loyalty, integrity, and devotion.

The Author — Anonymous

No. 257

If You Could Hie to Kolob

Words by W. W. Phelps   **Music by Joseph J. Daynes**

The Hymn

"If You Could Hie to Kolob"[*]challenges the finite mind to understand the infinite. What is the meaning of "Everlasting?" Nothing is final. Everything is intermediary between two other things. The beginning is as illusive as the end. There is no end-only eternity.

The Composer — Joseph J. Daynes (See No. 232)

The Author — William W. Phelps (See No. 213)

No. 258

In Remembrance of Thy Suffering

Words and Music by Evan Stephens

The Hymn

Evan Stephens shows his ability as a poet in this very lovely sacramental hymn. The rhythmical flow of the music in this hymn, induced by the ever-recurring triplets, makes it a likable song to sing as well as to hear.

The Composer and Author — Evan Stephens (See No. 144)

[*]See *The Pearl of Great Price* for information concerning Kolob. *Book of Abraham*, pp. pp. 34-35; Abraham 3:3-9.

No. 259

Jesus, Lover of My Soul

Words by Charles Wesley   Music by Joseph P. Holbrook

The Hymn and The Author — (See No. 84)

The Composer

It is this compiler's opinion that the Holbrook tune for "Jesus, Lover of My Soul" has had much to do with its popularity. The two-line duet for alto and tenor with which the hymn begins is immediately appealing and the musical phrase "Hide Me, O My Savior, Hide," has an impact of lasting proportions. Notwithstanding the fact that the tune is of the sentimental gospel song tradition, it is a beloved hymn of many a sincere worshiper. No information is available concerning the life of Joseph P. Holbrook except that in 1862 he appeared on the musical horizon with the publication of some hymns and hymn arrangements. He was born in 1822, and died in 1888.

No. 260

Lean on My Ample Arm

Words by Theodore E. Curtis   Music by Evan Stephens

The Hymn

This choir hymn is almost of anthem proportions. It is somewhat dramatic in its harmonic content, reaching an imposing climax in the fourth line. The final measures which reiterate the first phrase are calm and impressively peaceful.

The Composer — Evan Stephens (See No. 144)

The Author — Theodore E. Curtis (See No. 294)

No. 261

I'm a Pilgrim; I'm a Stranger

Words by H. H. Petersen   Music by Leroy J. Robertson

The Hymn

The following is quoted from Leroy J. Robertson, the composer of this hymn, "The music to this hymn was written to some other words as a class assignment when this composer was a student at the New England Conservatory of Music in 1921. It was later adapted to the Peterson words for publication in the 1927 hymnal where it is listed as No. 414. It has become well-known because of the impressive renditions over the CBS network given it by the Tabernacle Choir under the effective direction of J. Spencer Cornwall."

The Author — Hans Henry Peterson (See No. 127)

The Composer — Leroy J. Robertson (See No. 45)

No. 262
Let Zion in Her Beauty Rise

Words by Edward Partridge   **Music by Lewis D. Edwards**

The Hymn

In August of 1831 while Edward Partridge lived in Kirtland he, with Martin Harris and other elders, was directed by the Lord to journey to the land of Missouri. They were told that the next conference of the Saints should be held there upon the land which the Lord would consecrate unto his people, it being the land of their inheritance where the city of Zion should be built. Sidney Rigdon dedicated the land to that end. It is undoubtedly this incident which inspired Bishop Partridge to write the hymn "Let Zion in Her Beauty Rise."

The Composer — Lewis D. Edwards (See No. 95)

The Author

Edward Partridge was born August 27, 1793 in Pittsfield, Berkshire, Massachusetts. He was a convert to Mormonism from the Campbellite faith and was baptized by the Prophet Joseph Smith. In February of 1831 he was made the first Presiding Bishop of the Latter-day Saint Church and in the Doctrine and Covenants, section 42 (p. 51) is recorded the revelations from the Lord outlining his work.

He died in Nauvoo, May 27, 1840, while he was still in the office of Presiding Bishop.

No. 263
He Died! the Great Redeemer Died

Words by Isaac Watts   **Music by George Careless**

The Hymn

"He Died! the Great Redeemer Died" is an exalted sacramental hymn and is a favorite with Latter-day Saint choirs. The musical aspects of the hymn reveal a practised composer of genuine worth.

The Composer — George Careless (See No. 269)

The Author — Isaac Watts (See No. 168)

No. 264
Lo! the Mighty God Appearing

Words by William Goode   **Music by Evan Stephens**

The Hymn

"Lo! the Mighty God Appearing" is an exultant hymn abounding with the joys of the gospel restoration.

Its exuberant musical phrases have attracted most ward choirs to the learning and performing of it.

The Composer — Evan Stephens (See No. 144)

The Author

No information is at hand concerning the life of William Goode.

No. 265
Lord, Thou Wilt Hear Me When I Pray

Words by Isaac Watts   Music by Joseph J. Daynes

The Hymn

"Lord, Thou Wilt Hear Me" is one of the thousand hymns that came from the pen of Isaac Watts. The hymn is an evening prayer with a tender touch. As a composition, the music is not in true hymn form. It has a lilting style, more pretty than profound.

The Composer — Joseph J. Daynes (See No. 232)

The Author — Isaac Watts (See No. 168)

No. 266
We're Not Ashamed to Own Our Lord

Words by William W. Phelps   Music by Joseph J. Daynes

The Hymn

The hymn "We're not Ashamed to Own Our Lord" is one filled with restored gospel truths; notably its reference to the second coming of Christ.

The Composer — Joseph J. Daynes (See No. 232)

The Author — William W. Phelps (See No. 213)

No. 267
Sometime We'll Understand

Words by Maxwell N. Cornelius   Music by James McGranahan

The Hymn

In the mysteries of life and the obscure subtleties of religion, there are many seemingly unanswerable questions. Everyone has them. Mary, the mother of Jesus, did not understand the events and happenings of her early life, for we read in Luke 2nd chapter, 18th - 19th verses "And all they that heard it wondered at those things which were told them by the shepherds. But Mary kept these things and pondered them in her heart."

The three great phenomena of the world—birth, life, and death, stagger the imagination for explanations. "Life is real" declared Longfellow, but what is reality? The firm religious believer feels that he has the answer in the Lord's words found in the scriptures, but his conviction is based on that first great principle of religion-faith. That principle is the underlying substance of the declaration in the first line of the hymn "Sometime We'll Understand." The above is ample evidence why "Sometime We'll Understand" has become our most widely used funeral hymn.

The Composer

James McGranahan was a self-made musician and composer. His sacred compositions were all in the gospel song idiom but they became very popular in revivalistic efforts of such men as P. P. Bliss, Ira Sankey, and Dwight L. Moody. For four years from 1881 to 1885 he toured England, Scotland, Ireland, and major cities in the United States in religious efforts. He had a beautiful tenor voice which was his "stock in trade" for missionary work. He was co-editor with Sankey and Moody as the publishers of fifteen *Gospel Hymn Collections.*

Latter-day Saints will remember him as the composer of "My Redeemer" to which the words of "O My Father" have been appended.

Mr. McGranahan was born in Adamsville, Pennsylvania, July 4, 1840.

He lived the later years of his life in Kinsman, Ohio, and died in 1907.

The Author

Maxwell N. Cornelius was born in a farm in Pennsylvania. He became a brick mason as a young man, and one day while erecting a house he fell and broke his leg which had to be amputated. Being maimed for life he turned to an education for the Ministry. His first appointment was a pastorate in Altoona, Pennsylvania. Later he went to California and built the largest church in Pasadena. At the death of his wife he wrote "Sometime We'll Understand" which was read at her funeral. Soon after it was given to James McGranahan who set it to music.

No. 268

Oh, Awake! My Slumbering Minstrel

Words by Eliza R. Snow   **Music by Evan Stephens**

The Hymn

The thematic line of this prophetic hymn "Zion Prospers, All is Well" has far-reaching and significant connotations.

In the midst of tribulation, "Zion" which stands for the Church of the Latter-day Saints, has always prospered and will never be overthrown. Such is the belief and testimony of the Latter-day Saints.

The Composer — Evan Stephens (See No. 168)

The Author — Eliza R. Snow (See No. 139)

No. 269

The Morning Breaks; the Shadows Flee

Words by Parley P. Pratt   **Music by George Careless**

The Hymn

"The Morning Breaks, the Shadows Flee"* is one of the best and most inspiring of Latter-day Saint hymns. It was written by Parley Parker Pratt, and has first place in the authorized collection called *Latter-day Saint Hymns*. It was not written in time to be included in Emma Smith's collection, and was first published on the first page of the initial number of *The Millennial Star*, in March, 1840. There was no dramatic incident connected with its writing as far as we know. It was one of those poems, which, in the author's own words, "were the melting strains of joy and admiration in contemplating the approaching dawn of that glorious day which shall crown the earth and its inhabitants with universal peace and rest." Its author was the most prolific hymn writer of the Church. Thirty-eight of his inspired songs appear in the new Church hymnbook.

The first two stanzas of the hymn "The Morning Breaks; the Shadows Flee" deal in metaphors. They picture the world in spiritual darkness until the Lord spoke to the Prophet Joseph Smith and opened up this Dispensation of the Fulness of Times, when—

---

*From George D. Pyper's *Stories of Latter-day Saint Hymns*.

Day from his quiver drew His shining shaft,
And thwart the night the flaming arrow flew—

and the gospel was established and the shadows of night dispelled by the dawning of a new day."

The third and fourth stanzas speak of the ushering in of the fulness of the Gentiles, the realization of Israel's blessings, and the return of the Jews to the promised land.

When we fully sense what is now going on in Palestine, these lines seem like a song-prophecy.

A new note of exultation is found in the first two lines of the fifth stanza:

Angels from heaven and truth from earth
Have met, and both have record borne.

These are poetic responses to one of the most beautiful of the revelations of the Lord to the Prophet on the coming forth of the Book of Mormon.

The Lord hath brought down Zion from above.
The Lord hath brought up Zion from beneath.
The earth hath travailed and brought forth her strength;
And truth is established in her bowels;
And she is clothed with the glory of her God;
And the heavens have smiled upon her;
For He stands in the midst of His people.

D & C 84:100, 101.

This hymn occupies first place in *Latter-day Saint Hymns* not only because of its restoration theme but also because of its effective imagery and its superior literary and poetic qualities. It will live forever in Latter-day Saint hymnology.

The Composer

"The Morning Breaks, the Shadows Flee" has had several musical settings. One by Haydn from the oratorio *The Creation*, another the hymn called "Duke Street," by John Hatton (1793). The tune published in *Latter-day Saint Hymns*, by George Careless, is the one now generally sung in our congregations. Is was composed under rather interesting circumstances. Brother Careless set sail from England on the *Hudson* June 3, 1864. When the ship neared Castle Gardens, New York, the captain came to George and said he had admired the singing of the Mormon group so much that he wanted one of the professor's hymn tunes.

264

"I am very sorry, captain, but my music is all packed up. I haven't even a bit of music paper, or I would write one for you." The captain said he must have one. So young Careless took a piece of writing paper out of his pocket, drew a staff across it. then looked for a quiet place. On an empty barrel, in a corner of the vessel, he sat down and wrote the tune called "Hudson" in honor of the boat upon which he had sailed and also of the Hudson River into which they were gliding. The tune he put to the words "The Morning Breaks, the Shadows Flee." After writing the music, Brother Careless assembled his choir and sang it for the captain, giving him the rough copy of the music, over which the captain seemed much delighted.

Space will not permit the publication, in detail, of the interesting story of the life of George Careless. Only a few of the high lights can be given here. His full name was George Edward Percy Careless. He was born in London, September 24, 1839. As a boy George exhibited such musical talent that he was sent as a student to the Royal Academy of London, afterwards playing under eminent leaders at Exeter Hall, Drury Lane, and the Crystal Palace. He became a convert to Mormonism and did valuable service in the Church as leader of the choir in London. He immigrated to Salt Lake in 1864. It was while crossing the Atlantic, as stated, that Brother Careless composed the tune to "The Morning Breaks."

Soon after arriving in Salt Lake he was invited by President Young to direct the Tabernacle Choir and the Salt Lake Theatre orchestra. Talking over the appointment, President Young said: "I like soft music. I have heard the angels sing so sweetly."

"But," asked the musician, "would you like to be fed on honey all the time?"

"No, certainly not," answered the president.

"Some of our hymns," the professor went on, "require bold, vigorous treatment; others, soft sweet strains. As a musician, President Young, I think I can please you, and shall be glad to sing any of your favorites whenever you wish."

Professor Careless took over from Professor Charles J. Thomas the Salt Lake Theatre orchestra of twenty volunteer, unpaid men, but concluded it would be well to reduce the number of men and pay them. This was finally consented to by President Young.

Until the railroad was built, Professor Careless composed all the dramatic curtain music for the plays produced at the Salt Lake Theatre. His experience in the theatre orchestra was unusual. A tempting offer was made him to go to Virginia City at a high salary, but Professor Careless said "No, I came here for my religion, and I am going to stay."

He directed with success the Gilbert and Sullivan operas *Mikado* and *Pinafore* by the Salt Lake Opera Company. He was the first music teacher of the author of these articles.

The first performance of *The Messiah* in the Rocky Mountains was given in the Salt Lake Theatre under his direction in 1875. An incident further showing the religious faith of George Careless ocurred that night. His wife, Lovinia Triplett Careless, who was a member of his London Choir and whom he married after his arrival in Salt Lake City, was to sing the soprano role, but when she arrived at the theatre she was completely incapacitated on account of a severe cold. Brother Careless was implored to postpone the performance, but his sense of duty to the public was so great that he refused. He then asked Joseph R. Morgan, Thomas C. Griggs, and Henry Evans, elders in the chorus, to take Mrs. Careless in the Green Room and administer to her in accordance with the custom of the Church. They did so, and Mrs. Careless sang, "I Know That My Redeemer Liveth" better than she had ever before rendered it. She was a remarkably talented singer, and her voice still rings in the memory of those fortunate enough to have heard her. Of her rendition of "I Know That My Redeemer Liveth" the Salt Lake *Herald* said: "Her singing was simply perfection. Her young, fresh voice seemed to defy all difficulties. If angels

Parley P. Pratt

George Careless

had human voices, surely hers would suggest heavenly music." This seemed almost a prophecy, for in a very few years Mrs. Careless joined the heavenly throng, passing away July 10, 1885.

With that first performance of *The Messiah*, came a successful demonstration of Latter-day Saint faith in "divine healing."

As leader of the Tabernacle Choir and as a composer of hymn music, George Careless rose to a high place. A number of his compositions are published in the new *Latter-day Saint Hymns*. Many of these compositions were inspired while in the Tabernacle listening to the sermons of the Presiding Authorities of the Church. His beautiful and popular sacramental compositions are among the most soul-satisfying in Mormon hymnody.

In 1898 Elder Careless married Jane Davis, who was a congenial and helpful companion to him until his death, which occurred March 5, 1932.

The Author — Parley P. Pratt (See No. 20)

No. 270

O My Father

Words by Eliza R. Snow   **Music by James McGranahan**

The Hymn   **Arranged by Evan Stephens**

"O My Father" as hymn No. 270 is arranged for solo voice with choir accompaniment by Evan Stephens. It is particularly effective, probably the best arrangement that has yet been made. For a complete write-up on the hymn see No. 139.

No. 271

O Lord of Hosts

Words by A. Dalrymple   **Music by George Careless**

The Hymn

This hymn is a choir sacramental hymn of impressive mien.

The Composer — George Careless (See No. 269)

The Author

A. Dalrymple author of "O Lord of Hosts" has contributed a valued sacramental hymn to the Latter-day Saint Hymnal.

The words of this poet, coupled with the elegant music of George Careless, make it one of the most effective choir hymns of the entire collection.

One Sweetly Solemn Thought

Words by Phoebe Cary   **Music by Robert Steel Ambrose**

The Hymn

One of the most sobering thoughts which can be penned or uttered is that of America's woman poet, Phoebe Cary, "I am nearer home today than I've ever been before." This solemn but startling line is followed by the ever-present prayer, "Father, be near when my feet are slipping o'er the brink."

The Composer

Robert Steel Ambrose set "One Sweetly Solemn Thought" to music for solo voice. It is most popular as funeral music. In the Latter-day Saint Hymnal it is in anthem form. Technically, it has no place in a hymn collection but was included in the 1950 edition at the insistence of a member fo the church music committee. Ambrose was born in 1824 and died in 1908.

The Author

It is difficult to individualize either of the famous Cary sisters - Alice and Phoebe. They published many of their poems in the same volumes. Their lives were one complete series of unbroken companion-ship. Phoebe became best-known for her poem "Near Home" or "One Sweetly Solemn Thought." They both died in 1871 just five months apart. Phoebe Cary was born in 1824.

On the Mountain's Top Appearing

Words by Thomas Kelly   **Music by Thomas Hastings**

The Hymn

"On the Mountain's Top Appearing" is not of Latter-day Saint origin although it is prophetic of the establishment of the Church in the "tops of the mountains."

The Composer — Thomas Hastings (See No. 382)

It is possible that Thomas Kelly wrote both words and music to this hymn as he was a musician as well as a poet, but a tune by Thomas Hastings called "Zion" has been associated with it. The composer of the tune in the Latter-day Saint Hymnal cannot be identified at this writing.

The Author — Thomas Kelly (See No. 212)

O Thou, Before the World Began

Words by W. B. Turton   **Music by Frank Asper**

The Hymn

The text of "O Thou, Before the World Began" clearly defines Jesus Christ the Savior as the God of this earth and its Redeemer.

The third stanza is a plea that "our faith in him may never move, but stand unshaken."

The Composer — Frank Asper (See No. 96)

The Author

No information is available at this writing concerning W. B. Turton.

No. 275

What Voice Salutes the Startled Ear?

Words by Henry W. Naisbitt   **Music by Ebenezer Beesley**

The Hymn

"What Voice Salutes the Startled Ear" stems from the prophetic statement in 1st Corinthians, chapter 15, verse 55. "O Death where is thy sting? O grave, where is thy victory?"

This scripture is a plain declaration of a resurrection and a hereafter.

The Composer — Ebenezer Beesley (See No. 94)

It is the opinion of your author that the original version of this hymn as written by Ebenezer Beesley with solo voice and four-part chorus, was more impressive than the all part version of the present hymnal.

The Author — Henry W. Naisbitt (See No. 278)

No. 276

O Thou Kind and Gracious Father

Words by Charles Denny   **Music by George Careless**

The Hymn

"O Thou Kind and Gracious Father" is a hymn of fervent prayer.

The Composer — George Careless (See No. 269)

The tune for "O Thou Kind and Gracious Father" was used also in hymn no. 284 "Softly Beams the Sacred Dawning."

The Author

Charles Denny, Jr. was born August 11, 1849 in Blacklane, Middlesex, England. His father was Charles Denny, Sr., and his mother was Mary Ann Dangerfield Denny.

Charles Denny emigrated to America in July of 1866 and in the same year crossed the plains in Captain Holliday's wagon train, arriving in Salt Lake City September 28th, 1866.

On December 2nd, 1872 Charles Denny married Sarah Ann Gould in the Endowment House. Twelve children were born to this union—ten of whom were raised to adulthood.

Brother Denny worked as a typesetter and proofreader at the Deseret News. He was musical and together with his wife sang in the Tabernacle choir for a number of years. He also led the Eleventh Ward choir. Brother Denny was always active in church activities. When he moved his family to Union, Salt Lake County, he became Sunday School superintendent. He went on two foreign missions, one to Germany and one to England, and one home mission to Bingham, Utah.

He wrote over one hundred poems—some were personal, others for friends and events in the ward.

"Oh, Thou Kind and Gracious Father" was written about the year 1887. Charles Denny, Jr. passed away Sept. 10th, 1937 at the age of 88. (This sketch was supplied by Mrs. Ruth Berrett one of Charles Denny's twin daughters).

No. 277

Praise Ye the Lord

Words by Isaac Watts   **Music by Evan Stephens**

The Hymn

The hymn "Praise Ye the Lord" is a fervent hymn of praise. It is distinct for the verve with which it presses forward as it progresses toward the strong ending.

The Composer — Evan Stephens (See No. 144)

The Author — Isaac Watts (See No. 168)

No. 278

Rest, Rest for the Weary Soul

Words by Henry W. Naisbitt   **Music by George Careless**

The Hymn

Blessed are the dead which die in the Lord, from henceforth:

270

Yea, saith the spirit, that they may rest from their labours and their works do follow them. (Rev. 14:13.)

The beauty of Henry W. Naisbitt's "Rest, Rest on the Hillside, Rest,"* is in its simplicity. It is poetic, rhythmic; a most beautiful, comforting song—full of solace and peace. It declares that death is a happy release from the battles of life and that one enters into a peace where no strife intrudes, no quarrels come; where the oppressed are free and the weary rest.

But Henry W. Naisbitt did not believe that the spirit of a deceased person was buried in the cemetery. He believed in the Mormon doctrine that only the mortal remains are placed there; that the Spirit, the intelligent part, is taken to the paradise of God to await the resurrection morn. This is beautifully told by the Nephite Prophet Alma as recorded in the Book of Mormon (Alma, 40:11, 12):

> Now, concerning the state of the soul between death and the resurrection—Behold, it has been made known unto me by an angel, that the spirits of all men, whether they be good or evil, are taken home to that God who gave them life. And then shall it come to pass that the spirits of those who are righteous are received into a state of happiness, which is called paradise, a state of rest, a state of peace, where they shall rest from all their troubles, and from all care and sorrow.

The Prophet Joseph Smith, speaking of death and the resurrection, said:

> How consoling to the mourners, when they are called to part with a husband, wife, father, mother, child, or dear relative, to know that, although the earthly tabernacle is laid and dissolved, they shall rise again to dwell in everlasting burnings in immortal glory, not to sorrow, suffer, or die any more; but they shall be heirs of God and joint heirs with Jesus Christ. (*Teachings of Joseph Smith*, p. 343.)

The Composer — George Careless (See No. 269)

George Careless added to the artistic simplicity of this hymn when he wrote the tune to "Rest, Rest on the Hillside, Rest." It was written for the funeral of Brigham Young's brother, Joseph, who died July 16, 1881. The music was then named "Repose." Both the hymn and the music were written for the Tabernacle Choir which sang the selection at the funeral. Brother Careless' music was probably written in the choir loft of the Tabernacle where he often composed his music.

---

*From George D. Pyper's *Stories of Latter-day Saint Hymns*.

The diapason of the great pipes of the organ must have inspired the bass in the harmony of the last line of his truly beautiful song. To hear it sung, on the hillside, in the red glow of an evening's setting sun carries one close to the gates of paradise where the righteous await the glories of the resurrection. Truly, Henry W. Naisbitt and George Careless, natives of England, in the combination of their poetic and musical genius, have given solace to thousands of bereaved Saints, and added a precious contribution to Latter-day Saint hymnody.

The Author

Henry W. Naisbitt was born in November, 1826, in the little hamlet of Romanby, England, so named because it was on the road made by the Roman invaders. He grew up to early manhood at the nearby town of North Allerton, Yorkshire. His father was a Wesleyan exhorter, and Henry was raised under that religious atmosphere— a Bible student at home and a faithful attendant at Sunday School. His love for reading amounted almost to a passion, his favorite authors in addition to the Bible being Gray, Thompson, Cowper, Mrs. Barbould, Mrs. Segourey, Elliott, Massey and Cooper. After joining the Athenaeum and Mechanies' Institutions, of London, he

Henry W. Naisbett

272

reveled in the works of Shakespeare, Milton, Byron, Burns, and Moore, later being especially attracted by the poems of Eliza Cook, Henry Kirk White, and Mrs. Hemans. Henry's father died when the son was only nine years old, and the widow with five children was left to meet life's responsibilities. Henry was a Wesleyan until 1850, when he first heard the gospel preached by Orson Pratt. He was doubtful at first but gradually became convinced of its truth and joined the Church in Liverpool, immigrating to Utah in 1854. In his mountain home Brother Naisbitt contributed many inspiring poems, among which was the hymn "Rest, Rest for the Weary Soul."

Brother Naisbitt filled two missions to his native land, one in 1876-78 when he labored as assistant editor of the *Millennial Star*, and the other in 1898-91, when he was counselor to Platte D. Lyman, in the presidency of the European Mission. He died February 26, 1908.

No. 279

Ring Out, Wild Bells

Words by Alfred Tennyson   **Music by Crawford Gates**

The Hymn

This hymn was written on Waipio Peninsula in Pearl Harbor in the Hawaiian Islands on a naval Amphibious Operating base, August 23, 1945, scarcely a week after the end of World War II. It was first played on an army piano for Latter-day Saint Chaplain Marsden Durham at his base on Oahu Island in September a few days before Elder Durham (son of George H. and Nellie M. Durham) was killed in a tragic accident in which he slipped over the edge of one of the waterfalls on the Island of Hawaii. "On the previous Friday Chaplain Durham and I," says Crawford Gates, "had spent a free day together, the hymn was played and sung and enjoyed by the chaplain. On the following Sunday night, after Elder Durham had given a most remarkable testimony and gospel sermon in Waikiki Ward, the two of us, while riding in a jeep to the base from which the chaplain would fly to Hawaii the next day, sang the newly composed hymn together and especially the alto and tenor parts with its melodic imitation in the fourth phrase, which pleased us both." So the last hymn that Elder Durham sang in this life were the words of Tennyson, in this new little hymn, which he sang with his missionary companion and fellow serviceman as their jeep scooted to its base under Hawaiian palms. The words of the hymn seemed almost prophetic, when the two young men sang: "Ring out the darkness of the land; Ring in the Christ that is to be!"

273

The Composer

Crawford Gates, the son of Gilbert Marion Gates and Leila Adair Gates, was born in San Francisco, California, December 29, 1921. His early schooling was in Palo Alto, California. He then attended College of the Pacific (1938-39), San Jose State (1942-43), North Dakota State Teachers College and Columbia University in the U.S. Naval Reserve Program during World War II. He earned his BA degree from San Jose State in 1944, MA degree from Brigham Young University in 1948, and Ph. D. degree from the University of Rochester in 1954. He was the composer of the Utah Centennial Play *Promised Valley*, also Symphony No. I, a Piano Concerto, two orchestral Suites, three major orchestral choral works, including the music for the *Hill Cumorah Pageant*, six motion picture scores for the BYU Motion Pictures, numerous smaller works and arrangements. He is Associate Professor of Music at Brigham Young University and a member of the general board of the MIA since 1949. He married Georgia Lauper of San Francisco in the Salt Lake Temple.

The Author

English Poet Laureate Alfred, Lord Tennyson was born in Somersly, Lincolnshire in 1809 and was educated at Trinity College, Cambridge. He succeeded William Wordsworth as poet Laureate of

Crawford Gates

274

England. His poem, which he was sixteen years writing; called "In Memoriam," made him immortal. He was elevated to the Peerage in 1884. He fought governmental tyranny and "the narrowness and dryness of college instruction." "Ring Out Wild Bells" with its insistent cry of "Ring Out the Old, Ring in the New" was Tennyson's most forceful demand for a changed social order where all manner of evil was extant throughout the land. Stanza no. 3 summarizes it all with the words:

> Ring in the Valiant Man and free
> Ring in the Christ that is to be.

Tennyson died in 1892.

No. 280
Reverently and Meekly Now

Words by Joseph L. Townsend   **Music by Ebenezer Beesley**

The Hymn

"Reverently and Meekly Now" is one of the most beloved sacramental hymns of the Latter-day Saints Church. It extends far beyond the limits of a simple congregational hymn, having in it a bass solo section and a three part ladies chorus passage. Being written as it was for the Tabernacle Choir, these innovations are quite in order.

The Composer — Ebenezer Beesley (See No. 94)

The Author — Joseph L. Townsend (See No. 64)

J. S. Townsend

Ebenezer Beesley

No. 281

Sacred, the Place of Prayer and Song

Words and Music by Evan Stephens

The Hymn

Another of Evan Stephens' hymns wherein he is the author and composer. In poetic verse he avows the sacredness and purpose of places of worship.

The Composer and Author — Evan Stephens (See No. 144)

"Sacred the Place of Prayer and Song" is an effective and well-sounding choir hymn.

No. 282

Savior, Redeemer of My Soul

Words by Orson F. Whitney　　　　　　　　**Music by Evan Stephens**

The Hymn

The hymn "Savior, Redeemer of My Soul" has never been popular. The musical setting is not one of Evan Stephens' best hymns.

The Composer — Evan Stephens (See No. 144)

The Author — Orson F. Whitney (See No. 292)

No. 283

Up! Arouse Thee, O Beautiful Zion

Words by Emily H. Woodmansee　　　　　**Music by Leroy J. Robertson**

The Hymn

The music of the hymn "Up! Arouse Thee" was written for the 1927 "Green" hymnal. In this 1948 edition, verses three and four are omitted because of the irregularity of their meter. It is essentially a choral number of a concert or festival character, but it might also be used in church where a good conductor and choir are available.

The Composer — Leroy J. Robertson (See No. 45)

The Author

Emily H. Woodmansee was born near Warminster, Wilts, England, March 24, 1836. She says in the words of a Mormon poet "I never knew what trouble was till I became a Mormon."

A cousin, Miriam Slade, persuaded her to go to a Mormon meeting on foot six miles from her home when she was only twelve years of age. She was convinced of the truth spoken by the elders but found much opposition from her family when she returned home. Later Elder John Halliday of Santaquin, Utah, visited the family at their home and by his words allayed the opposition that was there. In May of 1856 Emily Woodmansee and her sister Julia sailed for America.

On reaching the body of the Saints she agreed to pull a handcart to Utah, a one thousand mile trip. When Emily reached Zion, she married. Her husband went on a mission for the Church but never returned to her, leaving her to battle life's troubles alone. In 1864 she married Joseph Woodmansee. She was the mother of a very large family. Being a gifted poetess, she made many contributions in that line.

No. 284

Softly Beams the Sacred Dawning

Words by John Jaques   **Music by George Careless**

The Hymn

Latter-day Saint gospel doctrine pervades this fine choir hymn. The theme of life after death and the resurrection are versified in its beautiful lines.

The Composer — George Careless (See No. 269)

Two hymn texts are used in the Latter-day Saint hymnal with this lovely tune of George Careless — No. 276 and No. 284.

The Author — John Jaques (See No. 143)

No. 285

Though Deep'ning Trials

Words by Eliza R. Snow   **Music by George Careless**

The Hymn

It was during these distressing times that Eliza R. Snow wrote the beautiful hymn the first line of which reads, "Though Deep'ning Trials Throng Your Way."* While there is no record of the date of this song was written, it first appeared in the *Times and Seasons,* January, 1841. It next appeared in the eleventh edition of the Latter-day Saint Hymnbook, published in 1856. Sister Snow had passed through the persecutions of Missouri and Nauvoo (being among those who were expelled from the City Beautiful), later drove an ox team from that city to Winter Quarters, walking beside them, the consequent exposure and hardships breaking down her health and bringing her close to the valley of death. She left Winter Quarters in June, arriving in Salt Lake City in October, 1847.

---

*From George D. Pyper's *Stories of Latter-day Saint Hymns.*

One would naturally think that on account of the shocking experiences through which she had passed there would be in her heart a vengeful spirit that would be reflected in her hymns; but such was not the case. On the contrary, all her songs breathe the essence of peace and forbearance of resignation to the providences of God, and a love for all his children. When the Saints left Nauvoo, she had a firm conviction that President Brigham Young was the divinely chosen leader of the Church as she had that her martyred Prophet and Seer was the instrument in the hands of God of ushering in the Dispensation of the Fulness of Times. With such a faith she wrote, "Though Deep'ning Trials Throng Your Way."

The song admonishes the Saints not to faint by the way but to press on in spite of tribulations; that ere long the light of truth would spread and envelop the nations of the earth; that though trials and vicissitudes await us in mortal life, the time would not be long before the Lord Jesus would come again, surrounded by a glorious and heavenly throng. Hearts, therefore, should be lifted up in praise to the Lord; rejoicings should never cease, though tribulations rage. The Saints should take courage in the words of Christ who said, *"Peace I leave with You.*

> *Peace I leave with you. My peace I give unto you. Not as the world giveth give I unto you. Let not your heart be troubled, neither let it be afraid. (John 14:27.) These things I have spoken that in me ye might have peace. (Ibid., 16:33.)*

Though stripped of our rights and despoiled of our property, the promises of Jehovah fail not; neither is he foiled in his purpose. Satan will rage in vain, for the words of the ancient prophets are as sure as the throne of God remains: Neither men nor devils can revoke them.

This graphic song-sermon ends with a paean of praise to the holy name of him who sends his missionaries to the nations of the earth, to proclaim salvation's tidings to every tongue and people.

The Composer — George Careless (See No. 269)

The tune to this song is among the best creations of the harmonious pen of George Careless, one of the most renowned composers of the Church. As the pen of Eliza R. Snow fashioned her hymn amidst the tribulations of the people, so, at a later date, George Careless composed the tune while under physical distress. He was very ill and needed encouragement—something to dispel his fears and raise him from the state of despondency into which he felt himself drifting. from searching the scriptures he turned to his loved hymnbook to which he had already contributed many notable tunes.

"Addie," he called to his eleven-year-old daughter, "bring me the hymnbook." She brought it to him. After scanning its pages for a few minutes he found what he was searching for—what his physical body as well as his spirit required. It was Eliza R. Snow's hymn. "Though Deep'ning Trials Throng Your Way." It gave him courage to fight his bodily ills and the faith that soon raised him from his bed of affliction. At the same time it inspired the muse that enabled him to pen one of the noblest of his compositions—one which, united with Eliza R. Snow's comforting poem, is among the most popular numbers in our Church hymnody.

When George Careless recovered from his illness, he took his composition to Horace G. Whitney and asked him if he could suggest a title for it. Mr. Whitney, after looking it over, said "Why not call it 'Reliance' " and as "Reliance" it was published in the *LDS Psalmody*, and remained there for nearly fifty years. The modern way, however, is to call a hymn by its first line, and so it now appears in our *Latter-day Saint Hymns*, under the title "Though Deep'ning Trials Throng Your Way."

The Author — Eliza R Snow (See No. 139)

No. 286

Unanswered Yet

Words by Ophelia G. Adams   **Music by Charles D. Tillman**

The Hymn

"Unanswered Yet" is a sentimental gospel song.

The Composer — Charles D. Tillman (See No. 188)

The Author

Ophelia G. Adams was an obscure writer of the early part of the twentieth century, whose hymns were perpetuated by the well-known publisher E. O. Excell.

No. 287

Lord of All Being, Throned Afar

Words by Oliver Wendell Holmes   **Music by Leroy J. Robertson**

The Hymn

This hymn can be used in any part of the church service for congregation or chorus. It is a cluster of metaphors, each suggesting an aspect of religion—the sun, the star, the moon, the night. Oliver Wendell Holmes, author of the hymn, said of it, "Forget for the moment the differences in the hues of truth we look at through our

279

human prisms, and join in singing (inwardly) this hymn to the source of the light we all need to lead us, and the warmth which alone can make us all brothers."

The Composer — Leroy J. Robertson (See No. 45)

The Author

Oliver Wendell Holmes was first of all a man of "letters" and secondly a great teacher. He tried law as a profession but did not like it. He became a medical doctor but gave that up also to teach anatomy at Harvard University. *Old Ironsides,* which saved the frigate *Constitution* from the scrap heap, and *The Autocrat at the Breakfast Table* established him in the literary field. When he visited Europe in 1886, he was showered with degrees. He was a deeply religious man. A colleague said of him, "No irreverent word ever escaped his tongue." He was born in 1809 and died in 1894.

No. 288

Ye Children of Our God

Words by Parley P. Pratt   **Music by George Careless**

The Hymn

"Ye Children of Our God" is a seldom used sacramental hymn.

The Composer — George Careless (See No. 269)

The Author — Parley P. Pratt (See No. 20)

No. 289

The Voice of God Again Is Heard

Words and Music by Evan Stephens

The Hymn

This hymn was written by Evan Stephens as a part of a cantata called *The Vision.* It was one of the Latter-day Saint hymns chosen for the Tabernacle Choir's repertoire on the 1955 European tour. Every line breathes the message of gospel restoration.

Composer and Author — Evan Stephens (See No. 144)

No. 290

Ye Simple Souls Who Stray

Words by Charles Wesley   **Music by Evan Stephens**

The Hymn

In the hymn "Ye Simple Souls Who Stray," Charles Wesley laments the state of those who "folly love" and "throng the down-ward road." These strong lines of the great hymn writer Wesley, make an intense appeal to the sinner to mend his ways.

The Composer — Evan Stephens (See No. 144)

The two line, three part beginning which composer Stephens wrote into this hymn with the alto and tenor duet plus bass gives an attractive musical effect which has much to do with the hymn's popularity with Latter-day Saint choirs and congregations. Evan Stephens the composer, struck a responsive melodic line which gives the hearer a long-lasting musical experience and one which calls for repetition.

The Author — Charles Wesley (See No. 10)

No. 291

A Voice Hath Spoken

Words by J. Marinus Jensen   **Music by J. J. Keeler**

The Hymn

"A Voice Hath Spoken from the Dust" is a pungent poetical expression referring to the coming forth of the Book of Mormon. It is one of the few hymns written on this topic in the Latter-day Saint Hymnal.

J. Marinus Jensen

The Composer

J. J. Keeler the composer of the music for "A Voice Hath Spoken from the Dust" is at this writing and has been for sometime the organist at the Brigham Young University. He is on the faculty of the school and teaches organ and other music classes.

281

The Author

J. Marinus Jensen was born in Provo, Utah, July 11, 1868.

He was a professor of English and journalism for many years at Brigham Young University, and with the exception of the years that he was away studying, he spent his entire life in Provo. He died there March 17, 1945. He was the grandfather of the composer of the hymn, J. J. Keeler.

No. 292

The Wintry Day

Words by Orson F. Whitney   **Music by Edward P. Kimball**

The Hymn

Induced by a calm wintry day, Elder Whitney meditates on the mountain home of the Saints. Written in miniature anthem form, "The Wintry Day" is a hymn of great favor with Latter-day Saint choirs.

The Composer — Edward Partridge Kimball (See No. 178)

The Author

Orson F. Whitney's life was one of consistant progress, consistant adherence to the things that he taught and was marked by untiring efforts in the cause of right. He gave his best to the Church.

Orson F. Whitney

282

He was a most effective speaker and famed as a writer. Elder Whitney could hold an audience spellbound by reading his own poems.

For twenty-eight years he served as bishop of the Eighteenth Ward of Salt Lake City, after which he was called to the Council of the Twelve Apostles.

Bishop Whitney, as he preferred to be called, was born in Salt Lake City, July 1, 1855 and was educated in the schools of Salt Lake and the University of Deseret. Later he became Chancellor of the University of Utah.

He filled three missions for the Church the last of which he presided over the entire European Mission.

Outstanding among his literary works is a *History of Utah*.

Elder Whitney was active in political circles.

In his youth he was much interested in dramatics and took prominent parts in the "Home Dramatic Company" productions. He was a rather good singer also.

Elder Whitney taught in the Brigham Young College in Logan, Utah, published two biographies, one on Heber C. Kimball and the other on Lorenzo Snow, and his poems are numerous.

He died of a heart attack May 16, 1931.

No. 293
When Dark and Drear the Skies Appear

Words by Emily H. Woodmansee   **Music by Joseph J. Daynes**

The Hymn

A hymn of trust with the assurance that "Providence is over all."

The Composer — Joseph J. Daynes (See No. 232)

The Author — Emily H. Woodmansee (See No. 283)

No. 294
I Wander through the Stilly Night

Words by Theodore Curtis   **Music by Hugh Dougall**

The Hymn

"I Wander through the Stilly Night" exemplifies without question, the fact that Theodore Curtis was a true poet. One has only to read any line to discover the beauty of his literary skill. His hymns in the hymnbook were written upon request of the Church music committee when the original book of hymns for choir was compiled.

The Composer — Hugh Dougall (See No. 86)

The Author

Theodore Edward Curtis (1872-1957) was the son of Theodore Walter Curtis and Flora Lydia Shipp. He was born the 27th of September 1872 in the 13th Ward, Salt Lake City. He married Bardella Shipp in August in 1901 in the Salt Lake Temple. He held many positions in the Church during his lifetime. Brother Curtis was ordained a patriarch June 16, 1946. His poetry appeared in all the Church magazines. He is the author of the following books of poetry: *In the temples of the Great Outdoors, Lyrics of the Westland, Sunbeams of Truth,* and the *Mother Heart of Gold* series.

His best known poem is in "The Trail Builder's Hymn." This was a request from the general Primary presidency.

Following is a tribute to Theodore E. Curtis which appeared in the editorial page of the *Deseret News:* "H. L. Mencken, the late famed literary critic of Baltimore, once observed that a secret ambition of every writer, is 'to get one line into the record that will stay.' Though writers produce millions of words in their lifetimes, rarely does one ever produce a line that is not soon forgotten.

But kindly T. E. Curtis of Salt Lake City who died Monday morning at the age of 85 was eminently successful in getting a "line into the record that will stay." Around the world and far away wherever there is an 11-year-old Trail Builder in the Primary Association of The Church of Jesus Christ of Latter-day Saints, there also will be a boy who knows and sings lustily, Patriarch Curtis' beloved "Trail Builder Song."

> Oh, we are the boy Trail Builders,
> Out West where the sunset glows;
> Where the brooks flow down like silver
> From the heights of the virgin snow.
> We build our trails through the valleys
> Where the heart beats light and free;
> Out here in the West.
> From the pine-clad crest
> To the shores of the rolling sea.

Back of the writing of this happy poet, was a long life of service with honor and diligence. His two sons, Theodore Jr., and R. Emerson, who are well-known to thousands of young men throughout the country because of their work as LDS chaplains at home and on foreign soils, successfully have carried on the heritage of unselfish service as personified by their father.

284

When Christ Was Born in Bethlehem

Words by Henry W. Longfellow **Music by Ebenezer Beesley**

The Hymn

"When Christ Was Born in Bethlehem" is a Christmas hymn from a great poet, Henry W. Longfellow.

The opening phrase of "When Christ Was Born in Bethlehem" composed by Ebenezer Beesley, follows practically the same pattern in the opening phrase as Handel's "Joy to the World"—that of the descending major scale. It was adjudged the best composition in a prize-winning competition.

The Composer — Ebenezer Beesley (See No. 94)

No. 296
The Seer, Joseph the Seer

Words by John Taylor **Music by S. C. Von Neukomm**

Arranged by Ebenezer Beesley

The Hymn

John Taylor loved the Prophet Joseph Smith with all the devotion that one man could possibly have for another.* His two poems written to the Prophet-"O Give Me Back My Prophet Dear" and "The Seer" have in them all the poetical fervor he could muster to portray his inmost feelings. John Kay was a favorite singer of Joseph Smith and often sang for him in Nauvoo. He often sang "The Sea" from which "The Seer" was arranged. When John Taylor wrote the present verses, Kay sang them to the Saints using the tune of "The Sea" by Neukomm-the first stanza of which is "The Sea! The sea! the open sea!"-whose author was Bryan Waller Procter.

The Composer

Sigismund Chevalier Von Neukomm was born in Salzburg in 1778. He studied with the Haydns, Michael and Joseph. Neukomm was sought after as a pianist and conductor by most of the European countries. In 1829, he went to England with Mendelssohn. Neukomm was a prodigious composer of oratorios, many of which he directed in Paris and London. He died in 1858.

The Author

President Taylor was a forceful writer. He was publisher and editor of several volumes of the *Times and Seasons*, and *The Nauvoo*

---

* From George D. Pyper's *Stories of Latter-day Saint Hymns.*

Neighbor, and subsequently sponsored the paper called *The Mormon.* A lover of hymns and a good vocalist, he was a favorite singer of the Prophet Joseph Smith, was in Carthage jail with him and cheered his last moments by singing "A Poor Wayfaring Man of Grief." When the Prophet and Patriarch were shot, Elder Taylor ran to the window through which Joseph leaped, and was met by a fusilade of bullets, four of which entered his body, and a fifth struck his watch, which was in his vest pocket, and forced him back into the room. Thus his life was providentially saved. But Brother Taylor carried some of these bullets in his body to the grave.

President Taylor was born November 1, 1808, in Milnthorpe, England, and died July 26, 1887, at Kaysville, Utah, while an exile for conscience' sake.

The second and last stanzas of "The Seer, Joseph the Seer" show the reverence in which the Prophet was held by President Taylor.

John Taylor

No. 297

Behold the Mountain of the Lord

Words by Logan   **Music by Joseph J. Daynes**

The Hymn

The text of "Behold the Mountain of the Lord" is based on the scriptures as found in Isaiah 2:2-5 inclusive;

"And it shall come to pass in the last days, that the mountain of the Lord's house shall be established in the top of the mountains, and shall be exalted above the hills; and all nations shall flow unto it."

The Composer — Joseph J. Daynes (See No. 232)

The Author

At sometime in the past century someone failed to give the printer of the hymn "Behold the Mountain of the Lord" the full name of the author. This fact makes it practically impossible for a subsequent historian to identify the person responsible for its writing.

No. 298

The Lord Imparted from Above

Words by Eliza R. Snow   **Music by George Careless**

The Hymn

This is one of the lesser-known hymns written by Eliza R. Snow and George Careless.

The Composer — George Careless (See No. 269)

The Author — Eliza R. Snow (See No. 139)

No. 299

What Was Witnessed in the Heavens?

Words by John S. Davis   **Music by Evan Stephens**

The Hymn

A question and answer form has been employed to good advantage, in this well-known hymn.

The Composer — Evan Stephens (See No. 144)

The Author

John S. Davis died at his residence after a lingering illness of four years, at the age of sixty-nine, in 1822. He was born in 1813.

No. 301

Brightly Beams Our Father's Mercy

Words and Music by Philip Paul Bliss

The Hymn

This number is a favorite gospel song with either of the above texts. "Brightly Beams Our Father's Mercy" was written by the composer P. P. Bliss. Philip Bliss heard the great evangelist, Dwight L. Moody relate a story about a boat nearing the Cleveland harbor. There was only one light in the lighthouse. The captain said to the

287

pilot, "Are you sure this is Cleveland?" "Quite sure," answered the pilot. 'Where are the lower lights?" asked the captain. "Gone out" said the pilot. "Can we make it?" asked the captain. "We must or we perish" answered the pilot. That night Bliss wrote both words and music to "Let the Lower Lights Be Burning." The author of the alternate text is unknown to this compiler at this time. The arrangement for male voices found in the Latter-day Saint Hymnal, is a splendid selection for a beginning male chorus.

The Composer and Author

Philip Bliss was born to poor parents in 1838 but developed a passion for music. While just a youth, he wrote a song and gave it to George F. Root, then one of America's best composers, asking him for a flute in return for the song. Mr. Root sent him the flute which started a companionship which together with Ira D. Sankey was to last and become extremely fruitful. Bliss was a man of handsome stature. Unlike his contemporary, Fanny Crosby, he could write the music to his hymns as well as the words. In 1870, he heard a story of the Civil War wherein General Sherman signaled a message to the garrison at Allatoona Pass, Georgia, to "Hold the Fort," Bliss at once wrote a gospel song on the command;

> Hold the fort, for I am coming
> Jesus signals all;
> Wave the answer back to heaven
> By thy grace we will.

When Bliss was only thirty-eight years old, he and his wife were killed in a railroad accident in 1876. A monument was erected to him in his home town of Rome, Pennsylvania.

No. 302

Come, All Ye Sons of God

Words by T. Davenport   **Music by O. P. Huish**

The Hymn

Come, All Ye Sons of God" is a hymn of threefold import:-first, an appeal to the sons of God to spread the gospel; second, an appeal to the "Scattered sheep" to listen to the voice of the shepherd; and third, a promise that all who are faithful shall enjoy heavenly bliss.

The Composer — O. P. Huish (See No. 85)

The Author

Thomas Davenport was born in Derbyshire, England in 1815. He joined the Church of Jesus Christ of Latter-day Saints in 1847.

He served as a local missionary in various parts of England. He estimated that he walked eighteen-hundred and forty-nine miles during his mission.

In 1849 he came to the United States, and three years later he crossed the plains to Utah, settling in Parowan. He lived in Parowan until his death in 1888.

Elder Davenport was a very spiritual man and held several church positions.

No. 303

Come, All Ye Sons of Zion

Words by William W. Phelps   Music by John Tullidge

The Composer

"Come, All Ye Sons of Zion" is a hymn for men and is arranged in the hymnbook for men's voices which, when the various parts are sustained, is rather effective.

The Composer — John Tullidge (See No. 224)

The Author — William W. Phelps (See No. 213)

No. 332

Rise Up, O Men of God

Words by William Pierson Merrill   Music by Frank W. Asper

The Hymn

"Rise Up, O Men of God" was written to aid the cause of the Brotherhood Movement in the Prebyterian Church. An article in a magazine entitled "The Church of Strong Men" induced its title. It was written by Dr. Merrill while returning to Chicago on a Lake Michigan steamer. This hymn is a clarion call to all religious men.

The Composer — Frank W. Asper (See No. 96)

The Author

William Pierson Merrill was born in Orange, New Jersey, in 1867. He was educated for the ministry in Union Theological Seminary in New York City. He served as pastor in Presbyterian churches in Philadelphia and Chicago. Merrill was an authority on hymnody and contributed many fine hymns to church hymnals. "Rise Up, O Men of God" is his outstanding hymn.

No. 335

O Home Beloved, Where'er I Wander

Words by Evan Stephens   Music by Joseph Parry

The Hymn

"O Home Beloved" is a missionary hymn and exhibits in a good way the fine ability of Evan Stephens as a poet.

The Composer

Joseph Parry was an American-born Welshman (1841-1903). His first instruction in music was in a class organized for iron-workers in Danville, Pennsylvania.

After he won a prize in composition, the Welsh colony in Danville sent him to New York City for further study. In 1865 he attended a Welsh Eistoddfod in Wales where the title of Pencerdd America was conferred on him. Later he received a Doctor's degree from the Royal Academy of Music in Cambridge.

After two extended trips to America he returned to Wales where he became professor of music in the Welsh University College at Aberystwyth. His compositions included two oratorios, several cantatas, four hundred hymn tunes, and many other numbers of varied assortment.

Concerning the tune to "O Home Beloved," Thomas Parry of the National Library of Wales writes, "The tune was first published in 1875 as a part song for male voices and has been very popular in Wales. The original words are of love song variety by a Richard Davies."*

The Author — Evan Stephens (See No. 144)

Evan Stephens wrote many hymn texts. For most of them he composed the music but in "O, Home Beloved" he adapted the music of Joseph Parry.

No. 337

O Happy Home among the Hills

Words and Music by Evan Stephens

The Hymn

" O, Happy Home among the Hills" was written and composed by Evan Stephens. This hymn, along with "The Morning Breaks,"

---

*Quoted from Wilkes in *Borrowed Music in Latter-day Saint Hymnals.*

(a setting for male voices) was popularized by the Pratt brothers, Noel and Wood, who sang it frequently when they were young men. The boys were trained by Conductor Stephens.

The Composer and Author — Evan Stephens (See No. 144)

No. 340
School Thy Feelings

Words by Charles W. Penrose   **Music by George F. Root**

The Hymn

"School Thy Feelings" is a hymn of exhortation toward self-mastery.

The Composer

George Fredrick Root (1820-1896) was an early American composer, teacher of singing, and an organist. In 1850, he went to Paris to study. On his return, he wrote several successful songs. Later, he met Lowell Mason with whom he organized a music school. Teachers in the school included William Bradbury and Thomas Hastings, some of whose compositions appear in the Latter-day Saint hymnal. In 1860 Root moved to Chicago where he went into the publishing business. Root became very successful until the great fire of 1871 almost ruined him financially. In 1881, he received a Doctorate from the University of Chicago. His compositions and writings on musical subjects were numerous. His most popular songs were those written about Civil War days of which "The Vacant Chair" was one. "School Thy Feelings" is adapted to the tune of the "Vacant Chair."

The Author — Charles W. Penrose (See No. 145 and Appendix, page 296.)

No. 344
Ye Elders of Israel

The Hymn

Words by Cyrus H. Wheelock   **Music Anonymous**

"Ye Elders of Israel" is a missionary hymn of exhortation.

The Composer

The anonymous tune to which "Ye Elders of Israel" is sung, was probably picked up by early Mormon missionaries in Great Britain.

The Author — Cyrus H. Wheelock (See No. 15)

Ye Who Are Called to Labor

Words by Mary Judd Page   Music Anonymous

The Hymn

The hymn "Ye Who Are Called to Labor" is especially directed to missionaries of the Church.

The Composer

This anonymous hymn was arranged for male voices by your compiler with the thought that missionaries would have more opportunity to use it than mixed voice groups.

The Author

Mary Judd Page was born November 26, 1818 in Leeds, Ontario, Canada. She was the daughter of Arza Judd and Lucinda Adams Judd. She was married to John E. Page, an early apostle of the Latter-day Saints Church.

No. 349

Bring, Heavy Heart, Your Grief to Me

Words by Herbert Auerbach   Music by Anthony C. Lund

The Hymn

This is a tender hymn of solace and comfort for the sorrowing.

The Composer — Anthony C. Lund (See No. 233)

The Author — Herbert S. Auerbach (See No. 233)

No. 370

Lift Thine Eyes

Words from the Scriptures   Music by Felix Mendelssohn

The Hymn

This hymn is a paraphrase of Psalm 121:1-5. It is one of several exhortations which the Lord gave to Elijah to arise and continue his mission, when he was so dejected that he cried out, "It is enough, O Lord, now take away my life."

This splendid ladies' chorus from the *Elijah*, is one of the most effective bits to be found in the entire oratorio. Being of subdued quality as an a cappella ladies' chorus in contrast to the elaborate mixed choruses of other sections, with their elegant orchestral accompaniments, it gives one a sense of ethereal repose when heard in its setting in the oratorio.

The Composer

We shall always remember Mendelssohn, first for his bringing to light the works of the great Bach; second, he was a great composer in his own right. Mendelssohn was born in an atmosphere of luxury and refinement in 1809 and was given every opportunity to become trained and skilled. His mother was his first teacher. At the age of thirteen years, he began to compose in the larger forms. He became a great conductor through the giving of concerts with choirs and orchestras in his father's house to members of his family and special friends. His home and garden on the outskirts of Berlin provided ample room for concerts of all kinds. In 1829, he paid a visit to England where he became an idol of the British people. While here, he composed some of his most famous works. He was a lifetime friend of the poet Goethe and spent much time with him.

Mendelssohn's travels took him to all parts of Europe where his music was warmly received. The lone exception was Paris, where his Reformation Symphony was rejected as being too pedantic. In 1840 he founded the Academy of Fine Arts in Berlin and later a conservatory in Leipzig. He was a prodigious worker in spite of the fact that he was comfortably wealthy. The composing of his greatest oratorio, the *Elijah,* was a strain on his health, but he lived to conduct it many times both on the continent and in England. With many unfinished plans, he was taken ill in October of 1847 and died a few weeks later.

Felix Mendelssohn

Rock of Ages Cleft for Me

Words by Augustus M. Toplady   **Music by Thomas Hastings**

The Hymn

"Rock of Ages Cleft for Me" is plagiaristic in that the opening lines in substance were written by John Wesley some thirty years before Mr. Toplady's hymn came out. "O Rock of Israel, Rock of Salvation, Rock struck and cleft for me, let those two streams of blood and water, etc," wrote Wesley. Strange to say, Wesley and Toplady were violent antagonists over religious conceptions. The hymn, however, is one of implicit faith in the saving power of a Divine Father.

The Composer

Thomas Hastings was a self-taught musician. He was born in Connecticut in 1784 but practiced his profession in New York City where he composed many hymns and anthems. He was a man of deep religious convictions and he believed and taught that religion has the same claim substantially in song as in speech. Hastings' *History of Forty Choirs*, 1854, consists of sketches illustrative of his own experiences with choirs, clergy, directors, and congregations.

In 1858, the University of the City of New York conferred on him the Ph.D. Music degree. He is said to have written six-hundred texts, and to have composed around one thousand tunes, besides issuing fifty volumes of music. For many years he was an integral part of the music life of New York, from which he guided much of the progress of sacred music throughout the country. Death came to him on May 15, 1872.

The Author

Augustus M. Toplady was a deeply religious child. He wrote hymns when he was in his teens, and published a volume of them at nineteen. He was first converted to Methodism but later became a minister in the Evangelical or Low Church. He was militant to the end against all who did not believe as he did. He was born in 1740 and died in 1778.

APPENDIX

No. 211

Ye Chosen Twelve

The Composer — Alfred Marshall Fox (See page 219)

Alfred Marshall Fox was born September 3, 1842 in Sheffield, Yorkshire, England. He emigrated to Utah in October, 1860 with his parents. On January 4, 1868 he married Mary Southwick in the Endowment house. Eleven children were born to them. They made their home in Lehi, Utah.

As a young man he made three trips east to the Mississippi River to bring back emigrants in the handcart companies. He was a gifted musician, playing several instruments, directing choirs and bands and composing.

He died May 28, 1920.

Alfred Marshall Fox

School Thy Feelings

The Author — Charles W. Penrose (See page 291)

This hymn was written in Birmingham, England, shortly before President Penrose was to leave England for the United States in 1861.

In a sacrament meeting a few years later, President Penrose made the following comments:

"This was written under peculiar circumstances just before I left England, after having traveled over 10 years in the ministry. A sort of quiet slander had been circulated concerning me in Birmingham by an elder from Zion and it had cut me to the quick.

"There was not a word of truth in the story. An accusation was made, but there was no bottom to it, and it ruffled me. I did not care how much I might be scandalized by enemies of the Church I had become accustomed to that. I used to say that my hide had got as tough as a hippopotamus; I did not care what an enemy said about me.

"But when an elder in the Church did that it cut me to the heart, and I felt like retaliating. But I sat down and wrote that little poem, 'School thy feelings, O my brother, Train thy warm, impulsive soul,' and so on. And that was for me.

"I did not intend it for anybody else, but it was giving a little counsel to myself."

INDEX

A

A'Becket Thomas 45
"Abide with Me" 59
"Abide with Me, 'Tis Eventide" 5
Adams, Ophelia G. 278
Adams, Sarah F. 128
Addison, Joseph 120-21
Adolphus, Gustavus 6
"Again, Our Dear Redeeming Lord" 254
"Again We Meet around the Board" 249
Alexander, Cecil F. 67, 214
Alford, Dean Henry 38
"All Creatures of Our God and King" 7
"All Hail the Glorious Day" 234
Alldredge, Ida R. 192
Alldridge, Richard 114, 228
Ambrose, R. S. 268
"America" 121
"America the Beautiful" 129
American Etude 80
American Guild of Organists 37, 114
American Tune Book, The 25, 149
Anderson, Edwrd H. 113
Anglican Hymnology 59
"An Angel from on High" 28, 140, 234
"Arise, My Soul, Arise" 237
"Arise, O Glorious Zion" 237
Arnold, Matthew 8
"As Swiftly My Days" 9
"As the Dew from Heaven Distilling" ..239
Asper, Frank W. 111, 137, 167, 185,
                        196, 202, 217, 262, 269, 289
Auerbach, Herbert S. 242-43, 292
"Author of Faith, Eternal Word" 238
"Awake! O Ye People, the Savior Is
   Coming" 199
"Awake, Ye Saints of God, Awake" 238

B

Bach, Johann Sebastian 6, 102
Baird, Robert B. 89-90, 103, 213
Baker, Mary Ann 117
Ballard, Melvin J. 5, 72, 245
Baring-Gould, Sabine 126, 133
Barnby, Joseph 126
Bates, Katherine Lee 129-30
"Beautiful Isle of the Sea" 9
"Beautiful Zion Built Above" 92
"Beautiful Zion for Me" 9
Beesley, Ebenezer ....vii, 58, 67, 75, 84,
      105, 106-7, 125, 149, 177, 201, 203, 204,
      211, 241, 243, 253, 254, 269, 275, 285
"Before Thee, Lord, I Bow My Head" ..239
"Behold the Mountain of the Lord" 286
"Behold the Mountain of the Lord" 286
"Behold the Royal Army" 10
"Behold Thy Sons and Daughters" 32
Beirly, A. 12
Bennett, Archibald F. 71-72
Bennett, John 43
Bennett, Wallace F. 42-45

Benson, Rev. Louis F. 59
Best Church Hymns 59
Bishop Sir Henry 201
Blenkhorn, Ada 12
"Blessed Are They that Have the
   Faith" 242
Bliss, Philip Paul 121, 175, 287-88
Bode, John E. 52-53
Bohemian Brethren's Songbook 174
Bone, Mary W. 42
Borrowed Music in Mormon Hymnals ..198
Bortniansky, Dimitri 120
Bowen, Emma Lucy Gates 161
Boyd, Audrey Petersen 132
Bradbury, William B. ....vii, 42, 54, 184, 219
"Break Forth O Beauteous Heavenly
   Light" 245
Bridges, Robert 156
Brief History of the Church 113
"Brightly Beams Our Father's Mercy" |287
"Bring Heavy Heart, Your Grief to Me"
  292
Brooks, Phillips 183, 184
Brown, Felicia D. H. 247, 248
Brown, Mary 91
Broyhill, Joel 136
Bullock, William 215-16
Burns, James D. 255-56

C

Cadman, Charles W. 83
Calkin, J. Baptiste 229
Callis, Charles 127
Calvin, John ix
Campbell, Alexander 147
Cannon, Annie Wells 157
Cannon, Clara C. 52
Cannon, George Q. 4, 36
Cannon, Tracy Y. 4-5, 37, 39, 42, 77,
                  118, 149, 165, 167, 186, 245
"Cantica Laudis" 198
"Captain of Israel's Host and Guide" ..244
Careless, George ....vii, 84, 105, 143, 149,
      193, 198, 230, 237, 238, 241, 249, 256,
      260, 263, 264-67, 269, 270-72, 277, 278
                                  279, 280, 287
Carey, Henry 121-22
Carr, Benjamin 31
"Carry On" 48-52
Carthage Jail 22, 169, 286
Cary, Phoebe 268
"Cast Thy Burden the Lord" 244
Chamberlain, John M. 204-6
Children Sing, The 4
Choir hymns ix
"Choose the Right" 119
"Christ the Lord Is Risen Today" 12
Church Chorals and Choir Studies 96
Church Music Comittee, *see* General
   Music Committee
Civil War 6, 79, 104, 106, 182
Clairvaux, Bernard of 164-65

297

304